The Path —
8 steps

MORE PRAISE FOR
EIGHT MINDFUL STEPS TO HAPPINESS

Sharon Stewart

"Bhante has an engaging voice and a straightforward delivery that's hard not to like, especially when he's enlivening the Buddha's map to enlightenment, the eightfold path. Each chapter in *Eight Mindful Steps to Happiness* explains the purpose and practice of an aspect of right conduct, pointing out some potential pitfalls in our modern-day context."
—*Shambhala Sun*

"Mentally evolved, elegantly presented, and beautifully simple."—*Midwest Journal*

"Bhante Gunaratana delves into the Buddha's most profound teachings, the Eightfold path. Appreciated as a 'teacher's teacher,' he offers generous and specific advice (still in plain English) towards developing mindfulness. Combining meaningful examples of each noble truth with direct, specific suggestions for related practices, this book will be a boon to all who aspire to follow in the Buddha's path toward contentment."—*NAPRA ReView*

EIGHT MINDFUL STEPS
TO HAPPINESS

Walking the Path of the Buddha

Bhante Henepola Gunaratana

WISDOM PUBLICATIONS • BOSTON

Wisdom Publications
199 Elm Street
Somerville MA 02144 USA
www.wisdompubs.org

Library of Congress Cataloging-in-Publication Data
Henepola Gunaratana, Bhante
    Eight mindful steps to happiness : walking the path of the
Buddha / Bhante Henepola Gunaratana.
        p.   cm.
    Includes index.
    ISBN 0-86171-176-9 (alk. paper)
    1. Eightfold Path. I. Title
BQ4320 H46 2001
294.3′444—dc21   00-068570

ISBN 0-86171-176-9

06 05 04 03
6   5   4   3

Designed by Gopa and the Bear
Back cover photo: ©2000 Lee J. Halfpenny, Jr., all rights reserved.

Wisdom Publications' books are printed on acid-free
paper and meet the guidelines for the permanence
and durability of the Production Guidelines for Book
Longevity set by the Council on Library Resources.

Printed in Canada.

Contents

Publishers' Acknowledgment

The publisher gratefully acknowledges the generous help of the Hershey Family Foundation in sponsoring the publication of this book.

Acknowledgments

THIS BOOK would not have seen the light if not for the initiative of my friend Douglas Durham, who transcribed my talks and created the first draft of this book. I thank him for his hard work on this project.

I acknowledge the assistance of my student Samaneri Sudhamma (whose name means "good Dhamma") for helping with revisions to bring out the good Dhamma of this book.

I must also express my great appreciation to my editors, Brenda Rosen and John LeRoy, and to my indexer, Carol Roehr.

Finally, I thank all my students residing at the Bhavana Society, who patiently endured my long absences while I worked on this book. May you all share in the merit of this little book as it reaches many thousands of people who seek happiness.

List of Abbreviations

IN ENGLISH-LANGUAGE WORKS, CITATIONS from the Pali Canon are typically referenced to the page numbers they appear on in the Pali-language edition from the Pali Text Society (PTS), Oxford. (You can find these citations in the various English translations using page number references that are inserted throughout the translated text.) Where possible in this book a more straightforward form of citation has been adopted for your convenience. The various genres of texts are organized differently, however, thus no one approach will work with all the books in the Pali Canon.

A   Anguttara Nikāya, or *Gradual Sayings*, available through the Pali Text Society (PTS), Oxford. (Example: A I (Threes). VII. 65 refers to volume 1, *The Book of Threes*, chapter 7, story number 65.)

D   Dīgha Nikāya, or *The Long Discourses of the Buddha*, available through Wisdom Publications, Boston. (Example: D 22 refers to Sutta number 22.)

Dh   Dhammapada, or *Word of the Doctrine*, available in translation through many publishers, including PTS. (Example: Dh 5 refers to verse number 5.)

DhA   Dhammapada Aṭṭhakathā, or the Dhammapada Commentary, available through PTS as *Buddhist Legends*. (Example: DhA 124 refers to part 124 of the Commentary, which analyzes Dhammapada verse 124.)

J   Jātaka, or *Jataka Stories*, available through PTS. (Example: J 26 refers to story number 26.)

M   Majjhima Nikāya, or *The Middle Length Discourses of the Buddha*, available through Wisdom Publications, Boston. (Example: M 80 refers to Sutta number 80.)

MA   Majjhima Nikāya Aṭṭhakathā, or Commentary to the Middle Length Discourses of the Buddha, not available in English. (Example: MA i 225 refers to volume 1, page 225 of the Pali edition.)

Mhvs   Mahāvaṃsa, or the *Great Chronicle of Ceylon*, available through PTS. (Example: Mhvs V refers to chapter 5.)

Miln   Milindapañho, or *The Questions of King Milinda*, available through PTS. (Example: Miln 335 [V], refers to the page number 335 of the PTS book in Pali; reference to chapter 5 is added to assist in locating the verse.)

S   Saṃyutta Nikāya, or *The Connected Discourses of the Buddha*, available through Wisdom Publications. (Example: S I.7.1 [2] refers to part 1, chapter 7, subchapter 1, story number 2.)

Sn   Sutta Nipāta, or the *Group of Discourses II*, available through PTS. (Example: Sn 657 refers to verse number 657.)

Thag   Theragatha, or *Poems of Early Buddhist Monks*, available through PTS. (Example: Thag 303 refers to verse number 303.)

Thig   Therīgathā, or *Poems of Early Buddhist Nuns*, available through PTS. (Example: Thig 213 refers to verse number 213.)

Ud   Udāna, or *Verses of Uplift*, available through PTS. (Example: Ud VI.2 refers to chapter 6, story number 2.)

V Vinaya, or *Book of the Discipline*, available through PTS. (Example: V ii 292 refers to volume 2, page 292 of the Pali edition.)

Vsm Visuddhimagga, or *The Path of Purification*, available through the Buddhist Publication Society, Kandy, Sri Lanka. (Example: Vsm I [55] refers to chapter 1, paragraph number 55.)

Introduction

SOON AFTER *Mindfulness in Plain English* was published, several of my friends and students asked me to write a book about the Buddha's path to happiness in the same straightforward style. This book is my response.

Mindfulness in Plain English was a meditation manual, a guide for students in the practice of mindfulness meditation. Yet mindfulness is only part of the Buddha's teachings. Mindfulness can much improve our lives, but the Buddha offered more. He gave us a complete guide to happiness, which he summed up in eight steps. Even a little effort to incorporate these eight steps into your life will yield happiness. Strong effort will transform you and bring you the happiest and most exalted states achievable.

The eight steps of the Buddha's path are easy enough to memorize, but their meaning is deep and requires an understanding of many related topics of the Buddha's teachings. Even those familiar with the Eightfold Path may not see how central it is to the whole teaching or how it fits their experience. As in *Mindfulness in Plain English,* I have tried to present this teaching plainly, so that anybody can practice the eight steps in their daily life.

I recommend that you do not read this book as you would a novel or the newspaper. Rather, while reading, continually ask yourself, "Am I happy?" and investigate what you find. The Buddha invited the people he taught to come and see. He invited all of us to look at ourselves, to come home, to come close to our own bodies and minds and examine them. Don't get lost in beliefs and suppositions about the world, he told us; try to find out what is really going on.

We are good at accumulating information, gathering data. Perhaps you have picked up this book to gather more information. If you have been reading popular Buddhist books, stop and ask yourself what you hope to get from this one. Do you just want to impress people with how well you know Buddhism? Do you hope to gain happiness through intellectual knowledge of the teachings? Knowledge alone will not help you find happiness.

If you read what follows with the willingness to put the Buddha's path to happiness into practice—to actually try out his advice, rather than just get an intellectual impression—then the profound simplicity of the Buddha's message will become clear. Gradually, the full truth of all things will be revealed to you. And gradually you will discover the lasting happiness that full knowledge of the truth can give you.

If you get upset by things that you read in *Eight Mindful Steps to Happiness*, then investigate why. Look within. Ask yourself what is currently happening in your mind. If something you read makes you miserable, ask yourself why. Sometimes we feel uncomfortable when someone points out how unskillful we are. You may have a lot of bad habits and other obstacles that keep you from greater happiness. Do you want to learn about them and make some changes?

So often we get upset by some tiny little thing and then blame it on someone—a friend, secretary, boss, neighbor, child, sibling, parent, the government. Or we get disappointed when we don't get what we want or lose something we value. We carry within our minds certain "psychic irritants"—sources of suffering—that are triggered by events or our thoughts. Then we suffer, and we try to stop the pain by changing the world. There's an old story about a man who wanted to cover the whole earth with leather so he could walk more comfortably. He would have found it much easier to make a pair of sandals. Similarly, instead of trying to control the world to make yourself happy, work to reduce your psychic irritants.

But you must actually train yourself, not just read or think about it. Even meditating won't get you far if you do not practice the entire path—especially its key aspects of developing right understanding, making strong, discerning effort, and practicing continuous mindfulness. Some of you sit on your meditation cushion for hours with your minds filled with anger, fantasy, or worry. Then you say, "I can't meditate, I can't concentrate." You carry the world on your shoulders as you meditate, and you don't want to put it down.

I heard that a student of mine was walking down the street while reading a copy of *Mindfulness in Plain English*. He wasn't being mindful of where he was, and he was hit by a car! The Buddha's invitation to come and see asks you to personalize what you read here. Put the Buddha's eight steps into practice, even while you are reading. Don't let your misery blindside you.

Even if you read this book a hundred times, it won't help you unless you put what's written here into practice. But this book surely will help you if you practice sincerely, investigate your unhappiness fearlessly, and commit yourself to doing whatever it takes to reach lasting happiness.

THE BUDDHA'S DISCOVERY

Rapid technological advances. Increased wealth. Stress. Stable lives and careers come under the pressure of accelerating change. The twenty-first century? No, the sixth century B.C.—a time of destructive warfare, economic dislocation, and widespread disruption of established patterns of life, just like today. In conditions similar to ours, the Buddha discovered a path to lasting happiness. His discovery—a step-by-step method of mental training to achieve contentment—is as relevant today as ever.

Putting the Buddha's discovery into practice is no quick fix. It can take years. The most important qualification at the beginning is a strong desire to change your life by adopting new habits and learning to see the world anew.

Each step along the Buddha's path to happiness requires practicing mindfulness until it becomes part of your daily life. Mindfulness is a way of training yourself to become aware of things as they really are. With mindfulness as your watchword, you progress through the eight steps laid down by the Buddha more than twenty-five hundred years ago—a gentle, gradual training in how to end dissatisfaction.

Who should undertake this training? Anyone who is tired of being unhappy. "My life is good as it is," you may think; "I'm happy enough." There are moments of contentment in any life, moments of pleasure and joy. But what about the other side, the part that you'd rather not think about when things are going well? Tragedy, grief, disappointment, physical pain, melancholy, loneliness, resentment, the nagging feeling that there could be something better. These happen too, don't they? Our fragile happiness depends on things happening a certain way. But there is something else: a happiness not dependent on conditions. The Buddha taught the way to find this perfect happiness.

If you are willing to do whatever it takes to find your way out of suffering—and it means confronting the roots of resistance and craving right here, right now—you can reach complete success. Even if you are a casual reader, you can benefit from these teachings, so long as you are willing to use those that make sense to you. If you know something to be true, don't ignore it. Act on it!

That may sound easy, but nothing is more difficult. When you admit to yourself, "I must make this change to be more happy"—not because the Buddha said so, but because your heart recognizes a deep truth—you must devote all your energy to making the change. You need strong determination to overcome harmful habits.

But the payoff is happiness—not just for today but for always.

Let's get started. We'll begin by looking at what happiness is, why it's so elusive, and how to start journeying on the Buddha's path toward it.

What Happiness Is and What It Isn't

The desire to be happy is age-old, yet happiness has always eluded us. What does it mean to be happy? We often seek an experience of sensual pleasure, such as eating something tasty or watching a fun movie, for the happiness it will bring us. But is there a happiness beyond the fleeting enjoyment of a pleasurable experience?

Some people try to string together as many enjoyable experiences as they can and call that a happy life. Others sense the limits of sensual indulgence and seek a more lasting happiness with material comforts, family life, and security. Yet these sources of happiness also have limitations. Throughout the world many people live with the pain of hunger; their basic needs for clothing and shelter go unmet; they endure the constant threat of violence. Understandably, these people believe that increased material comfort will bring them lasting happiness. In the United States the unequal distribution of wealth leaves many in poverty, but the starvation and deprivation commonly found in much of the world is rare. The standard of living of most U.S. citizens is luxurious. So people elsewhere assume that Americans must be among the happiest on earth.

But if they were to come to the United States, what would they see? They would notice that Americans are constantly busy—rushing to appointments, talking on cell phones, shopping for groceries or for clothes, working long hours in an office or in a factory. Why all this frantic activity?

The answer is simple. Although Americans seem to have everything, they are still unhappy. And they are puzzled by this. How can they have close, loving families, good jobs, fine homes, enough money, richly varied lives—and still not feel happy? Unhappiness, they believe, results from the lack of such things. Possessions, social approval, the love of friends and family, and a wealth of pleasurable experiences ought to make people happy. Why, then, do Americans, like people everywhere, so often experience misery instead?

It seems that the very things that we think should make people happy are in fact sources of misery. Why? They do not last. Relationships end, investments fail, people lose their jobs, kids grow up and move away, and the sense of well-being gained from costly possessions and pleasurable experiences is fleeting at best. Change is all around us, threatening the very things we think we need to be happy.

It's a paradox that the more we have, the greater our possibility for unhappiness.

People today are ever more sophisticated in their needs, it's true, but no matter how many expensive and beautiful things they collect, they want more. Modern culture reinforces this wanting. What you really need to be happy, as every TV ad and billboard proclaims, is this shiny new car, this superfast computer, this gorgeous vacation in Hawaii. And it seems to work, briefly. People confuse the buzz of excitement gained from a new possession or a pleasurable experience with happiness. But all too soon they're itching again. The suntan fades, the new car gets a scratch, and they're longing for another shopping spree. This incessant scrambling to the mall keeps them from discovering the source of true happiness.

The Sources of Happiness

The Buddha once described several categories of happiness, placing them in order from the most fleeting to the most profound.

THE LESSER HAPPINESS OF CLINGING

The Buddha lumped together almost everything that most of us call happiness in the lowest category. He called it the "happiness of sensual pleasures." We could also call it the "happiness of favorable conditions" or the "happiness of clinging." It includes all the fleeting worldly happiness derived from sense indulgence, physical pleasure, and material satisfaction: the happiness of possessing wealth, nice clothes, a new car, or a pleasing home; the enjoyment that comes from seeing beautiful things, listening to good music, eating good food, and enjoying pleasant conversations; the satisfaction of being skilled in painting, playing the piano, and the like; and the happiness that comes from sharing a warm family life.

Let us look more closely at this happiness of sensual pleasures. Its lowest form is the wholehearted indulgence in pleasure from any of the five physical senses. At its worst, overindulgence can lead to debauchery, depravity, and addiction. It's easy to see that indulging the senses is not happiness, because the pleasure disappears almost immediately and may even leave people feeling wretched or remorseful.

The Buddha once explained that as one matures spiritually, one comes to understand that there is more to life than pleasure through the five senses. He used the metaphor of a tender little baby tied down by thin strings in five places: both wrists, both ankles, and the throat. Just as these five strings—the five sense pleasures—can hold down a baby but not a mature adult, who easily breaks free, so a discerning person breaks free from the idea that indulging the five senses makes life meaningful and happy. (M 80)

Worldly happiness, however, goes beyond sense indulgence. It
includes the joys of reading, watching a good movie, and other forms of
mental stimulation or entertainment. It also includes the wholesome
joys of this world such as helping people, maintaining a stable family
and raising children, and earning an honest living.

The Buddha mentioned a few of these more satisfying forms of happiness. One is the happy, secure feeling you get from possessing wealth
earned through honest, hard work. You enjoy your wealth with a clear
conscience and no fear of abuse or revenge. Better than this is the satisfaction of both enjoying the wealth that you earned honestly and also
sharing it with others. Another especially gratifying form of happiness
comes from reflecting that one is completely free of any kind of debt to
anyone. (A II (Fours) VII.2)

Most of us, even the most discerning, view these things as the
essence of a good life. Why did the Buddha consider them part of the
lowest form of happiness? Because they depend on conditions being
right. Though less fleeting than the transient pleasures of sensual indulgence, and less potentially destructive to long-term happiness, they are
unstable. The more we trust them, seek them, and try to hang on to
them, the more we suffer. Our efforts will create painful mental agitation and ultimately prove futile; conditions inevitably will change. No
matter what we do, our hearts will break. There are better, more stable
sources of happiness.

Higher Sources of Happiness

One of them is the "happiness of renunciation," the spiritual happiness
that comes from seeking something beyond worldly pleasures. The classic example is the joy that comes from dropping all worldly concerns and
seeking solitude in peaceful surroundings to pursue spiritual development. The happiness that comes from prayer, religious rituals, and religious inspiration is also part of this category.

Generosity is a powerful form of renunciation. Generously sharing
what we have, and many other acts of renunciation, make us feel happy.
There is a sense of pleasure and relief every time we let go. It stands to

reason that if we can let go completely of grasping at anything in the world, then this great relinquishment will bring even more happiness than occasional acts of renunciation.

Higher than relinquishment of material things is the "happiness of letting go of psychic irritants." This kind of happiness arises naturally when we work with the mind to quickly let go of anger, desire, attachment, jealousy, pride, confusion, and other mental irritations every time they occur. Nipping them in the bud allows the mind to become unobstructed, joyful, bright, and clear. Yet there is no guarantee that the negativities will stay away and stop irritating the mind.

Even better is the refined pleasure and happiness of the various states of deep concentration. No sorrow can arise in these states. Powerful and transcendent as these states of concentration can be, however, they have one big drawback: the meditator must emerge from them eventually. Being impermanent, even states of profound concentration must come to an end.

The Highest Source of Happiness

The highest happiness is the bliss of attaining stages of enlightenment. With each stage, our load in life is lightened, and we feel greater happiness and freedom. The final stage of enlightenment, permanent freedom from all negative states of mind, brings uninterrupted, sublime happiness. The Buddha recommended that we learn to let go of our attachments to the lower forms of happiness and focus all of our efforts upon finding the very highest form of happiness, enlightenment.

But he also urged people to maximize their happiness at whatever level they can. For those of us who cannot see beyond the happiness based on the sense pleasures, he offered sage advice for avoiding worldly troubles and for finding optimal worldly happiness, for example, by cultivating qualities leading to material success or a satisfying family life. For those with the higher ambition to be reborn in blissful realms, he explained just how to accomplish that goal. For those interested in reaching the highest goal of full enlightenment, he taught how to achieve it. But whichever kind of happiness we are seeking, we make use of the steps of the Eightfold Path.

The Trap of Unhappiness

The Buddha knew that the relentless search for happiness in pleasurable worldly conditions traps us in an endless cycle of cause and effect, attraction and aversion. Each thought and word and deed is a cause that leads to an effect, which in turn becomes a cause. Pointing out how the cycle of unhappiness works, the Buddha said:

> Because of feeling, there is craving; as a result of craving, there is pursuit; with pursuit, there is gain; in dependence upon gain, there is decision-making; with decision-making, there are desire and lust, which lead to attachment; attachment creates possessiveness, which leads to stinginess; in dependence upon stinginess, there is safeguarding; and because of safeguarding, various evil, unwholesome phenomena [arise]—conflicts, quarrels, insulting speech, and falsehoods. (D 15)

We each experience versions of this cycle every day. Say you're shopping in the grocery store. You see a delicious-looking pie with red filling and fluffy white topping. It's the last pie left. Though only a moment before, your mind was quiet and content, this sight, which the Buddha calls "contact between sense organ and sense object," causes a pleasant feeling and pleasant thoughts to arise.

Craving arises from the pleasant feeling. "Mmmm…strawberry," you say to yourself, "with real whipped cream topping." Your mind pursues and expands upon these pleasant thoughts. How delicious strawberry pie is! How good it smells! How wonderful whipped cream feels on the lips and tongue! A decision follows: "I want to have some of that pie." Now comes attachment: "That pie is mine." Maybe you notice some aversion as your mind hesitates for a moment while it considers the negative effects of the pie on your waistline or your pocketbook.

Suddenly you realize that someone else has stopped at the display and is admiring this pie. Your pie! Seized with stinginess, you snatch it up and hurry to the checkout while the other shopper glares. In the unlikely event that the other shopper were to follow you into the parking lot and try to take your pie, imagine what unwholesome actions might take place—insults probably, maybe a shoving match. But even if there is no direct confrontation, your actions have caused another person to develop negative thoughts and to see you as a greedy person. Your contented state of mind has also been destroyed.

Once craving arises in the mind, selfish and stingy behavior is usually inevitable. In our drive for any kind of small pleasure—a piece of strawberry pie—we may act rudely and risk making an enemy. When the craving is for something major, such as someone's valuables or an adulterous sexual contact, the stakes are much higher, and serious violence and endless suffering may result.

If we can reverse this cycle, starting from our negative behavior and moving backward step by step to its emotional and mental causes, we may be able to eliminate our unhappiness at its source. It only makes sense that when our craving and grasping is wiped out—completely eradicated—happiness is assured. We may have no idea how to accomplish such a feat, but when we recognize what we have to do, we have started our journey.

The Gradual Training

Now you see why we say that true happiness comes only from eliminating craving. Even if we think that attaining the highest happiness is unrealistic, we will still benefit from reducing craving. The more we let go of craving, the greater our sense of happiness. But how do we reduce craving? The idea of lessening craving—much less eradicating it—may seem daunting. If you think that making the effort to force craving out of existence by sheer willpower will end in frustration, you are correct. The Buddha came up with a better way: the gradual training of the Eightfold Path.

The Buddha's path of gradual development impacts every aspect of your life. The process begins at any point, at any time. You start wherever you are and move forward, step by step. Each new wholesome change in behavior or understanding builds upon the last.

Among the crowds of people who heard the Buddha teach, some had such receptive minds that they achieved lasting happiness after hearing his step-by-step instructions in a single discourse. A few were so ready that upon hearing only the highest teaching—the Four Noble Truths— their minds were completely freed. But most of the Buddha's disciples had to work their way through the teachings, mastering each step before moving on to the next. Some disciples took years to work through obstacles in their understanding before they could move on to the next level of inquiry.

Most of us must do a lot of personal work to disentangle ourselves from years of destructive and self-defeating attitudes and behavior. We must work slowly along the Buddha's path of gradual training with much patience and encouragement. Not everybody gets full understanding overnight. We all bring differences from our past experiences and the intensity of our dedication to spiritual growth.

The Buddha was a profoundly skillful teacher. He knew that we need some basic clarity before we can absorb the higher teachings. His Eightfold Path to happiness consists of three stages that build upon each other: morality, concentration, and wisdom.

The first stage, morality, consists of adopting a core set of values and living our lives according to them. The Buddha knew that thinking, speaking, and acting in ethical ways are preliminary steps to take before progressing to higher spiritual development. But of course we must have at least some wisdom to discern what is ethical. Thus he began his teaching by helping us to cultivate a basic level of Skillful Understanding (step one) and Skillful Thinking (step two). These mental skills help us distinguish between moral and immoral thoughts and actions, between wholesome behaviors and those which hurt us and those around us.

As we develop the right mind-set, we can begin to put our evolving understanding to work by practicing Skillful Speech (step three), Skillful Action (step four), and Skillful Livelihood (step five). These practical steps of good moral conduct help make our minds receptive, free from hindrances, elated, and confident. As the distractions that come from destructive behavior begin to fade away, concentration can arise.

Concentration has three steps. The first is Skillful Effort (step six), which brings mental focus to every other step of the path. Such effort is especially necessary if many unwholesome thoughts spring into awareness when one sits down to meditate. Next is Skillful Mindfulness (step seven). To have mindfulness there must be some wholesome concentration at every moment, so that the mind can keep in touch with changing objects. Skillful Concentration (step eight) allows us to focus the mind on one object or idea without interruption. Because it is a positive state of mind, free from anger or greed, concentration gives us the mental intensity we need to see deeply into the truth of our situation.

With morality as the foundation, concentration arises. Out of concentration, the third stage of the Buddha's path—wisdom—develops. This brings us back to the first two steps of the path: Skillful Understanding and Skillful Thinking. We begin to experience "aha!" insights into our behavior. We see how we create our own unhappiness. We see how our thoughts, words, and deeds have hurt ourselves and others. We see right through our lies and face our life as it truly is. Wisdom is the bright light that shows us the way out of the tangle of our unhappiness.

Though I have presented the Buddha's path as a series of sequential stages, it actually works more like a spiral. Morality, concentration, and wisdom reinforce and deepen each other. Each of the eight steps on the path deepens and reinforces the others. As you begin to practice the path as a whole, each step unfolds, and each wholesome action or insight gives impetus to the next. Along the way, everything about you changes, especially your tendency to blame others for your unhappiness. With each turn of the spiral, you accept more responsibility for your intentional thoughts, words, and deeds.

For instance, as you apply your increasing wisdom to understanding moral conduct, you see the value of ethical thought and behavior more profoundly and are led to make even more sweeping changes in the way you act. Similarly, as you see more clearly which mental states are helpful and which you should abandon, you apply effort more skillfully, with the result that your concentration deepens and your wisdom grows.

SUPPORTS FOR PRACTICE

As you get started on the Buddha's path, you will naturally wish to modify your lifestyle and attitudes to support your practice. Here are a few changes that many have found useful in advancing along the path; they will help you overcome obstacles in the work you undertake as you read the following chapters. Do not be dismayed; some of these suggestions present great challenges that you may work with for quite a long time.

Simplify Your Life

A good place to begin is by honestly assessing your habitual daily activities. Look also at how you spend your time. Make a habit of asking yourself, "Is this task or behavior really necessary or is it just a way to be busy?" If you can reduce or eliminate some activities, you will achieve greater peace and quiet, which is essential to advancing in the training.

Right now you may have many responsibilities to your family or others who depend upon you. This is good, but be careful not to sacrifice opportunities to calm your mind and develop insight. Helping others is important, but as the Buddha stated clearly, tending to your own development is a priority.

Cultivate the inclination to spend time each day in solitude and silence, rather than always being in the company of others. If all your time is spent with other people, it's easy to get caught up in unnecessary activities and conversations. That makes it harder to maintain a contemplative practice. No matter where you live, if you wish to deepen your understanding and wisdom, from time to time get away from your commitments and spend time alone.

Of course, outer quiet is not always enough. Even in a quiet and solitary place, we sometimes find ourselves besieged by anger, jealousy, fear, tension, anxiety, greed, and confusion. We've also experienced times when our minds are completely quiet and peaceful despite all the commotion around us.

The Buddha explained this paradox. If we have little attachment and craving, he said, we can live in solitude in the midst of a crowd. We can let go of our sense of possession and ownership. Our loved ones, our possessions, our jobs, our obligations and ties, our views and opinions—all these we cling to. As we reduce our grasping, we move closer to inner freedom, the essence of solitude. Real solitude is in the mind. A person whose mind is free of the bonds of possessiveness and attachment, said the Buddha, is "one living alone." And someone whose mind is crowded with greed, hatred, and delusion is "one who lives with a companion"— even in physical solitude. The best support for our practice, then, is a well-disciplined mind.

Some people may find that traditional rituals help them calm the mind and remind them of what is really important. You and your family can chant together, light incense or a candle, or offer flowers to a Buddha image every day. These simple, beautiful practices will not bring enlightenment, but they can be useful tools to prepare the mind for a daily mindfulness practice.

Exercise Self-Restraint

A well-disciplined life can also be a source of happiness. Take a good look at your physical surroundings. If your bedroom is strewn with dirty laundry, if your desk is a jumble of books, papers, computer disks, and old magazines, and if last week's dishes are still in the sink, how will you be able to organize your mind? Practice develops from the outside in. Clean up your house first and then move inside to sweep away the dust of attachment, hatred, and ignorance.

Practice also benefits from a healthy body. Yoga and other forms of physical exercise contribute to our mental health. At least take a long walk each day. Walking is both good exercise and an opportunity to practice mindfulness in solitude and silence.

A healthy and moderate diet also supports spiritual practice. Eating a good breakfast, a reasonably substantial lunch, and a light supper will make you feel comfortable the next morning. There is an old saying, "Eat your breakfast like a king, share your lunch with your friend, and give your dinner to your enemy." (I would add, however, that you should not do something that could hurt your enemy!) Junk food, alcohol, coffee, and other stimulants make it more difficult to concentrate. Eat to live, don't live to eat. Try not to make eating a mindless habit. Some practitioners engage in an occasional fast, which quickly demonstrates that much of what we think of as hunger is really just habit.

Finally, discipline yourself to meditate every day. A session of meditation in the morning as soon as you get up and in the evening before you go to bed will help you progress. If you find that you are unable to maintain a regular practice, ask yourself why. Perhaps you doubt the importance of meditation, or fear that it will not help you solve your problems. Examine your doubts and fears carefully. Read the life stories of the Buddha and others who have used meditation to achieve permanent happiness. Remember that you alone can change your life for the better and that meditation has proven effective for countless others. Then apply a bit of self-control, especially at the beginning, to maintain the discipline of regular, daily meditation.

Cultivate Goodness

The cultivation of goodness—generosity, patience, faith, and other virtues—is the beginning of spiritual awakening.

Generosity is taught in every religious tradition, but it is a natural state of mind that all living beings possess inherently. Even animals share their food. When you are generous, you feel happy, and you delight in remembering the recipient's joy.

Also practice patience. Being patient does not mean giving someone free rein to abuse you. It means biding your time and expressing yourself effectively at the right time, at the right place, with the right words and the right attitude. If you impatiently blurt out something, you may regret what you say and cause pain.

Patience also means trying to understand others as best you can. Misunderstanding, misinterpretation, and suspicion cause pain and dissatisfaction. Remember that others have as many problems as you—maybe more. Some very good people are sometimes in a bad place and may say or do things unmindfully. If you remain patient in spite of provocation, you can avoid getting upset, and your understanding of the human situation will deepen.

Try not to blame others for your pain or expect others to make you happy. Look within, discover why you are unhappy, and find a way to be content. Unhappy people tend to make others unhappy. But if you're surrounded by unhappy people, you can maintain your peace of mind by keeping your mind as clear as possible—and your patience and understanding might cheer them up.

Finally, have faith in your potential for lasting happiness. This includes confidence in your religious teaching, in yourself, in your work, in your friends, and in the future. Faith or confidence leads to an optimistic attitude to life. You can increase your confidence through examining your own experience. You already have evidence of your many abilities. Have faith as well in those you have not yet manifested.

Find a Teacher and Explore the Teachings

A good meditation center and a meditation teacher who is sincerely willing to assist you are important aids. You don't want a teacher who requires submission or promises magical powers. You are looking for someone who knows more than you, whose life is exemplary, and with whom you can develop a long-term relationship. The Buddha's path may take several years—in some cases, several lifetimes. Choose your guide wisely.

The Buddha described the perfect teacher as "a good friend." Such a person speaks gently, kindly, and earnestly, respects you, and is caring and compassionate. A good friend never asks you to do anything wrong, but always encourages you to do the right thing and helps whenever you need assistance. A good friend is learned and resourceful, ready to share knowledge with you without hesitation.

Observe a potential teacher carefully. Deeds are more important than words. Daily contact with someone who has followed the Buddha's path for at least ten years is a good way to see for yourself whether the teachings work. Beware of teachers who charge high fees; they may be more interested in your money than your spiritual development.

Just as a master craftsman trains apprentices, not just in the techniques of the craft, but also in the personal characteristics needed to apply those skills, so, too, a good teacher both guides your practice and helps you make the lifestyle changes necessary to support it. If you are really seeking happiness, take the time and make the effort to apprentice yourself to such a master.

Next, follow the course of gradual training that the Buddha prescribed. The gradual training essentially involves learning how to quiet down and observe your thoughts and behavior and then to change them into something more conducive to meditation and awareness. It is a slow process, not to be hurried. One reason why so many people drop meditation is that they haven't taken the time to lay the foundation for effective practice.

Finally, make time to read and discuss the Buddha's teachings. Books are readily available, as are discussion groups and classes. You can even talk about the Buddha's message online and via email lists. Reading about and discussing the Buddha's teachings is never a waste of time.

While these requirements for progress might seem obvious, very few of us live quietly, eat moderately, exercise regularly, and live simply. Even fewer study with a qualified teacher, discuss the Buddha's teachings regularly, and meditate daily. This emphasis on simplicity and moderation does not mean that you cannot start to follow the Buddha's path right now, whatever your lifestyle. It simply tells you what you may need to do over a period of years—or even lifetimes—in order to advance toward the highest happiness.

BEGINNING A PRACTICE OF MINDFULNESS

The lifestyle changes mentioned in the previous section have one goal: to help you make mindfulness a part of your daily life. Mindfulness is a unique method of cultivating moment-by-moment awareness of the true nature of everything experienced through the body and mind. You may have heard it called "vipassana meditation." It is a skill that you will develop and use throughout every stage of the Buddha's path to happiness. Here are some suggestions for beginning a practice of mindfulness meditation.

Sitting Meditation

A good time to start your practice of sitting meditation is early in the morning, before you begin your day's activities. A quiet place is preferable, but as there are few noiseless places in the world, choose a place that is congenial for concentration and arrange a comfortable cushion there.

Next, choose a posture for your sitting practice. The best—but most difficult—posture is the full-lotus. Cross your legs and rest each foot on the upper part of the opposite thigh, the sole turned upward. Place your hands just below the level of the navel, with the bend of the wrists pressed against the thighs, bracing the upper part of the body. Your spinal column is straight like a stack of coins, each vertebra atop another. Your chin is up.

If you cannot sit in the full-lotus posture, try the half-lotus. Put your right foot over the left thigh (or the opposite), resting your knees on the floor. Then bend forward and tug the cushion behind. If touching the floor with your knees is difficult, then rest one thigh on the bend of the other foot.

You may also sit with the left or right lower leg in front of the other on the floor. Or, you may sit on a small bench, such as those provided in meditation halls. If all of these are difficult, you may sit on a chair.

After selecting one of these positions, straighten your back and make sure it is perpendicular so your chest can expand easily when you breathe. Your posture should be natural and supple, not stiff.

Settle into your posture carefully, because it's important not to change your position until the end of the meditation period. Why is this important? Suppose you change your position because it is uncomfortable. After a while, the new position becomes uncomfortable, too. Then you want another, and soon it too becomes uncomfortable. So you go on shifting, moving, changing from one position to another for the whole time you are on the cushion rather than gaining a deeper level of concentration. Exercise self-control and stay in your original position.

Determine at the start how long you are going to meditate. If you have never meditated, begin with about twenty minutes. As you repeat your practice, you can gradually increase your sitting time. The length of your session depends on how much time you have available and how long you can sit without pain.

When you are seated, close your eyes; this will help you concentrate. The mind before meditation is like a cup of muddy water. If you hold the cup still, the mud settles and the water clears. Similarly, if you keep quiet, holding your body still and focusing your attention on your object of meditation, your mind will settle down and you will begin to experience the joy of meditation.

Dealing with Pain

Suppose you have followed the instructions on posture and are sitting in the most comfortable position. Soon you realize that your comfort has vanished. Now there's pain, and you lose your original determination, your patience, and your enthusiasm for sitting in meditation.

It can be discouraging. But rest assured that the pain is mostly due to lack of practice. With practice, it diminishes, and you also find it easier to tolerate. So let pain become a signal to renew your determination to practice more.

If pain occurs due to a physical defect such as a dislocated disk or a past injury, then you should change your posture—perhaps moving to a bench or a chair. If, however, you are feeling pain in a normal, healthy part of the body, I suggest you try the following.

The most effective but most difficult way to deal with pain is to watch it. Be with the pain, merge with it. Experience it without thinking of it as my pain, my knee, my neck. Simply watch the pain closely and see what happens to it.

At first the pain may increase, which may cause fear. For example, your knee may begin to hurt so much that you fear you'll lose your leg—it will get gangrene and have to be amputated—which leads you to wonder how you'll get by with only one leg. Don't worry. I have never seen anybody lose a leg to meditation! When that pain that you're watching comes to its most excruciating point, if you wait patiently for, say, another five minutes, you will see this frightening, life-threatening pain begin to break up. The pain will change to a neutral sensation, and you will discover that even a painful feeling is impermanent.

You can use a similar technique with psychological pain, perhaps due to some guilt or traumatic memory. Don't try to push the pain away. Welcome it. Stay with it, even if some awful scenario plays out in your mind. Without getting lost in the story line, keep watching that psychological pain and see it eventually break up, just like physical pain.

When the breakthrough happens and the pain disappears, you may feel great relief, a peaceful and relaxing calm. Of course, the body pain or the painful memory may arise again. But once you have broken through a particular physical or psychological pain, that particular pain will never recur with the same intensity. And the next time you sit, you'll probably sit longer before the pain arises.

The second strategy for dealing with pain is to compare it with the pain you have experienced throughout your life. This present pain, although it seems so difficult now, is only a small portion of the pain you have experienced, and you have endured far worse. And don't forget the subtle, background feeling of dissatisfaction that haunts you day and night. Compared to these other pains, this small pain in your leg is not so great. It's worth bearing with it so that you can overcome the greater and more pervasive pains of life. This pain is like a splinter. Removing a splinter hurts a lot, yet you accept that hurt to avoid greater pain later on. In the same way, you can endure the pain of sitting meditation to save yourself from worse troubles in the future.

Another approach is to think of the pain that others are experiencing. Right now, many people are suffering physical and psychological pain due to sickness, exposure, hunger, separation from loved ones, and other serious problems. Remind yourself that compared to this misery, your pain is not so bad.

The fourth approach is to ignore the pain. You deliberately divert your attention to the breath. To help you stay with the breath, you may breathe quickly several times.

My final suggestion, only when all else fails, is to move—very mindfully. Slowly shift the muscles to see if the pain can be reduced with a minimum of change to your posture. If the pain is in your back, note that the back will begin to ache if you have slouched forward. If tension arises in the back, first make a mental survey of your posture, relax, and then gently straighten the back.

Pain in the ankles and knees needs a special approach, because you do not want to create damaging stress on the tendons. If you think the pain may come from a tendon, first try mindfully flexing and relaxing the muscles above and below that joint without changing or shifting your posture. If that does not bring relief, move the leg slowly just enough to alleviate stress on the tendon.

You may wonder what is to be gained from enduring pain. "I started this practice to get rid of my suffering. Why should I suffer more in sitting meditation?" Remember, this is the kind of suffering that can lead to the end of all suffering. When you mindfully observe pain as it arises and disappears and experience the blissful feelings that follow its disappearance, you gain confidence in your ability to withstand pain. More important, because your experience of pain is voluntary and focused, it is a good training ground. You break through your resistance to greater pain in life.

Have patience. Perhaps you have never assumed a meditation posture before, or have done so only occasionally. Perhaps you are accustomed to sitting on chairs and couches. Naturally you will feel some pain when you first sit on the floor in meditation. Have you ever climbed a mountain or ridden a horse? Remember how the body felt the first time you did it, or how sore it felt the next day? If you climb mountains or ride horses daily, however, you soon enjoy it pain-free. It's the same with meditation: you just have to do it again and again, sitting in the same posture every day.

Focus Your Mind

A good way to settle the mind is to focus on the breath. The breath is readily available. You don't have to work hard to find the breath, for it's always flowing in and out through the nostrils. The breath is not involved in any emotion, any reasoning, any choice-making. Keeping your mind on it is a good way to cultivate a neutral state.

You should begin every sitting meditation session with thoughts of loving-friendliness. Sometimes people can directly tap into them and send them to all living beings. More often, you need a method to do so. Begin with yourself and then slowly expand your thoughts of loving-friendliness to include all living beings. I recommend reciting (mentally or aloud) the following passage:

May I be well, happy, and peaceful. May no harm come to me; may no difficulties come to me; may no problems come to me; may I always meet with success. May I also have patience, courage, understanding, and determination to meet and overcome the inevitable difficulties, problems, and failures in life.

After reciting this passage, repeat it, replacing the words "I" and "me" with others, beginning with your parents: "May my parents be well, happy, and peaceful. May no harm come to them..." and so forth. Next recite this passage for your teachers: "May my teachers be well..." Then recite it for your relatives; then for your friends; then for "indifferent persons" (people toward whom you have neutral feelings); then for your adversaries; and finally for all living beings. This simple practice will make it easier to gain concentration in meditation and also help you to overcome any resentment that may arise as you sit.

Next take three deep breaths. As you breathe in and out, notice the expansion and contraction of the lower abdomen, the upper abdomen, and the chest. Breathe fully to expand these three areas of your body. After taking three deep breaths, breathe normally, letting your breath flow in and out freely, effortlessly, and gracefully, focusing your attention on the sensation of the breath on the rims of your nostrils. Most people notice the breath easily at the rims of the nostrils; however, some may prefer to focus on the sensation of the breath touching the upper lip, or in the nose, or in the sinus area, depending on their facial structure. Having chosen a place of focus, simply notice the feeling of breath going in and out.

When you focus your attention on the breath, you feel the beginning, middle, and end of each inhalation and each exhalation. You do not have to make any special effort to notice these three stages of breathing. When one inhalation is complete and before exhaling begins, there is a brief pause. Notice it, and notice the beginning of the exhalation. When the exhalation is complete, there is another brief pause before the next inhalation begins. Notice this brief pause, too. These two pauses occur so briefly that you may not be aware of them. But when you are mindful, you can notice them.

At the beginning, perhaps both the inhalation and the exhalation are long. Notice that, but without thinking or saying "long inhalation, long exhalation." As you notice the feeling of long inhalations and exhalations, your body becomes relatively calm. Then perhaps your breath becomes short. Notice how the short breath feels, again without saying "short breath." Then notice the entire breathing process from beginning to end. Now, perhaps, the breath becomes subtle. Mind and body become calmer than before. Notice this calm and peaceful feeling.

In spite of your efforts to keep focused on your breathing, your mind may wander away. You may find yourself remembering places you visited, people you met, friends you have not seen for a long time, a book you read long ago, the taste of food you ate yesterday. As soon as you notice that your mind is no longer on your breath, mindfully bring it back and anchor it there.

Some people make use of labeling, which is putting words to phenomena that come up in meditation. For example, the meditator may notice thoughts and then say mentally, "Thinking, thinking, thinking." On hearing a sound, the meditator thinks, "Hearing, hearing, hearing."

I don't recommend this technique. The occurrences you may want to label take place so quickly that you have no time to label them. Labeling takes time—time for the thought to arise or the sensation to occur, time to think of words to conceptualize what you are aware of. You cannot label something while it is happening. You can only label something after it has already past. It is sufficient to watch things as they happen and be aware of them.

Mindfulness teaches you direct awareness. It helps you to eliminate intermediaries such as concepts and words. Concepts and words arise after awareness to help you communicate ideas and feelings. In meditation, however, you're not expressing anything to anybody. You're just knowing that seeing should be limited to seeing, that hearing is hearing, touching is touching, knowing is knowing. That's sufficient.

Practice One-Minute Mindfulness

When you get up from your sitting meditation, make a determination to meditate for one minute of every hour throughout the day. You may wonder what you can do in one minute—that's hardly time to find your cushion. Don't worry about finding a cushion. Stay where you are, sitting, standing, lying down—it doesn't matter. Spend fifty-nine minutes of every hour doing whatever you do during the day. But for one minute of that hour, stop whatever you are doing and meditate. You might even set your wristwatch or computer to beep every hour as a reminder.

When you hear the beep, put whatever you have been doing out of your mind and close your eyes. Stay focused on your breathing. If you think you won't know how long a minute is, breathe in and out fifteen times giving undivided attention to the breath. If you spend longer than a minute, don't worry about it. You're not losing anything.

When the minute is up, before opening your eyes resolve to meditate again for a minute at the end of the next hour. Look forward to that minute and build up enthusiasm for it. Also ask yourself, "When am I going to sit and meditate again?"

If you repeat this simple method, by the end of the day, you will have done ten or fifteen minutes of additional meditation. Moreover, by the end of the day, your wish to sit in meditation—strengthened by your thinking of it every hour—will help you find the motivation to sit for a while before bed.

End your day with half an hour of sitting meditation. When you go to bed, keep your mind on your breath as you fall asleep. If you wake up at night, bring your mind to the breath. When you wake up the next morning, your mind will still be on your breath, reminding you to begin your day with sitting meditation.

STEP 1

Right View

Skillful Understanding

THE STORY OF THE BUDDHA'S LIFE is familiar to many of us. We know that Prince Siddhattha left his father's lavish palace, took up the homeless life of a wandering spiritual seeker, and after years of rigorous practice, attained enlightenment while meditating under the Bodhi Tree. When the Buddha arose from meditation, he walked to the city of Benares, now called Varanasi. There, in the Deer Park, he taught for the first time what he had discovered about the path to permanent happiness.

The Buddha's message was simple but profound. Neither a life of self-indulgence nor one of self-mortification can bring happiness. Only a middle path, avoiding these two extremes, leads to peace of mind, wisdom, and complete liberation from the dissatisfactions of life.

The message of the Buddha is traditionally known as the Four Noble Truths. The last of these four truths sets out eight steps to happiness. He taught us to cultivate skillfulness in our understanding, thinking, speech, action, livelihood, effort, mindfulness, and concentration.

In this and the following chapters we will examine these steps in detail. You'll notice that three aspects—understanding, effort, and mindfulness—come up repeatedly in each step. These are the cardinal points of the path. All the steps are intertwined, but no step functions without the strong application of understanding, effort, and mindfulness.

You walk this path by bringing mindful awareness to every aspect of your daily life, continually working toward greater wholesomeness and applying proper understanding. As the mind settles down, insights begin to arise.

Some insights feel like a gentle "aha!" when some part of your life or the world suddenly becomes clear. Other insights feel profound, as though the whole earth has been shaken by your new knowledge. There may be a feeling of release, followed by a powerful sense of well-being or bliss that can last for hours or even for days. These wonderful experiences are not enlightenment. They just hint at what full enlightenment may be like.

But there may come a moment when all the factors of the eight steps are in place. Morality is perfected; concentration is deep and strong; the mind is bright and clear without any hindrances present. Then you may have a most profound insight—that all experience is impersonal and impermanent in every way, that nothing is worth clinging to. At that moment, all your doubts disappear, and the way you see everything changes.

From that time on, you walk the path on a whole new level. Before this point, you must already have had a good, clear intellectual understanding of the way all the parts of the path fit together. After that profound insight, your understanding reaches a higher level, called the "beyond worldly" level, and you proceed with supreme confidence. You know that no matter what, you will reach your goal.

In anything we do, the first step is to know why we're doing it. That's why the Buddha made Skillful Understanding the first step on his path to happiness. He wanted us to understand that the Buddhist path is not some abstract notion of "promising to be good" so that we can get some reward, not some mysterious code of behavior we have to follow to belong to a secret club.

Rather, the Buddha's path is grounded in common sense and in careful observation of reality. He knew that if we open our eyes and look carefully at our lives, we will understand that the choices we make lead either to happiness or unhappiness. Once we understand this principle thoroughly, we will make good choices, because we do want to be happy.

As the Buddha explained it, Skillful Understanding has two parts: understanding cause and effect, and understanding the Four Noble Truths.

UNDERSTANDING CAUSE AND EFFECT

Buddhists may describe actions as being right or wrong, good or bad, moral or immoral, but they intend a somewhat different meaning than these words usually convey. "Skillful or unskillful" probably explains the idea best. The basis of Buddhist morality is that acting in unskillful ways leads to unhappy results, and acting in skillful ways leads to happy results. This simple principle of cause and effect is an aspect of what Buddhists call kamma (or karma).

Even though unskillful deeds may bring temporary happiness—when, for example, a drug dealer is pleased with his shiny new car, or when you feel self-righteous gratification in causing pain to someone who has hurt you—the Buddha pointed out that wrong actions always lead to harm. Our own observations confirm this truth. Some of the harm may not be visible, such as the mental suffering of guilt and remorse. Other kinds of harm may not manifest immediately. The results of skillful and unskillful actions, the Buddha explained, may come to someone far, far in the future, even beyond this lifetime.

You may think, "I'm not worried about a future lifetime, I just want what I can get out of this life." The Buddha advised us to consider these possibilities: Even if there is no future life, doing wholesome things will bring me happiness and a clear conscience in this life. If it turns out that there is a future life beyond death, I will be doubly rewarded—now and again later. On the other hand, if there is no future life, acting in an unwholesome way will make me feel miserable and guilty in this life. And if it turns out that there really is a future life beyond death, I will suffer again later. Thus, whether there is a future life or not, letting go of unwholesomeness and cultivating wholesomeness guarantees our happiness.

Once we understand that everything we think, say, or do is a cause that leads inevitably to some effect, now or in the future, we will naturally want to think, say, and do things that lead to positive results and avoid those thoughts, words, and deeds that lead to negative ones. Recognizing that causes always lead to results helps us accept the consequences of past actions. It also helps us focus our attention on making choices that can lead to a happier future.

Skillful actions are those that create the causes for happiness, such as actions motivated by loving-friendliness and compassion. Any action that comes from a mind not currently filled with greed, hatred, or delusion brings happiness to the doer and to the receiver. Such an action is, therefore, skillful or right.

Suppose, for example, that you consistently cultivate generosity and loving-friendliness toward all. This good behavior is a cause. Of what results? You'll make lots of friends, many will love you, and you'll feel relaxed and peaceful. People around you may be angry and unhappy, but you won't be.

Your positive behavior has generated two types of immediate results. The first is internal—how you feel. Since you have been consistently generous and loving and have reflected upon your acts of generosity and love, your mind is peaceful and happy. The second is external: other people appreciate you and care for you. While their caring is certainly pleasant, it is less important than how you feel. Since external effects are dependent on the response of others, they are less reliable.

Once we understand this principle, its opposite also becomes clear. The Buddha pointed to ten actions that are always unskillful because they inevitably cause suffering. Three are actions of the body: killing, stealing, and sexual misconduct. Four are actions of speech: lying, malicious words, harsh language, and useless talk. The last three are actions of the mind: covetousness, ill will, and wrong view of the nature of reality.

What is meant by each of these ten actions and how we can avoid them is explained in detail in later steps of the path. Before we can even begin to practice the Buddha's path, however, we need enough basic understanding to see that these ten actions are unskillful because they inevitably bring deep suffering both to the doers and the recipients.

Refraining from these ten actions is not a list of commandments but a set of voluntary principles to follow out of conviction. Nobody can force them upon you. You have to find out for yourself, from your own experience and from your observations of the experiences of others, whether such actions lead to positive results or negative ones. Your experience will tell you that unskillful behaviors bring about physical and psychological pain to yourself and others.

Moreover, people engage in such misdeeds only when their understanding is faulty and their minds are polluted by greed, hatred, or delusion. In fact, any action that comes from a mind filled with greed, hatred, or delusion leads to suffering and is thus unskillful or wrong.

Buddhist morality is rational behavior based on this principle of cause and effect. You have to be lying to yourself about causes and effects to act wrongfully. The worse your behavior, the bigger your lie has to be. What deep insight, what release, will you ever reach if you deliberately feed your delusions with behavior that goes against this basic truth that actions have consequences? If you engage in seriously wrongful behavior, you won't gain much clarity—let alone liberating insight—from the Buddha's path. You must embrace this morality. That's essential.

Mindfulness meditation increases awareness of the devastating consequences of immoral behavior. The meditator vividly experiences the painful effects of unwholesome thoughts, words, and deeds and urgently feels the need to give them all up.

You alone are the author of your future—experience teaches you that. Your behavior is not an unchangeable law of nature. At every moment, you have the opportunity to change—to alter your thoughts, your speech, your actions. If you train yourself to be mindful of what you do, and ask yourself whether it's likely to lead to positive results or negative, you'll be guiding yourself in the right direction.

Repeated good intentions can generate a powerful inner voice that will keep you on track. It will remind you—whenever you trap yourself in a cycle of unhappiness—that you can get out of that trap. Periodically you will have glimpses of what it is like to be free. You make this vision a reality by acting in positive ways and letting go of misery.

Thus morality—defined as actions in accordance with reality—is the foundation of all spiritual progress. Without this, nothing of the path will work to reduce suffering.

The idea that actions have their corresponding results is the first part of Skillful Understanding. Now you must add to it a good comprehension of the Four Noble Truths.

UNDERSTANDING THE FOUR NOBLE TRUTHS

The Buddha himself said that he taught only four ideas: dissatisfaction, cause, end, and path. "Dissatisfaction" refers to the unhappiness we feel in our lives. "Cause" is the reason for this unhappiness: our undisciplined, grasping mind. "End" is the Buddha's promise that we can end suffering by eradicating our craving. "Path" is the eight steps we must take to reach this goal.

In his forty-five years of teaching, from the time of his first sermon in the Deer Park until his death, the Buddha explained these four words hundreds of times. He wanted to make sure that these essential ideas could be understood by people with different temperaments at various stages of spiritual growth.

On one occasion, he explained that dissatisfaction with the suffering of life is a burden. We cause our dissatisfaction by taking up the burden. We end it by putting the burden down. The path tells us how to unburden ourselves. Another time, he called dissatisfaction a sickness. Like a doctor, the Buddha diagnoses the cause of the sickness. The end of the sickness is Dr. Buddha's cure, and the path is the medicine he prescribes to make us well.

Understanding the First Truth: Dissatisfaction

The Buddha's first truth tells us that dissatisfaction is unavoidable. You may wonder, "Is this teaching on dissatisfaction relevant to the modern world in which so many discoveries have made our lives more comfortable? In the time of the Buddha, people must have suffered from the elements, disease, and natural disasters. But doesn't our current technological know-how allow us to do whatever we want, go anywhere we wish, and manufacture anything we need?"

Yet, no matter how easy and safe our modern lives may seem, the truth of dissatisfaction has not changed. It is as relevant now as it was in the Buddha's time. People back then were dissatisfied, and so are we.

We may call the Buddha's first truth any number of names depending on the situation: suffering, stress, fear, tension, anxiety, worry, depression, disappointment, anger, jealousy, abandonment, nervousness, or pain. All human beings, no matter when or where they live, are subject to these problems.

We may fall ill at any time. We may be separated from our loved ones. We may lose what we have or be forced by circumstances to put up with conditions we despise. Parents and children, husbands and wives, brothers and sisters, neighbors and friends, communities and countries—all quarrel over wealth, position, power, and boundaries. Some of these problems are created by greed, some by hatred, others by ignorance. All of them relate to conditions both in the world—social, political, economic, educational, environmental—and in ourselves.

Recognizing the inevitability of these problems triggers pain in our minds. Acknowledging them and accepting them as they really are, without blaming others, is the essence of the Buddha's first truth. To get started toward happiness, he told us, we need to look at dissatisfaction straight on—with stable emotions and a steady mind—without getting angry or feeling depressed or pessimistic. We must look squarely at our predicament: every experience of life brings some degree of suffering to anyone not fully enlightened.

The suffering may be extremely subtle, perhaps an underlying subtle restlessness. Or it may be more obvious, some strong attachment to a person, possession, or opinion. It all depends on how much greed, hatred, and delusion we have, and on our personalities and past experiences.

Consider, for example, two people who witness the same event but have completely different impressions. One finds the event happy and agreeable; the other, frightening and terrible. Happiness and its opposite are mind-made. Our minds create our life experiences, and our minds either enjoy those creations or suffer because of them. That is why the Buddha spoke of our creating heaven and hell in this very life.

Until we attain enlightenment, many kinds of experiences cause powerful dissatisfaction for us all. Let's look at three: the life cycle, change, and having no control of our lives.

THE LIFE CYCLE

The inevitable round of the human life cycle—birth, aging, sickness, death—gives rise to dissatisfaction.

Babies are not born with big smiles on their faces. As we grow, the cry with which we first greeted the world becomes less audible. We might say that it changes to an inward cry that continues for the rest of our lives. We cry for so many gallons of milk; so many tons of food; so many yards of clothes; so many square feet of land for housing, schools, and hospitals; so many trees for making books, papers, furniture; so many pills for various sicknesses; so many people to love us; so many ways to try to fill our neediness. If we had not been born into this unsatisfactory world, all other kinds of dissatisfaction would not come into existence. With every baby, it seems, unhappiness, too, is born.

Society as a whole also suffers as a result of birth. As the earth's population increases, the pollution of our air, water, and land grows alarmingly. With so many mouths to feed, resources are depleted, and hunger stalks many parts of the planet. More forests are cleared to build roads and houses. Overcrowded living conditions contribute to the spread of terrible diseases. These are but a few examples. You can, no doubt, think of many more.

The aging process also gives rise to dissatisfaction. We've probably forgotten the adjustments we made in childhood to a new neighborhood or a new teacher, but we can remember the difficulties we had as teenagers adjusting to our changing bodies and emotions. In adulthood we have to adjust to new jobs, new relationships, new technologies, new diseases, new social conditions, often before we are fully at ease with existing ones. Uncomfortable changes seem to be common to every stage of life.

As we grow old, the problem of adjusting to change becomes more conspicuous. It is painful to lose the physical well-being we had when we were young. We know that aging is inevitable, but we wish it were not. Thus we suffer.

When the Buddha said that aging gives rise to unhappiness, he was really talking about growth and decay generally. We know that every cell in our body is decaying or dying, and new cells are continually taking their place. Every state of mind also disappears and a new one arises.

Eventually, this process of decay and change weakens the body and mind, causing our physical death.

Illness is obviously another cause of dissatisfaction. Everybody knows how painful sickness is. Sickness actually causes two kinds of pain: fear of sickness and its direct experience. Thus sickness is a continuing source of anxiety, causing suffering when we are ill and fear when we are healthy.

People generally think that pain and dissatisfaction are synonymous, but they are not. Though you can't avoid the pain of injury and disease, it is possible to avoid dissatisfaction as a result of the pain. As you grow less attached to your body feeling a particular way, you become less dissatisfied when it feels different. For instance, when Devadatta threw a rock and wounded the Buddha's foot, the Buddha experienced pain. But because he understood the nature of pain, he did not suffer like ordinary people. Pain sensations are usually manageable. Dissatisfaction with "what is" is more profound and harder to overcome.

The fourth form of suffering in the life cycle is death—not just the moment of death but also everything that leads up it. We all fear death and worry about how and when we might die. We also know that when we die, we will have to leave everything behind. Can we bear that? When a loved one dies, we experience shock, grief, and loss which can last for years if not forever.

But the dissatisfactions of the life cycle do not end with death. The Buddha taught that death does not bring the cycle of dissatisfaction to a close. Someone who has gone through a lot may say, when nearing death, "I don't want any more of this." But that mere wish cannot stop the life cycle from continuing. As long as we are ignorant of the true nature of reality, this life links to another. As long as desire, hatred, and ignorance exist in our consciousness, the endless round of rebirth—the cycle of past, present, and future lives—will continue.

Within that cycle, the dissatisfactions that we have mentioned recur again and again. The energy of all these experiences is like a backpack that we carry from life to life through countless rebirths. In each new life, its contents are simply transferred into new baggage. When we die, nothing material goes with us. Yet that same backpack of energy—the imprints of all the mental activities and all the intentional words and deeds of this and previous lifetimes—not only travels with us but actually initiates the new life.

Until we have emptied our backpacks—until we have exhausted the results of all we have created through desire, hatred, or ignorance over countless lifetimes—we cannot escape perpetual death and rebirth. We can use this thought to motivate us to do whatever we can in this lifetime to achieve the permanent happiness of liberation.

We have already mentioned desire and hatred as strong motivations for our actions, but what does the Buddha mean by ignorance? And why is it so critical to the dissatisfactions we feel?

Ignorance in the Buddhist sense is both "not knowing"—as in not knowing what the Buddha meant by the Four Noble Truths—and "wrong knowing"—believing that we understand the way the world works when we do not.

Ignorant of the truth of dissatisfaction, we believe that a new job, a new house, or a new partner will bring us genuine happiness. Ignorant of how the energy of our words and deeds travels with us from this life to the next, we allow greed, hatred, doubt, and jealousy to motivate us. Ignorant that a simple and disciplined life, good friends, meditation, and mindful investigation of the true nature of our experience will bring us happiness in this life and in lives to come, we make millions of excuses for not engaging in these positive activities.

We are ignorant even of our ignorance. After a particularly deep teaching on the nature of reality, the Buddha's attendant Ananda said to him, "Venerable sir, this teaching appears to be very deep, but it is as clear to me as clear can be."

The Buddha replied, "No, no, do not say that! It not only seems to be deep, but it is deep." (D 15)

Because of his ignorance, Ananda's understanding of the Buddha's message was not yet complete, and thus he did not attain liberation at that moment. Like Ananda, our ignorance keeps us spinning through the life cycle's many dissatisfactions.

CHANGE

Change also dissatisfies us. No matter what we do, change separates us from what we love and presents us with what we hate. Death and distance divide us from people we love. Friends move away. Partners reject us. Such separations hurt a lot. Losing anything to which we are attached makes us angry and sad. Even something trivial can cause grief when it breaks or disappears.

Once when I was four years old I drew a perfect circle around me with my finger tip as I sat in the sand. Was I pleased! My sister, who was about seven, came by and rubbed away my circle with her foot. I became so angry I chased her, picked up a small but heavy wooden bench, and threw it at her. She still has a scar on one of her toes. All that upset and rage, all those tears and pain, caused by something so silly and transient as a circle in the sand!

Not only do we lose things we love, we are continually confronted by people and conditions we wish did not exist—at least not here, not right now. Living or working day in, day out with someone we do not like causes much unhappiness. Even something we cannot control, like the weather, makes us dissatisfied. At the Bhavana Society in West Virginia where I teach, people complain when it is hot and sticky. But they also complain when it is rainy and cool. When it is dry, they complain that their skin or their sinuses are affected. When it is cold, they complain because they fear they will slip on the ice. And when the weather is perfect, they complain that they do not have time to enjoy it!

When we look around us, it's clear that everything that exists causes dissatisfaction. Why is this so? Actually, everything in the world exists as the result of a cause. Changes in the barometric pressure, winds, and temperature are causes of rain. A tree is caused by the seed from which it grows and the sunlight, soil, and water that nurture it. Our lives, too are the product of causes and conditions—the direct physical cause of our parents' procreation and the cause of the energetic imprints we accumulated during our previous lifetimes.

The Buddha called these and everything else that arises from causes "conditioned things." He explained that all conditioned things are characterized by three qualities. First, they are impermanent. Over time, everything—mountains and mayflies, marshmallows and microchips—breaks down, changes, or dies. Second, because of these changes, all conditioned things are unsatisfactory. As we have seen, every changing thing can give rise to suffering. Third, all conditioned things are selfless or soulless. This last quality is the most difficult to understand, so let's put it aside for a moment.

Impermanence is pretty easy to understand. The fact that things are temporary is not the problem. Rather, it's the attachment we have to people and things—like my circle in the sand—that makes us unhappy. Say we have a new jacket that we like enormously. After wearing it only a few times, we get some wet paint on it, or we tear it on something, or we leave it on a bus. We feel annoyed.

A ruined or lost jacket is no great tragedy, of course, and we can easily replace it. But what if the jacket was a gift from someone we love? What if we bought it to remember a special birthday, anniversary, or trip? Then we're really attached to it, and its loss or damage saddens us deeply.

Sometimes people get upset when they hear discussions like this. "How about happiness?" they ask. "Why don't we talk about that? Why don't we talk about joy, delight, and pleasure instead of dissatisfaction all the time?"

The answer, my friends, is change. Because of impermanence, anything that is pleasant, happy, or delightful, does not remain so. As intelligent, mature people, we must talk about what's really happening without getting upset. We must look it right in the eye, this dissatisfaction caused by change, and acknowledge it. Why hide it and pretend that everything's rosy?

When we look at change head on, we may begin to see that it has an up side as well. We can count on the fact that whatever conditions exist in our lives will also change. Things may get worse. But they may also improve. Because of impermanence, we have the opportunity to learn, develop, grow, teach, memorize, and make other positive changes, including practicing the Buddha's path. If everything about us were set in concrete, none of these changes would be possible. The uneducated would stay uneducated. The poor and hungry would stay poor and hungry. We would have no chance to end our hatred, greed, or ignorance and their negative consequences.

Okay, we understand impermanence and the dissatisfaction it causes. Now, what about this selflessness or soullessness? What do they have to do with change? The Buddha taught that the things and beings of this

world are selfless or soulless precisely because they are always changing. We and everything around us are not static, permanent entities. We
cannot affix a "me" or "mine" label to anything in the universe. It all
changes too quickly.

With our changing body and our changing feelings, perceptions,
thoughts, consciousness, habits, and intentions, how can we point to
something and say, "This is mine" or "This is me"? Even the idea or
belief "this is me" changes right away. For convenience, we may say "I
am here" or "this belongs to me," but we should say these words wisely
and not be fooled into thinking that they imply the existence of an
unchanging entity, the "I" or "me." Physical objects also change continually. We may use conventional labels and say "this is a chair" or
"this is a chimpanzee," but these labels barely fit the changing reality
that we experience.

Rather, we and everything else are in process, in a continual flux of
growth and decay, buildup and breakdown. Nothing about our world or
ourselves is separate or enduring. Watch your mind for one minute and
you'll see what I mean. Memories, emotions, ideas, sensations flicker
across the screen of consciousness so quickly we can hardly catch them.
Therefore, it makes no sense for the mind to grab on to any of these
passing shadows with attachment or to push them away with hatred.
When our mindful attention is quick and sharp, as it is in a state of deep
concentration, then we can clearly see the changes—so clearly that there
is no room left for belief in a self.

Some people feel depressed and disappointed when they hear about
the doctrine of non-self. Some even become angry. They mistakenly
conclude that life has no meaning. They don't understand that a life
lived without a sense of self is most pleasant and meaningful.

Once I gave a manuscript of an article to a friend to edit. He was a
professional editor, and I figured that the job would take him about an
hour. Yet for six months I heard nothing from him. He finally came for
a visit, and we went for a walk. When he said nothing about my article,
I sensed this would be a delicate topic. Very gently and hesitantly I
broached the subject. I asked, "Have you had time to take a look at my
article?" He remained silent for a long moment and then replied,
"Bhante G, I looked at it. When I came across the teaching of non-self,

I became so angry I threw away the whole manuscript!" I was amazed, but I did not get upset with him. Instead I let go of my attachment to the article I had written. He had thrown away my manuscript because of non-self, so I threw away the self associated with the manuscript. I was able to stay relaxed, friendly, and peaceful. This man, however, became rigid, uptight, and unhappy, due to his clinging to self.

So you see how hard it can be to accept this notion of non-self. Yet so long as you retain this notion of self you'll feel uncomfortable, rigid, and grasping, and people will find your egotistical self unpleasant. You'll get upset or angry when someone disagrees with you or blames you for something, when things disappoint you or don't go your way, and even when somebody offers you constructive criticism. Correctly understanding this idea of non-self, you'll feel relaxed and comfortable. You'll mix easily with people of any nationality, you won't feel any more or less important than others, you'll adapt easily to any situation, and everyone will feel comfortable around you.

By truly understanding selflessness you can feel happy and comfortable wherever you go, whether you are treated well or ill. Don't let this teaching make you depressed and don't let it make you angry.

For now, we must be content with trying to accept this idea intellectually. As our practice of mindfulness continues, however, we can look forward to the day when we will perceive the selflessness and soullessness of all phenomena directly. When we do, the unhappiness that comes as a result of change will end for us, forever.

The Buddha and the other great beings who have attained full enlightenment are proof of this. The Buddha was completely free of the concept of "I." Of course, the Buddha continued to live in society after he achieved enlightenment. For conventional purposes and to make communication easy, he continued to use conventional terms, such as "I" or "me." It's okay if you do as well. The name on your driver's license may not be an absolutely accurate label, a guarantee of your permanent identity, but it's a convenient handle for the conventions of everyday life.

But when mindfulness leads you to realize that the "self" you have been protecting so vigorously is, in fact, an illusion—a stream of constantly changing sensations, emotions, and physical states, with no permanence or fixed identity—then there will be no "you" to attach to the impermanent things of this world, and thus no reason for you to be dissatisfied or unhappy.

No Control

If we were really in control of our lives, we'd have no reason to be dissatisfied. But we're not in control. Time after time we don't get what we want, and we get what we don't want.

We want our perfect job, perfect office, perfect boss, and perfect pay to continue forever, but they change, and we have no say about why or when. We want to keep our loved ones, but no matter how tightly we cling to them, someday we'll be separated. To stay healthy we take herbs and vitamins, work out, and eat right, but we still get sick. We want to remain young and strong and hope that old age will happen only to others, but years pass and we discover that our body has other plans. Whatever ideal situation we're in, we naturally wish to hold on to it. But we have no control over the law of impermanence. Everything exists by consent of this law, and we have no protection against it.

It's also painful to have things happen to us that we never wished for. You're stung by a bee. Your favorite TV show is canceled. Someone breaks into your car. You lose your job. A loved one gets cancer. Your precious wedding pictures or baseball memorabilia are lost in a fire. Your child has an accident or gets involved in drugs. Scandal, blame, shame, failure, hunger, loss of goods, loss of love, physical deterioration—so many bad, unwanted things happen to us and to the people we wish to protect. And we have no control over any of it.

"All right!" you may be saying. "Enough already!" But there's one more piece to this picture. If we look carefully, we can see that even getting our wishes fulfilled is also unsatisfying.

Say what you wish for is a beautiful house. So, you buy it, and look at the trouble you have to go through. You have to pay the mortgage, pay the taxes, protect it, secure it, insure it, decorate it, repair and maintain it. And then, you're not home very much anyway. Early in the morning, you go to work. In the evening, maybe you go to a party or a movie, come home to sleep for five or six hours, and then off you go again. The house is very big and very beautiful, no doubt. And you keep paying the bills and cutting the grass and fixing the roof and cleaning out the garage. You have gotten what you wished for, but are you happy?

Look at another example. A boy likes a girl, and she likes him. Each works very hard to attract the other. But from the moment they start their relationship, they are afraid. He fears that she'll fall for some guy who is more handsome, and she fears a more attractive woman will steal him. Jealousy, suspicion, worry. Is this happiness?

You can think of other examples. Just read the newspaper. Read about the lucky fellow who wins the lottery and lives miserably ever after! That's why it is said that there are only two tragedies in life: not getting what one wants, and getting it.

REALISTIC PERCEPTION

The Buddha tried to make it very clear that every single thing in life brings suffering for the unenlightened person. He listed "five aggregates" that include every possible aspect of reality: form, feelings, perceptions, volitional formations, and consciousness. "Form" refers to all material existence—including the body and things that are contacted through the senses.

The other four aggregates cover all mental experience. At the end of a list of all the things that bring suffering, the Buddha said, "In short, the five aggregates of clinging are suffering." (D 22)

What's going on here? Why is it that dissatisfaction touches absolutely every aspect of our lives? As the Buddha explained, our dissatisfaction comes from how we perceive and think about what we experience. How this works is very subtle.

We know that we perceive the world through our senses. We generally talk about five senses, through which we see, hear, smell, taste, and touch. The Buddha also spoke of a sixth sense, the mind, for our minds can also perceive ideas, thoughts, mental pictures, and emotions. So far, so good.

What our senses actually perceive is the raw data of experience or, in the case of the mind, mental pictures of experience—color, shape, size, intensity, pitch, hardness, and grossness or subtlety. We know, of course, that perception can differ from person to person depending on the perceiver's state of mind and senses. A person with a bad cold may have difficulty smelling or tasting. A person whose hearing is impaired may not hear low-pitched sounds. So perception is subjective, depending on the faculties of the person perceiving.

We're aware of these differences, but our mind plays a trick on us. It convinces us that our perception is solid and reliable. It encourages us to take for granted that the qualities we notice are actually part of the thing we're looking at, rather than the result of ever-changing conditions, including the changing conditions of our own senses.

Not only that. After we perceive something, our mind immediately categorizes or judges whatever it is and puts the thing or experience into one of three boxes. The first box is labeled pleasant perceptions—the smell of fresh baked bread, a violin concerto, a brilliant sunset. The second holds unpleasant perceptions—the memory of our father's death, a headache, the wail of a police siren. Into the third go neutral perceptions—all those things and experiences about which we have a neutral reaction.

Then, of course, because our minds are not completely free of attachment, we cling to the pleasant. Because of aversion, we push away the unpleasant. And because of ignorance, we ignore the neutral, and we regard all objects—pleasant, unpleasant, or neutral—as permanent, as possessing a self or soul, and as capable of giving us permanent happiness or causing us permanent misery.

The Buddha explained the effect of this mistaken or unwholesome perception this way:

> Depending on the eye and forms, eye consciousness arises. The meeting of the three is contact. With contact as a condition, there is feeling. What one feels, that one perceives. What one perceives, that one thinks about. What one thinks about, that one mentally proliferates. With what one has mentally proliferated as the source, perception and notions tinged by mental proliferation beset a man with respect to the past, future, and present forms cognizable by the eye [the same regarding the ear, nose, tongue, body, and mind]. (M 18 [translated by Bhikkhu Bodhi])

Realistic or wholesome perception, on the other hand, neither clings nor pushes away. It perceives impermanence as it is, dissatisfaction as it is, and selflessness as it is. When we perceive the world in a wholesome way, we cultivate wholesome thoughts. Realistic perception is powerfully therapeutic. If we could see objects and people as they truly are—as impermanent, unsatisfactory, and selfless or soulless—nothing that we perceive could make us unhappy.

Realistic perception is the goal of mindfulness meditation. Being realistic means not running away from unpleasant facts about ourselves and our world.

Through mindful awareness, we learn to look realistically at existence, which is not always beautiful, pleasant, or happy. We see that life is a mixture of pain and pleasure. We notice physical or mental suffering at its very birth and watch how it arises. We also observe how long it remains and how it disappears. Mindfulness meditation acts like a shock absorber. If you've grown accustomed to facing the dissatisfactions of everyday life and know that they are natural occurrences, when some difficult or painful situation comes your way you'll face it bravely and calmly.

When we can look into the face of suffering without flinching, we will also be able to recognize true happiness.

Understanding the Second Truth: The Cause of Dissatisfaction

The Buddha's second truth tells us that the cause of our dissatisfaction is desire, which we might also call attachment, greed, or grasping. It doesn't seem to matter what it is—a fine meal, a dear friend, an exalted spiritual goal—if we're attached, we'll feel dissatisfied and suffer.

Where, you might ask, does desire come from? Most obviously, it comes from the impulses of the body—the desire to stay alive, the desire for food, clothing, shelter, warmth, variety, pleasure. Desire is built into humans. It is also built into animals. Even plants seem to have some kind of desire, for they turn toward the sun for light and warmth. Another source of desire is social conditioning—all those views and values that we learn from parents, family, friends, schools, advertising, and books that condition us to believe that some things are good and others are bad.

STEP ONE: SKILLFUL UNDERSTANDING

The strongest desire is that based upon pleasurable feelings. Life provides us with overwhelming pleasure through each of our senses. Take, for instance, the sense of sight: your eyes are agreeable and pleasurable. So, too, is eye consciousness agreeable and pleasurable, and so are visual objects, eye contact, feelings about what we see, visual recognition, desire for visual things, thoughts of them, deliberations, fantasies, and so on. Similarly agreeable and pleasurable sensations arise from the ear, nose, tongue, body, and mind. Every single day you have opportunities to get involved in agreeable and pleasurable objects through your senses. Yet you are not happy.

In his second truth, the Buddha asked us to recognize that our attachment to sensual pleasure is dangerous to our happiness. He compared sensual pleasure to a bone with no meat thrown to a hungry dog. Though the dog gnaws on the bone for a long time, the bone never satisfies his hunger. On reflection you may find that you are like that, too. No matter how much sensual pleasure you have, you're still hungry for more.

How many potato chips are enough? How many pieces of chocolate? How many video games must you play or novels must you read to fulfill your longing for such experiences? How much sex would it take for your sexual craving to be satisfied forever? How much alcohol or drugs? Sometimes people stay up and party all night until they pass out. Did they get enough? You can always think of some pleasurable thing that you haven't yet tried.

The Buddha compared sensual pleasures to a razor-sharp sword with honey smeared on the blade. To taste the honey, people are willing to risk great pain. We can all think of examples of people who hurt or even kill themselves seeking pleasure. There was a story in the newspaper a few years back about a worker who was repairing a roof when, looking down through a skylight, he caught sight of the woman of the house walking around in the nude. To get a better view, he leaned so far over the skylight that it gave way; he tumbled into the house and was badly injured.

Alcohol, drugs, adventure travel, dangerous sports—to say nothing of careless sexual behavior—cause many people much suffering.

Moreover, sensual pleasures don't last. Like a dream, pleasures are fleeting. They slip away from you quickly, leaving you nothing to hold on to but your feelings and memories. Like borrowed goods, they are not yours to keep. The more attached you are to a pleasure, the more it hurts when time, change, or circumstance inevitably snatches it away.

Desire arises from feelings of pleasure and pain. When pleasure arises, there is a desire to cling to it and perpetuate it. When pain arises, there is a desire to reject it or turn away from it. Because of your attachment to pleasant feelings and your aversion to unpleasant feelings, you constantly seek experiences that perpetuate the pleasant or reject the unpleasant. Once you have found something that accomplishes this goal, you become biased and prejudiced. This state of mind makes people cling. To protect or hold on to what they have, people are willing to lie, abuse or insult others, and even take up arms to defend what they believe is theirs.

Desire also leads to mental suffering. Due to feelings arising from contact with what is pleasurable—sights, smells, sounds, tastes, touches, and ideas—people think and rationalize, theorize, philosophize, speculate, and conceptualize. They come to hold wrong views and wrong beliefs. Recalling past pleasant sensations, they concoct even more desirous thoughts, beliefs, and theories.

Some people become so obsessed with their desires that they hope to be reborn to enjoy all the pleasant things again. Others, because of unpleasant experiences they have had, desire not to be reborn: "This is it," they say. "One life is enough. I don't need any more of this."

At bottom, desire comes out of ignorance—ignorance that nothing lasts and ignorance that desire creates discomfort. When the senses contact something pleasurable, the ignorant mind develops the intention to grasp and hold on to it. The reverse also occurs. When the senses contact something unpleasant, the ignorant mind develops the intention to escape and avoid it. Because of these intentions, people engage in unskillful actions of body, speech, and mind, despite the consequences. Because of desire, people distort reality and avoid taking personal responsibility for their actions.

ACCEPTING RESPONSIBILITY FOR OUR ACTIONS

The Buddha's teaching on causes and their results makes clear that accepting responsibility for our actions is the foundation for personal well-being and fulfillment. Denying your shortcomings and blaming the world for your discontent keeps you mired in unhappiness. Bad things happen to everyone. As long as you blame your parents or society for your problems, you give yourself an excuse not to change. The moment you accept responsibility for your situation, even though others may have contributed to it, you begin to move in a positive direction.

It seems to me that we distort reality and excuse ourselves from taking personal responsibility in at least three ways. First, we think that our unhappiness is caused by the outside world. As a result, we direct all of our energy and our mental capabilities outward. We get engrossed and sometimes even obsessed in trying to straighten out the people around us, as if their perfection would bring us relief. Or we try to straighten out society, assuming that correcting society's ills will solve our own problems: "When hunger, war, and pollution are eliminated, then I'll be happy."

The desire to improve society is, of course, commendable. We see how dissatisfied people are, we feel compassion, and we act to alleviate their suffering. But often we don't recognize that while trying to correct others people's problems, we forget or suppress our own. Our excuse: there are so many social wrongs that need to be fixed, we have no time to improve ourselves.

In reality, we may lack the honesty and courage to examine our real intentions. While people involved in social action may be very compassionate and service-minded, some of us fail to admit our real motivation. We all know that helping the less fortunate can give us a sense of power that we would not get from working with people who are not dependent on us. The desire for power is a basic instinct. It takes much honesty to see how much of what we do for others springs from this desire. Recognizing the intentions behind our actions can help us focus on the all-important task of putting our own house in order before we try to save others.

The second excuse we use to avoid accepting responsibility for our actions is to insist that there is no problem with us. We focus on our own ends and pleasures and have little regard for how what we do affects others. Deep inside, we may believe that the outside world is unimportant, in a certain way even imaginary. If we could listen to our own thoughts, we'd hear ourselves say, "I alone exist, and only what I care about is important—nothing else matters."

We can all think of public figures who declare certain values while privately acting against those values.

These people focus on helping themselves. Some who are a bit honest admit that they are driven by the desire for financial success, power, or popularity. Still, they have found a way to avoid taking responsibility for the results of their actions. They fool themselves into thinking that the personal goal they pursue is more important than anything else. They fool themselves into believing that if they reach their goal they'll be happy, no matter who gets hurt along the way.

The third way we avoid our personal problems is simply running away from them. We all do this. Watching television or raiding the refrigerator for chocolate ice cream are typical ways to avoid honest self-reflection. You lull your mind and body into comfort and relaxation, and then you go to bed. Time passes. Except for getting older and fatter, nothing changes. The challenge is to have the courage to ask why.

At one time or another, we have all indulged in these kinds of escapes from responsibility, and they have given us some temporary solace, some very brief comfort. But none offer a genuine or lasting solution to our problems. Whether you try to change the world, ignore the world, or distract yourself from the world, you cannot avoid ultimate responsibility for your actions. Life has its ups and downs, and we create them. This vehicle of ours—our mind-body combination—is full of difficult moments. The only thing that works, according to the Buddha's teaching, is to find a way to improve the only instrument that has the power to make ourselves and the world happy. That instrument is our own mind.

Understanding the Third Truth: The End of Dissatisfaction

The Buddha's third truth is his promise that there is an end to dissatisfaction. That end comes from our completely eradicating all attachment, all desire. Now that we are beginning to understand the causes and consequences of our own behavior and to accept responsibility for our thoughts, words, and deeds, we can see that we have an important part to play in ending our own unhappiness. Yet it is hard for us to imagine at this point what total happiness might feel like. What would it be like never to experience desire or hatred?

This very question came up among Buddha's disciples. One day the Venerable Sariputta, one of the Buddha's two chief disciples and himself an enlightened teacher, was having a discussion with a group of monks. They asked him, "Venerable Sir, this state of permanent happiness, which the Buddha calls nibbana [or nirvana], is said not to be experiential happiness. How can something that is not experienced be called happiness?"

Sariputta answered, "That is why it is called happiness."(A IV (Nines) IV 3)

In other words, happiness consists of what is not experienced. The third truth teaches us that happiness is wiping out all negative states of mind—all desire, all hatred, all ignorance. When we at last succeed in putting out the internal fires that burn our eyes, ears, nose, tongue, body, and mind, then we experience total happiness, total peace. It may be hard to imagine what such a state feels like, but the only way to find out is by following the path toward this goal.

Like many of us, the monks talking to Sariputta wanted to know right at the beginning of the path what its end is like. This is like asking a young girl, "How does it feel when you give birth to a child?" The young girl has never given birth. She has to grow and mature in order to have that experience. She may be able to say something about childbirth from what she's read or heard, but she cannot express the entire experience.

Even her mother might not be able to capture what it's like to give birth. She can describe her own experience, but listeners who have never given birth will still not be able to understand how a mother feels.

The permanent happiness of enlightenment is like this. It can be understood only by those who have completed the preliminary work and gone through the experience themselves.

Suppose that same young girl goes to her father and asks, "Daddy, what is your relationship to Mommy?"

He might reply, "Darling, go out and play. I will tell you later."

Perhaps, when she grows up and is ready to be married, her father says to her, "Long ago you asked me what my relationship with your mother was. Do you want me to answer that question now?"

The daughter replies, "No, Daddy, I know the answer."

The daughter has matured in her understanding. She knows the answer to the question herself. If a worldly experience such as the relationship between a man and a woman is so difficult to explain, imagine how difficult it is to understand the permanent happiness of freedom from dissatisfaction!

At present, our mind is full of ideas, opinions, and views, many of them motivated by desire, hatred, or ignorance. Trying to understand the bliss of permanent happiness before we have eliminated our negative states of mind is impossible. All we can do is quote the similes, parables, and analogies told to us by those who have reached enlightenment and try to come to some inferential understanding. For instance:

> Once a tortoise living among the fish and other sea creatures suddenly disappeared. When he returned, the fish asked him questions about where he had been.
>
> "I went to the land," the tortoise told them.
>
> They asked him, "What is the water there like?"
>
> He replied, "There is no water on the land."
>
> "How did you swim?"
>
> "I didn't swim. I walked."
>
> "Walked? What do you mean 'walked'? And did you find many fish there?"
>
> When the tortoise tried to explain, the fish said, skeptically, "No water; no fish; you can't swim; and you say you 'walked.' How can this be?"
>
> The tortoise answered, "You seem satisfied with your speculations. Let me go back to the land." And with that, he disappeared.

Just as the fish could never conceive of the idea of land, a person who suffers from greed, hatred, and delusion cannot make sense of nibbana. To understand, you must transcend all negative states of mind and experience enlightenment for yourself.

Until you do so, the nearest you can come to experiencing the happiness of enlightenment is the bliss you sometimes achieve when you have momentarily let go of your burden, when the mind is just "mind" with nothing else in it. The inferential understanding you get at such times may be compared to being in the desert and feeling tired and thirsty. You come upon a deep well with some water at the bottom but there is no bucket or rope. You're too weak to hoist up a bucketful anyway. So although you can see the water, you can't taste it, let alone drink any. Similarly, when your mind is temporarily free of greed, hatred, and delusion, you can perceive the peace of nibbana, but you don't necessarily have the tools to reach it. Getting rid of greed is like finding the rope of generosity. Freeing the mind from hatred is like attaching the rope to the bucket of loving-friendliness. Strength in your hands is like wisdom, free of ignorance. When you put these three together, you have the means to taste, at last, the bliss of nibbana.

The bliss of this state is indescribable. Its single characteristic is peace. It is not born, not created, not conditioned. The best we can do is to say what this state does not have. It does not have desire or attachment or grasping after things, people, and experiences. It does not have hatred or aversion or anger or greed. It does not have the fault of seeing things as permanent, as satisfactory, or as possessing an inherent self or soul.

People who are still under the delusion that they are enjoying life as it is here in this unsatisfactory world might hear this description and say, "Enlightenment does not sound like much fun. I'm not sure I want to attain that state. Are there houses there? What about families, schools, medical insurance, hospitals, good roads, and so forth?" I have been asked this question.

We would have to answer no. One who remains attached to life, this endless existence, does not have the clarity of mind to want to attain the state of permanent bliss. This person has not understood the Buddha's first truth, that dissatisfaction is unavoidable, or his second truth, that to whatever degree we desire, to that degree we suffer. Without Skillful Understanding of these essential points, it is impossible to understand the Buddha's third truth—that dissatisfaction ends when we cease all attachment, all desire.

You might be wondering whether it is all right to have the desire to achieve enlightenment and escape the endless round of rebirth.

The answer is yes, this is very good desire—called "the desire to be desireless."

Understanding the Fourth Truth: The Path

The Buddha's fourth truth is the path that leads to the end of dissatisfaction. Its eight steps bring peace and happiness to those who follow them. Later we'll examine each step in detail, but let's look at them quickly:

- Step one: Skillful Understanding of the Buddha's message requires that we understand skillful behavior in terms of cause and effect and the Four Noble Truths and how they fit into the overall scheme of the Buddha's teachings.

- Step two: Skillful Thinking introduces us to three positive thoughts—generosity or letting go, loving-friendliness, and compassion.

- Step three: Skillful Speech explains how telling the truth and avoiding malicious talk, harsh language, and gossip can help us advance on the path.

- Step four: Skillful Action lays out the principles for leading an ethical life—especially abstaining from killing, stealing, sexual misconduct, and intoxication.

- Step five: Skillful Livelihood explains why choosing an appropriate job or profession is important to our spiritual practice and how we should approach questions of business ethics.

- Step six: Skillful Effort lays out four steps we can take to motivate our practice—preventing negative states of mind, overcoming negative states of mind, cultivating positive states of mind, and maintaining positive states of mind.

- Step seven: Skillful Mindfulness refers to the practice of mindfulness meditation—specifically, cultivating mindfulness of your body, feelings, mind, and thoughts.

- Step eight: Skillful Concentration refers to four stages of deep absorption we can reach in meditation.

These eight steps are not merely an interesting list of ideas taught by the Buddha. They are your best hope for enlightenment. If the eight steps are something you have just skimmed through quickly and then set aside, you have missed their potential. No other teaching is more profound and more central to the Buddha's message. In fact, these eight steps are the Buddha's message.

These eight steps are often represented as a wheel—the wheel of clarity, as opposed to the wheel of endless birth, death, and rebirth. Clarity stops the cycle of repeated births and deaths. The spokes on the wheel of clarity are the eight steps of the Buddha's path. Its hub is the combination of compassion and wisdom. By contrast, the spokes of the wheel of endless birth, death, and rebirth are the many lives we have led and will lead in the realms of suffering. The hub of this wheel is the combination of desire, hatred, and ignorance.

Both wheels are always in motion. We see all around us the endless cycle of birth and death. Plants, animals, people are always being born and dying. It's harder to see the motion of the wheel of clarity, yet it is there. All around us, people are practicing the Buddha's path to happiness. This wheel is in motion because spiritual practice is dynamic, always active and moving. The circular shape of both wheels symbolizes perfection. The wheel of life and death is a perfect closed system—it is the perfect system to stay miserable. Whereas the circular shape of the wheel of clarity symbolizes that the Eightfold Path is complete and perfect.

To liberate yourself from dissatisfaction, you should put into practice every aspect of the wheel of clarity. Simply reading about the eight steps of the wheel will not help you make your life happy. If you try to make a bicycle wheel stand upright, it will fall over. However, if you set the wheel spinning by riding the bicycle, the wheel will stand upright as long as the motion lasts. To benefit you, the wheel of clarity also needs to be put in motion through daily practice. *Recognition* *Acceptance* *Interest* *Non-attachment*

MINDFULNESS OF SKILLFUL UNDERSTANDING

As an example of how you might practice the first step—Skillful Understanding of the Four Noble Truths—imagine that while sitting on your cushion one morning you get a pain in your leg. Instead of just noticing the arising and passing away of the sensation, on this occasion you become unhappy about the pain, and your unhappiness makes the pain worse. If your mindfulness had been skillful, this problem would not have happened, but now you are stuck. What should you do?

You can overcome the suffering caused by this pain by using the Buddha's eight steps. Here is an opportunity to see the Four Noble Truths in action.

Although we have described the eight steps in a particular order, you do not need to exercise them in that order. It is not so neat and tidy as that. If you are cooking in a kitchen where all the pots are hung according to size and all the utensils neatly arranged in some kind of logical order, you don't use these implements in the order in which they are arranged. Instead, you grab whatever spoon or pot you need at the moment. Similarly, incorporating the eight steps into your daily life requires that you select and use whatever step is needed.

First you simply become mindful of the pain and your resistance to it. Thus you make use of Skillful Mindfulness, the seventh step of the path. With mindfulness, you become aware that "this is suffering." When you thus see the truth of your suffering, you are seeing the First Noble Truth. It becomes real to you, and you begin working with Skillful Understanding, which is the first step of the path.

With mindful attention, you will likely notice that the more you resist the pain, the worse it feels. So you make an effort to overcome your aversion. This involves Skillful Effort, the sixth step. You let go of aversion by relaxing and cultivating a friendly attitude. You may, for example, realize that the pain in your leg is as worthy of loving-friendliness as any other bodily sensation. In this way, you develop an aspect of Skillful Thinking, the second step.

Then you may notice that your suffering arises not just because of aversion but because you want to feel better. You may think, for example, "If only I could have a peaceful sitting, without this pain!" Seeing the connection between your desire and your suffering brings direct insight into the Second Noble Truth, the truth that desire causes suffering. Now you have developed further Skillful Understanding.

As you sit with the awareness of the Second Noble Truth, becoming increasingly mindful of the connection between your desire and your suffering, you also further develop Skillful Mindfulness. Because you see so clearly how desire leads to suffering, determination arises to do something about desire. Rousing energy, you again apply Skillful Effort, this time, in order to let go of your craving and clinging to pleasant feeling. The thought of letting go, also known as renunciation, is another aspect of Skillful Thinking.

Perhaps you initially reacted to the pain with a sense of disappointment and frustration. If self-blame or other uncompassionate thoughts directed toward yourself have arisen, you now make a Skillful Effort to let go of them. In doing so, you again exercise Skillful Thinking. Please notice that if you make excessive effort, it will create more pain and tension. With mindfulness, however, you see that problem. Then the step of Skillful Thinking again becomes useful, this time to cool your mind with thoughts of loving-friendliness toward yourself.

Such successes in cultivating Skillful Understanding, Thinking, Effort, and Mindfulness let your mind settle down. The mind becomes more concentrated; this is an expression of the eighth step of the path, Skillful Concentration. When there is good concentration, the physical and mental pain goes away. As the pain disappears you feel joyful, tranquil, peaceful, and happy. These qualities, in turn, lead to even deeper concentration.

Deeper concentration causes mindfulness to strengthen, and you continue to examine your experiences. You see that the pain disappeared because you let go of your desire for pleasurable sensations. Then your Skillful Understanding increases as the logic and power of the Third Noble Truth become clear: with the ending of desire comes the ending of suffering.

You may notice that in this example we have not mentioned the "morality" aspects of the path: Skillful Speech, Skillful Action, and Skillful Livelihood (steps three, four, and five). But they too play a role, for they are key aspects of a good life. Immorality unsettles the mind, making meditation difficult even in comfortable circumstances. You need a good moral foundation before you can remain focused and maintain strong determination in the face of physical or mental pain.

Thus, when you correctly apply the steps of the Buddha's path, you find in them the way to let go of suffering. In doing so, you witness the last of the Four Noble Truths, the truth that the way to end suffering is to follow the Eightfold Path. Now you have touched upon all four basic aspects of Skillful Understanding.

By seeing for yourself how the Four Noble Truths function in this kind of situation, you glimpse how they work in your life generally. Thus the wheel of clarity spins on.

KEY POINTS FOR MINDFULNESS OF SKILLFUL UNDERSTANDING

The following points will help you gain happiness through Skillful Understanding:

- Skillful Understanding leads us to act with a comprehension of cause and effect and the Four Noble Truths.

- In accordance with the principle of kamma (karma), acting in skillful ways causes happy results and acting in unskillful ways causes unhappy results.

- Any action that comes from a mind under the influence of greed, hatred, or delusion leads to suffering and is thus unskillful or wrong.

- Any action that comes from a mind not under the influence of greed, hatred, or delusion brings happiness and is thus skillful or right.

- The Four Noble Truths proclaim dissatisfaction, its origin, its cessation, and the Eightfold Path that leads to the cessation of dissatisfaction.

- Facing the truth of dissatisfaction helps us recognize true happiness.

- Birth, old age, sickness, and death; separation from what we love and association with what we hate; not getting what we want and getting what we don't want—these are all dissatisfaction.

- Dissatisfaction arises when we fail to accept the impermanent, inherently unsatisfying, and selfless nature of all phenomena.

- Desire is the underlying cause of dissatisfaction. To the degree we have desire, to that degree we suffer.

- We must take responsibility for our desire and the intentional actions it motivates.

- When we take responsibility for the results of our intentional actions, we change our behavior.

- There is an end to dissatisfaction.

- The eight steps of the Buddha's path to happiness show us the way to end dissatisfaction and achieve total happiness.

- Mindfulness can help us understand the Four Noble Truths and the eight steps of the path to happiness.

STEP 2
Skillful Thinking

I<small>T'S NO MYSTERY</small> that thinking can make us happy or miserable. Let's say you're sitting under a tree one fine spring day. Nothing particular is happening to you, except perhaps the breeze is ruffling your hair, yet in your mind you're far away. Maybe you're remembering another spring day several years back when you were feeling terrible. You had just lost your job, or failed an exam, or your cat had wandered off. That memory turns into a worry. "What if I lose my job again? Why did I ever say such-and-such to so-and-so? No doubt this or that will happen, and I'll be out on my ear. Now, I'm really in for it! How will I pay my bills?" One worry brings up another, which brings up yet another. Soon you feel your life is in shambles, but all this while you've been sitting under the tree!

Fantasies, fears, and other kinds of obsessional thinking are a big problem for us. We all tend to lock into unhealthy thought patterns— grooves we have worn into our consciousness that keep us circling in familiar tracks leading to unhappiness.

The second step of the Buddha's path offers us an escape from this pattern, a way of redirecting our thoughts in positive and helpful directions. When we begin to understand things rightly—through mindfulness of the key points of the first step of the path—our mind naturally flows into Skillful Thinking. Thinking here refers not only to thoughts but to any intentional mind state. As we come to understand that desire is the cause of dissatisfaction, we see that thoughts connected to attachment and aversion always lead to unhappiness. Skillful Thinking consists of abandoning negative thoughts, such as grasping, hatred, and cruelty, and replacing them with wholesome thoughts, such as letting go, loving-friendliness, and compassion. These skillful thoughts work as antidotes to obsession and worry and move us along on the path toward permanent happiness.

LETTING GO

Letting go is the opposite of desire or attachment. Think of it as generosity in the highest sense. Along the Buddha's path, we will have the opportunity to give away or let go of everything that holds us back from our goal of the highest happiness—possessions, people, beliefs and opinions, even our attachment to our own mind and body.

When people hear this, they sometimes start to worry. They think that to follow the Buddha's teachings they have to give everything away and join a monastery. Though becoming a monk or a nun is indeed one way of practicing generosity, most people can let go in the midst of busy, family-centered lives. What we need to reject is not the things we have, or our family and friends, but rather our mistaken sense that these are our possessions. We need to let go of our habit of clinging to the people and the material things in our lives and to our ideas, beliefs, and opinions.

Material Generosity

Letting go is a gradual process. Before we actually give anything away, we have to cultivate the thought of generosity. We do this by considering carefully what generosity means and by looking at the pitfalls and advantages of practicing it. A good place to begin is with the easiest type of generosity, giving away material things.

Notice first of all how our mind tricks us into avoiding the thought of generosity. We tell ourselves that in order to be generous, we first must have a lot to give. "Just wait until I get rich," we say, "then I'll build shelters for the homeless and hospitals and beautiful meditation centers. Think of all the people I'll be able to help!" So we collect, accumulate, and invest a little bit here and there. As our investments grow, we get busier and busier taking care of them, and more and more attached to what we have. Somehow there doesn't seem to be any time to practice generosity.

Another trick the mind plays is attaching an ulterior motive to our generosity. Giving someone a gift, we discover, makes us feel good. Sometimes we enjoy the experience of giving a gift even more than the recipient enjoys getting it. Giving makes us feel proud. Our ego is pleased by how beautiful or expensive the gift is, by the message it carries about our good taste or our sense of style. Moreover, we may secretly feel that the person who gets the gift now has an obligation to us. We may even be using our excessive generosity to demean the recipient. When we give something away, some element of seeking enjoyment is generally present. Giving so that we feel good, or so that someone will think well of us or owe us a favor, corrupts our generosity.

Another kind of less-than-skillful giving occurs when we make a gift to avoid painful feelings. For example, a family may donate money so that a park or public building is named after a lost loved one. The gift may be a way of transferring their grasping from the loved one to the idea of a permanent monument. True generosity lets go not only of wealth or possessions but of clinging to a person who has died and to feelings of sorrow or anger. A wealthy couple I knew once gave away everything they owned after the death of their only child. Though they made a show of giving their money to charity, they really gave out of anger. They wanted to blunt the feeling of pain over losing their child by punishing themselves. Monasteries and charities may benefit greatly from such gifts, but the giver does not fully benefit. On the other hand, people may make such gifts in order to transform their grief into generous, loving, friendly thoughts. This generosity is skillful and brings healing.

The best giving occurs when we have no expectations of any return, not even a thank-you. We give while knowing that we already have in our hearts everything we need to be happy. Such giving is motivated by a sense of fullness, not loss. Giving anonymously, and without knowing the recipient, is a wonderful way to be generous. Giving quietly, without fanfare, lessens our desire and reduces our attachments to the things we have.

The highest form of material giving happens when we respond to others' needs at the risk of our own lives. On television news I once saw a man do this after there had been a terrible accident. On a cold winter day in 1983 an airplane leaving Washington, D.C., for Florida never managed to gain altitude because of ice on the wings. It crashed into the Fourteenth Street bridge. Most on board were killed. Many fell to the ice-covered Potomac River, smashing through the ice into freezing water.

At one spot where people were crawling out of the water onto the broken ice, a rescue helicopter approached and dropped a cable within reach of a man. But instead of grasping it and saving his life, he helped a woman grab the line. She was flown to safety. The helicopter returned, and, even though the man was freezing, he again passed the cable to a woman, and she too was saved. When the helicopter returned a third time, this man had died from the cold.

But we do not need an opportunity to act heroically, nor do we need great wealth, to practice generosity. All we need is the willingness to give of ourselves, even in some small way. With that thought we can, for example, spend time with people, helping them to overcome their loneliness. Better yet, we can help them to overcome dissatisfaction by sharing with them what we have learned of the Buddha's path and what we know about the practice of mindfulness and meditation. Such sharing excels all other gifts.

Clinging to People, Experiences, and Beliefs

As we are coming to discover, pain arises from clinging to anything—form, feelings, perceptions, volitional formations, and consciousness. Letting go of our tendency to cling to people, experiences, and beliefs is more difficult than giving away material things, but it is even more important to our ultimate happiness.

Clinging to bodily form has two aspects. Most obviously, we cling to other people in our lives. Clinging is not the same as loving. It is not the same as caring for someone's welfare and wanting that person to be happy. It is, rather, a jealous or obsessive possessiveness that seeks to own another person. We can all think of examples of husbands and wives who try to possess each other, or of friends who are so bossy and controlling

that they strangle the friendship. Practicing generosity in human relationships means trusting another person and allowing him or her to
enjoy space and freedom and dignity.

However, even good relationships can have an element of clinging.
All happy married couples hope that their marriage will last. An element of fear is always there: "He will leave." "She will die." It may be
painful to think of this, but we must remember that every marriage, no
matter how happy, ends in separation. Even if a couple lives together for
fifty years and dies together in bliss, at the time of death, they must
part and go their separate ways according to their past deeds.

A more subtle kind of clinging to the body is our attachment to our
physical form and to our belief that we are in control of it. No matter
how healthy and strong our body is now, we know that it will deteriorate with age and become weak and sick. Moreover, we cannot control
what happens to our bodies. We cannot control whether our next sensation will be pleasant or unpleasant. Nor can we control the stream of
thoughts entering our minds. For instance, try not to think of the image
of a dog. Any luck? We cannot control even this much.

We try to defend ourselves against the onslaught of constant change
by building up concepts and images and hanging on tight—to my house,
my car, my job, my partner, my body—as if these things had their own
existence that we could depend upon. At the bottom of our holding on
to these things is terror. With time, no matter how tightly we hold on,
everything in this world shifts and changes. The images we hold so
tightly will shatter like glass. Then how we suffer!

Possessing, clinging, or holding on to anything makes life more
painful. Using a material possession without clinging helps us avoid
heartbreak when it is lost, broken, or stolen. Also, holding on to our
families and friends or to our sense of personal identity—my title or
occupation, my family background, my position in the world—leads to
suffering when, as is inevitable, these concepts dissolve. When we do
not cling, our mind is always at peace. This relaxed attitude consoles us,
comforts us, and reduces our tension, anxiety, worry, and fear.

Developing an attitude of not clinging requires, at first, that we spend
a certain amount of time alone. Many of us cling to the experience of being
with others out of fear of being lonely. But aloneness is not loneliness.

Rather, it is singleness that creates space for us to think, reflect, meditate, and free the mind from noise and attachment. As our greed, hatred, and delusion diminish through our solitary practice of mindfulness and meditation, we strengthen our ability to be with others without clinging. When the mind is at peace, we can be in company with many people without attachment and the suffering it brings.

The Buddha walked many miles every day with thousands of monks, nuns, and laypeople around him. Some came to live with him. Some came to talk to him. Some came to discuss their problems with him. Some came to ask him questions. Some came to argue with him. Some came simply to listen to his discourses. The Buddha carried his aloneness within him, even in a crowd. His attitude of nonattachment was total. Occasionally, some of the monks, nuns, or laypeople who followed the Buddha spent time alone in the forests perfecting their practice of nonattachment. But they did not live in the forest forever. As they let go of attachment, they learned to live with other people while maintaining a solid, well-grounded state of mind.

That state of mind is called renunciation. Renunciation is not only for monks and nuns but for anyone who loves solitude or who longs to live without bondage. All renounced people, even monks and nuns, live with others some of the time. Mindfulness of Skillful Thinking helps us create a stable psychological state so that we are not bothered by the changing conditions of our physical environment or by other people. Like the Buddha, we learn to carry our renunciation within ourselves.

Letting go of clinging also requires that we renounce attachment to our beliefs, opinions, and ideas. This is difficult. We tend to derive our sense of personal identity—to define ourselves—by what we think about various issues. Often we get so caught up in this identification that we feel personally attacked when someone criticizes the political candidate we are supporting or our opinion about some question of public policy. Yet our ideals, opinions, or views are also subject to the law of impermanence. Think back to what you believed at age sixteen or at age thirty, and you'll see just how changeable your personal beliefs are.

On a larger scale, throughout history people all over the world have gone to war in the name of their cherished opinions or beliefs. The amount of killing we humans do to protect our material possessions is insignificant as compared to the killing we do to protect unwholesome beliefs, such as racial or religious bigotry. Bring to mind the cherished beliefs that have led to war and ask whether protecting them was worth war's terrible cost.

Letting go of unwholesome thoughts, words, and deeds creates the space for us to cultivate wholesome thoughts such as loving-friendliness, appreciative joy, nonviolence, and equanimity. But we should not be attached even to these wholesome thoughts. Letting go requires us to go beyond good and evil. In the end, the Buddha told us, even his teachings must be cast aside: "These teachings are like a raft, to be abandoned once you have crossed the flood. Since you should abandon even good states of mind generated by these teachings, how much more so should you abandon bad states of mind!" (M 22)

I am not suggesting that you will be able to give up your clinging all of a sudden or become liberated overnight. Seeking "instant enlightenment" can be just a big ego trip. As I travel and teach, sometimes people approach me and inform me that they have quickly reached enlightenment. I respond by quoting the Buddha's description of the attributes of someone who has attained stages of enlightenment. Since the people speaking to me do not have these attributes, they sometimes become very disappointed or even angry with me because my response does not please their egos.

Attachment is built into our psyches and strengthened over many lifetimes. It is impossible to let it go quickly or easily. We do not have to wait lifetimes to make a start, however. With proper understanding, patience, effort, and mindfulness, we can begin to free ourselves from our bondage and even attain full enlightenment in this lifetime. To achieve happiness, we must start today to develop the skillful thought of letting go of attachment and replacing it with open-minded generosity, flexibility, and detachment.

Dealing with Fear

When we begin to practice mindfulness of letting go, we often stumble on fear. Fear arises because of an insecure, emotional, or greedy attachment to ideas, concepts, feelings, or physical objects, including our own body. It can also be caused by coming into contact with something that we do not understand or whose outcome is uncertain.

Say, for example, that you have recently been told that you have cancer. You are scheduled to have surgery, after which your doctors will decide whether more treatment is needed. Now you are trying to meditate. So many thoughts run through your mind. The thoughts and feelings build on each other, and you become increasingly agitated, upset, and very afraid. What should you do?

As you sit in meditation, watch as each mental state arises. If many thoughts and feelings come up at once, try to distinguish between them: "What is going to happen to me?"—fear. "How dare the nurse say that to me!"—anger. "They need me! I can't be sick! I can't die!"—attachment. "This is the same diagnosis my friend had. His wife still cries when we talk about him."—sadness. "I hate needles!"—aversion. "Who should go with me to the next appointment?"—restlessness and worry. "How many people survive this thing?"—fear.

As you begin to sort them out, your thoughts and feelings become more manageable. You stop being so caught up in the frightening stories that the mind is conjuring up, and you can start to reason with yourself. You can bring to mind consoling thoughts—the skill and compassion of your doctors and nurses, the recent advances in treatment, the people you know who are living full lives despite a diagnosis like yours.

As you counter the ideas that have been feeding your fear, you are practicing mindfulness in action. You can see how the mind plays games with itself, using thoughts to create fear, and fear to create more thoughts. This may also be a good time for self-reflection. You might examine your past behavior for times when fear caused you to act in unskillful ways. You can resolve to remain mindful and not allow fear to cause you to act in such ways in the future.

Now that your mind is calm and clear, you can go back to meditating on the breath or other meditation object. Accept the fact that fearful thoughts will arise in your meditation from time to time. With the experience you have gained, you can ignore their specific content and just witness what happens to all thoughts and feelings. You see that every mental object rises and peaks. No matter how intense it is, if you stay with it—as if it were a friend who wants to hold your hand while walking through a difficult experience—you will also see every mental object fall away. Now that you have noticed the thinking process itself, you gain confidence that no matter how frightening a train of thought may be at the time, it eventually comes to an end.

Once you have managed to sit with strong fear completely, you will no longer see fear the same way. You'll know that fear is just a natural mind state that comes and goes. It has no substance and cannot hurt you. Your attitude around fear begins to soften. You know that you can observe and let go of whatever arises. As you lose the fear of fear, you gain a sense of freedom.

The same strategy works with other unpleasant states of mind, including memories, imaginings, daydreams, or worries about problems you are facing. Sometimes you may be afraid of unpleasant memories because you think that you may not be able to handle them. But now you know that you can handle any state of mind that you might ordinarily want to repress.

Your practice of mindfulness has taught you that it is not the mental states themselves that make you uncomfortable, but your attitude toward them. You may have the idea that mental states are part of your own personality, part of your existence. Then you try to reject the unpleasant ones as if they were foreign bodies. But you cannot really reject any of them, because they were not yours in the first place. Your best response is to maintain a steady practice of observing your mind, without reacting with clinging or aversion to anything that comes up, but skillfully working to free the mind from all unwholesome states.

LOVING-FRIENDLINESS

As you let go of negative states of mind, you create the space in your mind for the cultivation of positive thoughts. Skillful Thinking means that we replace angry or hostile thoughts with thoughts of loving-friendliness. Loving-friendliness, or *metta*, is a natural capacity. It is a warm wash of fellow-feeling, a sense of interconnectedness with all beings. Because we wish for peace, happiness, and joy for ourselves, we know that all beings must wish for these qualities. Loving-friendliness radiates to the whole world the wish that all beings enjoy a comfortable life with harmony, mutual appreciation, and appropriate abundance.

Though we all have the seed of loving-friendliness within us, we must make the effort to cultivate it. When we are rigid, uptight, tense, anxious, full of worries and fears, our natural capacity for loving-friendliness cannot flourish. To nurture the seed of loving-friendliness, we must learn to relax. In a peaceful state of mind, such as we get from mindfulness meditation, we can forget our past differences with others and forgive their faults, weaknesses, and offenses. Then loving-friendliness naturally grows within us.

As is the case with generosity, loving-friendliness begins with a thought. Typically, our minds are full of views, opinions, beliefs, ideas. We have been conditioned by our culture, traditions, education, associations, and experiences. From these mental conditions we have developed prejudices and judgments. These rigid ideas stifle our natural loving-friendliness. Yet, within this tangle of confused thinking, the idea of our friendly interconnection with others does come up occasionally. We catch a glimpse of it as we might glimpse a tree during a flash of lightning. As we learn to relax and let go of negativity, we begin to recognize our biases and not let them dominate our minds. Then the thought of loving-friendliness begins to shine, showing its true strength and beauty.

The loving-friendliness that we wish to cultivate is not love as we ordinarily understand it. When you say you love so-and-so, what you conceive in your mind is generally an emotion conditioned by the behavior or qualities of that person. Perhaps you admire the person's appearance, manner, ideas, voice, or attitude. Should these conditions change, or your tastes, whims, and fancies change, what you call love might change as well. In extreme cases, your love might even turn to hate. This love-hate duality pervades all our ordinary feelings of affection. You love one person and hate another. Or you love now and hate later. Or you love whenever you feel like it and hate whenever you feel like it. Or you love when everything is smooth and rosy and hate when anything goes wrong.

If your love changes from time to time, place to place, and situation to situation in this fashion, then what you call love is not the skillful thought of loving-friendliness. It may be erotic lust, greed for material security, desire to feel loved, or some other form of greed in disguise. True loving-friendliness has no ulterior motive. It never changes into hate as circumstances change. It never makes you angry if you do not get favors in return. Loving-friendliness motivates you to behave kindly to all beings at all times and to speak gently in their presence and in their absence.

When fully matured, your net of loving-friendliness embraces everything in the universe without exception. It has no limitations, no boundaries. Your thought of loving-friendliness includes not only all beings as they are at this moment but also your wish that all of them, without any discrimination or favoritism, will be happy in the limitless future.

Let me tell you a story of the powerful, far-reaching effects that an act of loving-friendliness can have:

In a little house in India lived an old lady and her young daughter. Nearby in a hut lived a meditating monk. Out of respect, the old lady called the monk her son and asked her daughter to treat him as her brother. Every morning the monk went to the village to collect cooked food for his midday meal. He never forgot to stop at the little house to get the small quantity of food that old lady and her daughter offered him with great affection and devotion. Every afternoon he returned to the village to see his supporters and encourage them to practice meditation and live peaceful lives.

One afternoon on his way to the village, the monk overheard a conversation between the old lady and her daughter. The old lady told her daughter, "Darling, tomorrow your brother will come to our house on his alms round. Here is ghee; here is honey; here is rice; here are spices; here are vegetables. Make sure that you prepare a delicious meal for him."

The daughter asked the mother, "Where will you go tomorrow?"

"I plan to spend the day in the forest meditating by myself."

"But what will you eat?"

"I will make a little rice soup from today's leftover rice. That is enough for me. But make sure that you make a good meal for your brother and offer it to him when he comes to our house."

Hearing this conversation, the monk thought, "This old lady loves and respects me so much that she ordered her daughter to make a delicious meal for me when she herself is going to eat a simple rice soup made out of stale rice. I don't deserve that delicious meal until I attain full enlightenment. I must make myself worthy of her loving gift. This is the time for me to make unremitting effort to liberate myself from all negative states of mind."

The monk hung up his upper robe. He decided not go to the village again to collect food until he attained full liberation of mind. He sat down on his meditation seat making the following resolution: "Let my blood dry up. Let my flesh wither. Let this body be reduced to a skeleton. I shall not get up from this seat without attaining the final stage of liberation."

With that vow, the monk meditated the entire afternoon, the entire night, and part of next morning. Just before the time came for him to go on his alms round, he attained his goal.

Then the monk put on his robes and went to the village taking his alms bowl. When he visited the little house, the daughter of the old lady offered him the delicious meal.

The young lady waited anxiously for her mother to return home from her day's meditation. That evening, as soon as the mother arrived home, the daughter ran up to her and said, "Mother I have never seen our monk so serene, so composed, so radiant, calm, so beautiful."

"My dear, he must have attained true freedom, liberation from negative states of mind. We are very fortunate to have such a monk so close to our home. But if we really honor him, we must follow in his footsteps. From now on, let us meditate more vigorously so that we might achieve the same state."

So both mother and daughter meditated until they, too, reached higher stages of attainment. Many villagers followed their example and attained stages of enlightenment. Such was the far-reaching effect of the loving-friendliness of an old lady. (MA i 225)

Loving Your Enemies

Some people wonder how they can extend the feeling of loving-friendliness toward their enemies. They wonder how they can say sincerely, "May my enemies be well, happy, and peaceful. May no difficulties or problems come to them."

This question arises from mistaken thinking. A person whose mind is filled with problems may behave in a way that offends or harms us. We call that person an enemy. But in actuality, there is no such person as an enemy. It is the person's negative state of mind that is causing us problems. Mindfulness shows us that states of mind are not permanent. They are temporary, correctable, adjustable.

In practical terms, the best thing I can do to assure my own peace and happiness is to help my enemies overcome their problems. If all my enemies were free of pain, dissatisfaction, affliction, neurosis, paranoia, tension, and anxiety, they would no longer have reason to be my enemies. Once free of negativity, an enemy is just like anybody else—a wonderful human being.

We can practice loving-friendliness on anyone—parents, teachers, relatives, friends, unfriendly people, indifferent people, people who cause us problems. We do not have to know or be close to people to practice loving-friendliness toward them. In fact, sometimes it's easier not to know people. Why? Because if we don't know them, we can treat all people alike. We can look at the many, many beings in the universe as if they were specks of light in space and wish them all to be happy and at peace. Though merely wishing may not make this so, cultivating the hope that others might enjoy loving-friendliness is a skillful thought that fills our own minds with contentment and joy.

If everyone holds the thought that everyone else enjoys loving-friendliness, we will have peace on earth. Say there are six billion people in the world, and each one cultivates this wish. Who will be left to cultivate hatred? There will be no more struggle, no more fighting. Every action comes from thinking. If the thought is impure, the actions that follow from that thought will be impure and harmful. The opposite is also true. As the Buddha told us, the pure thought of loving-friendliness is more powerful than hatred, more powerful than weapons. Weapons destroy. Loving-friendliness helps beings live in peace and harmony. Which do you think is more lasting and more powerful?

Dealing with Anger

The main obstacle to loving-friendliness is anger. When anger and hatred consume us, there is no room in our minds for friendly feelings toward ourselves or toward others, no space for relaxation or peace.

We each react to anger in our own way. Some people try to justify their angry feelings. They tell themselves again and again, "I have every right to be angry." Others hold on to their anger for a long time, even months or years. They feel that their anger makes them very special, very righteous. Still others lash out physically against those who anger them. Whatever your style, you can be sure of one thing: Your anger ultimately hurts you more than it hurts the person you're angry with.

Have you noticed how you feel when you are angry? Do you experience tension, pain in your chest, burning in your stomach, blurred eyesight? Does your reasoning become unclear, or your speech turn harsh and unpleasant? Doctors tell us that these common manifestations of anger have serious consequences for our health—high blood pressure, nightmares, insomnia, ulcers, even heart disease. The emotional toll of anger is equally grim. To put it bluntly, anger makes us feel miserable.

Anger also disrupts our relationships. Don't you generally try to avoid people who are angry? In the same way, when you are angry, people avoid you. No one wants to associate with someone in the grip of anger. An angry person can be irrational, even dangerous.

Moreover, anger often does no damage to the person toward whom it is directed. In most cases, your anger with someone who insulted you harms that person not at all. Rather, it's you who are red in the face, you who are shouting and making a scene, you who look ridiculous and feel miserable. Your adversary may even find your anger entertaining. An attitude of habitual ill will and resentment can adversely affect your health, your relationships, your livelihood, your future. You yourself may even experience the terrible things you wished upon your adversary.

Since it's clear that anger can hurt us, what can we do about it? How can we let go of anger and replace it with loving-friendliness?

In working with anger, we must first determine to restrain ourselves from acting on angry impulses. Whenever I think about restraint, I remember my uncle's elephant. When I was a little boy, my uncle had a big, beautiful elephant. My friends and I used to like to tease this animal. We would throw stones at her until she became angry with us. The elephant was so big, she could have crushed us if she had wanted to. What she did instead was remarkable.

One time when we threw stones at her, the elephant used her trunk to grab a stick about the size of a pencil and to spank us with this little stick. She showed great self-restraint, doing only what was needed to make us respect her. For a few days after that, the elephant held a grudge against us and would not let us ride her. My uncle told us to take her to the big creek, where we scrubbed her skin with coconut shells while she relaxed and enjoyed the cool water. After that, she completely let go of her anger toward us. Now I tell my students, when you feel justified in reacting violently out of anger, remember the moderate response of my uncle's big, gentle elephant.

Another way of dealing with anger is to reflect on its results. We know very well that when we are angry, we do not see the truth clearly. As a result, we may commit many unwholesome actions. As we have learned, our past intentional actions are the only thing we really own. Our future life is determined by our intentional actions today, just as our present life is heir to our previous intentional behavior. Intentional actions committed under the influence of anger cannot lead to a happy future.

The best antidote to feelings of anger is patience. Patience does not mean letting others walk all over you. Patience means buying time with mindfulness so that you can act rightly. When we react to provocation with patience, we speak the truth at the right time and in the right tone. We use soft, kind, and appropriate words as if we were speaking to a child or a dear friend to prevent him from doing something harmful to himself or others. Though you may raise your voice, this does not mean that you are angry. Rather, you are being skillful in protecting someone you care about.

A famous story illustrates the Buddha's patience and resourceful-
ness when confronted by an angry person:

> Once there was a Brahmin, a person of high rank and authority.
> This Brahmin had a habit of getting angry, even for no reason. He
> quarreled with everyone. If someone else was wronged and did
> not get angry, the Brahmin would get angry at that person for not
> being angry.
>
> The Brahmin had heard that the Buddha never got angry.
> One day he went to the Buddha and abused him with insults. The
> Buddha listened compassionately and patiently. Then he asked
> the Brahmin, "Do you have any family or friends or relatives?"
>
> "Yes, I have many relatives and friends," the Brahmin replied.
>
> "Do you visit them periodically?" the Buddha asked.
>
> "Of course. I visit them often."
>
> "Do you carry gifts for them when you visit them?"
>
> "Surely. I never go to see them without a gift," said the Brahmin.
>
> The Buddha asked, "When you give gifts to them, suppose
> they do not accept them. What would you do with these gifts?"
>
> "I would take them home and enjoy them with my family,"
> answered the Brahmin.
>
> Then the Buddha said, "Similarly, friend, you gave me a gift.
> I do not accept it. It is all yours. Take it home and enjoy it with
> your family."
>
> The man was deeply embarrassed. He understood and admired
> the Buddha's compassionate advice. (S I.7.1 [2])

Finally, to overcome anger you can consider the benefits of loving-
friendliness. According to the Buddha, when you practice loving-
friendliness, you "sleep in comfort, wake up in comfort, and dream sweet
dreams. You are dear to human beings and to nonhuman beings. Deities
guard you. [If you are filled with loving-friendliness, at that moment]
fire, poison, and weapons cannot affect you. You concentrate easily. Your
face is serene. You die unconfused and…are reborn in the highest realm
of existence." (A V (Elevens) II.5) Aren't these prospects more pleasant
than the misery, poor health, and ill will we get as a result of anger?

As your awareness of your mental states increases, you will recognize more and more quickly when you are becoming angry. Then, as soon as angry thoughts arise, you can begin to apply the antidotes of patience and mindfulness. You should also take every opportunity to make restitution for your angry actions. If you said or did something to someone in anger, as soon as that moment has passed, you should consider going to this person to apologize, even if you think the other person was wrong or acted worse than you did. Spending a few minutes apologizing to someone you offended produces marvelous and immediate relief for both of you.

In the same spirit, if you see that someone is angry with you, you can approach this person and talk in a relaxed way to try to find the cause of the anger. You might say: "I am sorry you're angry with me. I'm not angry with you at all. Perhaps we can work this out as friends." You might also give a gift to the person you think is angry with you. A gift tames the untamed and makes friends of foes. A gift can convert angry speech into kind words and harshness into gentleness.

Here are some practical steps you can take to overcome anger:

- Become aware of your anger as soon as possible.

- Be mindful of your anger and feel its strength.

- Remember that a quick temper is extremely dangerous.

- Bring to mind anger's miserable consequences.

- Practice restraint.

- Realize that anger and its causes are impermanent.

- Recall the example of the Buddha's patience with the Brahmin.

- Change your attitude by becoming helpful and kind.

- Change the atmosphere between you and a person with whom you are angry by offering a gift or other favor.

- Remember the advantages of practicing loving-friendliness.

- Remember we all will die one day, and we don't want to die with anger.

COMPASSION

Compassion is the third skillful thought the Buddha encouraged us to cultivate. Compassion is a melting of the heart at the thought of another's suffering. It is a spontaneous, wholesome reaction, coupled with a wish to alleviate another's pain.

Compassion requires an object. In order to cultivate compassion, you must reflect on the suffering you have personally experienced, notice the suffering of others, and make the intuitive connection between your own painful experiences and theirs. Suppose, for example, you hear of a child being beaten or abused. You open your mind to this child's suffering by perhaps recalling the pain you felt in your heart when you were mistreated. You develop the prayerful wish, "May such pain not happen to anybody in the world. I wish that no child be abused the way I have been abused." Or, when someone is ill, you reflect on how unpleasant and painful it is to suffer from sickness, and you wish that no one else suffer similar pain and anxiety. Or you recall the heartbreak of separating from someone you love. This memory leads to compassion for anyone separated from a loved one by death, distance, or rejection, and to the wish that no one need go through such pain.

Compassion and loving-friendliness are mutually supportive. When you are full of loving-friendliness, your heart is open and your mind is clear enough to see the suffering of others. Say, for instance, that someone treats you in a snobbish or disdainful way. An attitude of loving-friendliness helps you to recognize that this harsh behavior must arise from some problem or inner hurt this person is experiencing. Since you also have suffered problems in your life, your compassion arises, and you think to yourself, "This person must be suffering. How can I help? If I get angry or upset, I will not be able to help in any way. I may even aggravate this person's problem." You are confident that if you continue to act in a loving and friendly way, this person will benefit, perhaps immediately and, if not, eventually. Perhaps at some later time, this person will admire how you remained loving in spite of provocation and begin to imitate this friendly way of dealing with others.

The compassion of those who walk the Buddha's path is extraordinary, as in this Mahayana legend:

Once there was a monk practicing meditation on compassion who wished to gain enough merit to see Metteyya, the Buddha of Loving-Friendliness. The monk's practice had so softened his heart that he would not hurt any living being.

One day, he saw a dog lying by the side of the road groaning in pain. A gaping wound on the poor animal was filled with maggots. This monk knelt down in front of the dog. His first thought was to remove the maggots from the dog's wound. But then he thought, "If I use a stick to remove the worms, I may hurt them. If I use my fingers, I may crush them, because they are very delicate creatures. And if I put them down on the ground, someone may step on them."

Then he knew what he must do. He cut a piece of flesh from his own thigh and put it on the ground. Then he knelt down and stretched out his tongue to remove the maggots from the dog's wound and place them on his own flesh.

As he did so, the dog disappeared. In its place was Metteyya, the Buddha of Loving-Friendliness.

We may consider ourselves to be compassionate people, but our level of compassion cannot compare to this! Suffering surrounds us. Every day we have many opportunities to practice compassion, yet we often find it difficult. Why? The answer is that pain—even the pain of others—is hard to endure. To avoid it, we move away, close down, make ourselves tight and rigid. Mindfulness practice helps us to relax and to soften into whatever life presents. When we allow our minds to become gentle and our hearts to open, the wellspring of our compassion can flow freely.

Practicing compassion for the people in our life is challenging to be sure, but it is critical to our happiness, now and in the future. Our parents, partners, and children need our compassion. We need compassion for ourselves as well.

Compassion for Ourselves

Some of you may wonder why you have to practice compassion toward yourself. "Caring for myself is selfish," you may say. "My needs are not important. True spiritual practice is compassion for others." This sounds nice, but you may be fooling yourself. When you investigate your mind carefully, you will discover that there is no one in the whole universe that you care for more than yourself.

There's nothing wrong with this. In fact, compassion for ourselves is the basis for our practice of compassion toward others. As the Buddha said: "Investigating the whole world with my mind, never did I find anyone dearer than myself. Since oneself is dearer than others, one who loves oneself should never harm others." (Ud V.1)

It is a mistake to think that it is more refined or "spiritual" to think harshly about yourself or to view yourself as unworthy. The Buddha found through his own experience that self-mortification does not lead to enlightenment. Of course, we do need to cultivate self-restraint, but we do so out of the determination to act in our own best interests. Seen rightly, kind and gentle self-discipline is actually an aspect of practicing compassion for ourselves.

Moreover, it is impossible to practice genuine compassion for others without the foundation of self-compassion. If we try to act compassionately out of a sense of personal unworthiness or the belief that others are more important than we are, the true source of our actions is aversion for ourselves, not compassion for others. Similarly, if we offer help out of a sense of cold superiority to those we are assisting, our actions may actually be motivated by pride. Genuine compassion, as we have seen, arises from the tender heart we feel for our own suffering, which we then see mirrored in the suffering of others. Self-compassion, grounded in wholesome self-love, motivates us to reach out sincerely to help.

Firefighters show a good example of this motivation. They are known for their great courage in willingly risking their lives to save people trapped in a burning building. They do not deliberately sacrifice themselves, however. They do not carelessly rush into the flames, unequipped to deal with the dangers of the situation. Instead, they take every precaution, putting on helmets and heavy gear, making careful plans, and relying on their judgment and skill to determine the best way to save others without endangering themselves. In the same way, we clothe ourselves with compassion and loving-friendliness toward ourselves, purifying our motives to the best of our abilities and allowing our minds to become clear and bright. From that place of clarity, we can help others effectively and also encourage our own spiritual progress.

Actually, the division between self and other is more blurred in our minds than we usually realize. Whatever attitudes we habitually use toward ourselves, we will use on others, and whatever attitudes we habitually use toward others, we will use on ourselves. The situation is comparable to our serving food to ourselves and to other people from the same bowl. Everyone ends up eating the same thing. So we must examine carefully what we are dishing out.

As we sit in meditation, we should examine how we act toward ourselves and others when things do not go the way we hoped, or when mistakes happen. Do we respond with blame or forgiveness? Anxiety or equanimity? Harshness or gentleness? Patience or fury?

Although it is important for us to notice our mistakes, feel their effects, and pledge to improve, self-blame and other harshness serves no useful purpose. No one feels peaceful after being scolded. Generally, people recoil and become angry, defensive, or stubborn. Think, for example, of a man who is exercising to lose weight. If one day he fails to do his daily exercise and compounds that failure by saying to himself, "You fat, lazy slob, you'll never change!" how likely is it that he'll do his workout tomorrow? The unenlightened mind is untrained. It is ignorant. It suffers. That is why we do regrettable things. Remembering that we make mistakes because of our own suffering helps us extend compassion to ourselves, rather than harsh judgment and self-abuse.

It is especially important that we approach our efforts to meditate and follow the path of the Buddha with a compassionate attitude. We practice the Buddha's eight steps to happiness to alleviate our suffering. If we add to our burden by holding an oppressive or judgmental attitude about our practice, we may soon decide—rightly!—that now we're suffering even more. We may even feel compelled to quit.

Western students in particular seem to fall into this mental trap.

From my Eastern perspective, they often seem ambitious, driven, goal-oriented, and insecure. When they first begin to meditate and discover the mind's monkey nature, they try right away to control it. They clamp down on the mind and try to make it behave by sheer force of will. But the mind does not follow anybody's command. Often, they get frustrated and become self-judging and harsh. A similar thing can happen to more experienced students who feel disappointed that they have not yet achieved their spiritual goals. It is important for any student of the Buddha's path to remember that there is a difference between watching the mind and controlling the mind. Watching the mind with a gentle, open attitude allows the mind to settle down and come to rest. Trying to control the mind, or trying to control the way that one's spiritual practice will unfold, just stirs up more agitation and suffering.

We can open and soften our minds. Nothing that arises in meditation is a sign of failure. There is only the failure to watch. If unwholesome thoughts arise and persist, we should not struggle with them or beat ourselves up. Instead, we should calmly and compassionately apply Skillful Effort to overcome them and to uplift the mind.

No one is uniquely bad. Everyone in the world has the same problems. Greed, anger, jealousy, pride, bad days, disappointments, and impatience come to all unenlightened beings. When we make a habit of meeting the mind's many changes with compassion, the mind can relax. Then, we can see more clearly, and we continue to grow in understanding.

Compassion for Our Parents

Many of us have hard, unkind feelings toward our parents. Some find it difficult to forgive things they did when we were children. Child abuse and other harmful actions may have caused us pain and suffering. These misdeeds cannot be excused; nor can they be forgotten easily. What they did can never be undone. But what we do in this moment can affect our current and future happiness.

One way to develop compassion is to think about how much your parents suffered in bringing you into the world and raising you. The Buddha said that even if you carry your parents, one on each shoulder, for the rest of your life, caring for all of their needs, still you would not have repaid them for what they have done for you. Parents sacrifice sleep, comfort, food, time, and energy, for days, months, years. Consider the utter helplessness of a baby, how demanding its needs are. Think of the fear your mother and father may have felt trying to protect you, how they nursed you through illnesses and worried over your troubles. Rather than blaming them for acting in confused ways, consider the pain and suffering their confused minds must have caused them as they wrestled with the challenges of caring for a child. Consider how hard they may have struggled to free themselves from addictions and other destructive behaviors motivated by desire, hatred, and ignorance.

Then consider that the parents who raised you are not identical to the parents you know today. Time has passed, and impermanence changes everyone. As your parents have grown older, they may have softened or developed greater wisdom. You have matured as well. Don't stay stuck in your childhood relationship. As your parents age, you may even need to switch roles and provide them with material, emotional, and spiritual support. Caring for your parents' needs can open your heart of compassion. Even if your parents never gave you anything but your life and endless pain, you can at least feel sorry for them and wish them happiness: "I wish I could help my parents to have a better state of mind." Compassion has no limit, no boundary.

Compassion for Children

Maintaining equilibrium in your life can be doubly hard when you are raising children. Bringing up children in a balanced manner can be compared to walking a tightrope five hundred feet above the ground. On the one hand, dealing with them in a harsh and rigid manner may earn your children's lasting enmity. On the other hand, without giving them structure and a sense of discipline, children will not learn about limits or the consequences of their actions.

If children are loved and taught, trained, and cared for with the honor and respect they deserve as human beings, they will mature into responsible, loving, and kind adults. Your children will shoulder the burdens of the world after you have gone. They can bring peace and happiness to you, to other members of the family, to society, and to the whole world.

But as any parent knows, children can try the patience of the most tolerant person. When you find yourself struggling with them, remind yourself to find a place of selflessness in your heart. Let go of your need for things to turn out the way you want. Put more effort into understanding your children's points of view, their needs, fears, or concerns; and when you have a better grasp of what they are struggling with, your heart will melt with compassion. With a compassionate state of mind, your actions will always carry a tone of kindness and softness, which is very useful in overcoming difficulty with anyone, child or adult.

If you lack compassion for your children, you can, fortunately, still cultivate it; it just takes practice. People are not born knowing how best to raise a child to become a healthy, responsible, loving adult. This skill must be learned. If you are a parent, it is incumbent upon you to learn as much as possible about how to bring up children in a wholesome way, without teaching them greed, hatred, and ignorance. These unwholesome influences are already abundant enough in the world. Above all, you can show compassion to children when you teach them letting go, loving-friendliness, and compassion.

Compassion for Your Partner

Practicing compassion for your partner requires generosity and patience. We each have a different personal style. Some of us are good at expressing emotions; we laugh and cry easily and often. Others find it hard to say what we're feeling and never cry at all. Some of us are happiest when we're working and enjoy putting in long hours on the job. Others get their work done quickly and prefer to spend their time reading, meditating, or visiting friends. None of these styles are right or wrong. A partner who likes to work enjoys life as much as a partner who prefers travel. Both are trying to avoid suffering and to be as happy as possible. Both can be good, kind human beings. Focus on your partner's good qualities.

Sometimes your heart may harden against your partner after a conflict. Angry thoughts may run repeatedly through your mind, building up your own case and judging your partner's shortcomings. You may need to do some hard inner work before your compassion can arise. In meditation, you can reflect on your own unskillful actions of body, speech, and mind, identifying all the ways in which you have been greedy, selfish, hateful, jealous, or proud. Then, with an open mind, you can look at how these actions may have affected your partner. If you are resentful, that is your own shortcoming, no matter what your partner did. Are you clinging to something? Attachment and genuine love are far apart.

If the situation with your partner is impossible to put up with and cannot be improved, then you may need to end it. But then leave in a loving way, acknowledging your own shortcomings and wishing your partner well. Why hurt your partner with more anger and blame?

It is very important that you do not compare your actions to your partner's or judge your partner's behavior as unskillful. Rather, focus on your own actions and take responsibility for them. Recall those times when you looked into your partner's eyes and saw the pain you caused. Remind yourself that you have caused this person you love to suffer. If you can admit your own faults, if you can see how hurtful your actions were and tap into a sense of concern for your partner's well-being, then compassion and loving-friendliness will flow.

You've had an ugly quarrel in the morning, let's say. Later your partner comes home, looking stiff and angry, and glances at you guardedly to see if you are angry. But you have examined your own faults and opened up your heart's wellspring of love and compassion, so you meet your partner's eyes with a soft, warm expression. Through your compassion, the relationship between the two of you heals.

MINDFULNESS OF SKILLFUL THINKING

As we sit in meditation many things go through our minds. We may hear sounds, feel an itch, and think about many kinds of things. We may even forget briefly that we are meditating and that we are trying to stay focused on the breath. This is normal; it happens to everybody. When something takes our attention away from the breath, we should examine it briefly, just long enough to notice its impermanence—how it arises, peaks, and falls away. Then we return to the breath.

Some thoughts or mental states, however, are tricky and require special attention: the unwholesome thoughts arising from greed, hatred, or delusion whenever we are not mindful. No wisdom develops while the mind is lost in unwholesome thoughts. Not only do we waste our time and create painful feelings, we also reinforce the mental habits that cause all our suffering. We must overcome unwholesome thoughts right away, quickly rebuking them with mindfulness before they overtake us, become entrenched, and dominate the meditation session.

Sometimes such thoughts go away by the simple act of giving brief attention to their impermanence. Other times, we must rouse strong effort to overcome them. We will examine various ways to do this when we discuss Skillful Effort. Once an unwholesome thought has been overcome, we go back to the breath with a slightly deeper level of focus. If another negative thought arises, we repeat our efforts. Each time an unwholesome thought has been overcome, we deepen our concentration.

Eventually, we find that our concentration is so steady that all thoughts stop coming. It may take many meditation sessions for this state of concentration to come about, or it may happen more quickly. Once we have achieved deep concentration, we can use that powerful state to return to our practice of mindfulness, again examining objects as they come to our attention. Since thoughts have vanished, we examine other objects, such as body sensations or positive mental qualities like bliss or equanimity. We focus on the impermanence and related characteristics of these objects, just as before, but with strong concentration, our insight grows dramatically. So long as the state of strong concentration lasts, no unwholesome thoughts arise to disrupt our meditation.

Until we reach that level of concentrated meditation, however, we must skillfully deal with unwholesome thoughts as they arise. We must tackle such thoughts whenever they come up, even outside meditation sessions. Mindfulness of Skillful Thinking refers to all these efforts.

One of the methods for overcoming an unwholesome thought is to examine the downsides of that thought. You see how it debases the mind. You see how your habitual negative thinking causes difficulties in your life. Then you can cultivate the opposite, a wholesome thought, such as the feeling of compassion. This is a great opportunity for you to look at yourself and change your life by changing your thinking.

People often ask me: "How can I integrate my meditation practice and my daily life?" I often respond with questions of my own: "What did you do on the cushion? Did you merely focus the mind on the breath?" If that is all you did, you have two different lives going on: your life on the cushion and everyday, ordinary life.

There is much work to be done in meditation. The same difficult mental states that create problems in our daily lives—greed, fear, anger, jealousy, self-criticism—come to us in meditation. They may emerge in the form of unwholesome thinking at any moment in which our mindfulness or concentration lapses.

First we make effort to simply let go of those thoughts. We do this both to purify the mind in this moment and to train the mind in the habit of self-purification. When a thought is so strong that it persists despite your best efforts, that is the signal to do more intensive work. Now you must look hard at these thoughts and put them to use to develop insight into your life.

For example, let's say that in meditation I get lost in angry thoughts about a stranger who insulted me. I've tried other methods for overcoming these thoughts, but the thoughts don't go away. So I examine them. First, I look at how this thought is affecting my practice, how it creates tension in my body and affects my blood pressure, how it generates a lingering sense of ill will toward this person. I see that such angry thoughts are no good, because they hurt me and affect my mind so negatively that I may even harm others. Next, perhaps, I consider how embarrassed I would be if others knew what I was thinking, and I develop a wholesome sense of shame that such thoughts dominate my mind. This kind of examination often creates enough distance to free the mind from the negative state.

Once the mind is clear, I may examine my thoughts more deeply, reflecting on what caused them. Why did I remain upset after being insulted? I ask myself. What did I cling to that made the insult stick in my mind? I may discover that the cause was something in my past that has nothing to do with the insult.

Next I think: Okay, it's true that this man insulted me, but what did I do to upset him? Was I too hasty or greedy? Too arrogant? Maybe I meant no harm, but I know I've upset people this way before. Let me do better next time. Reflecting thus upon my unskillful motives and actions, I resolve to improve. Once I see my own part in the conflict, I can even develop compassion for this man who suffered so badly that he needed to strike back at me with an insult.

This kind of self-reflection is a critical part of meditation practice. Before his enlightenment, the Buddha himself practiced in this way, using his unwholesome thoughts as a means to look inside and correct his faults. As he meditated in the forest before his enlightenment, the Buddha said to himself, "I have this weakness. I have done that in the past. From now on, my behavior must be different."

You can do the same. If you recall an occasion when you spoke harshly to a child and saw hurt and puzzlement in her eyes, you can resolve to apologize to her and to speak more compassionately in the future. Or if you recall a conversation when you held on stubbornly to your views, even when they were shown to be mistaken, resolve to let go of grasping more gracefully next time.

If a persistent desire arises, such as for ice cream or a new CD, you can use the opportunity to cultivate its opposite, generosity. You can think, "I don't need that right now. I can let go of this desire." If your perspective is generous and open-hearted, eventually the desire for that sense pleasure will diminish. You can then recognize how petty or self-centered your desire really was. By so doing, you come to better understand the nature of craving. After using this new understanding to correct your thinking, return to the breath.

Another good strategy when your thinking has spun out of control and your mind is filled with pain, restlessness, and worry is to use your own suffering to cultivate wholesome thoughts of compassion. Seeing the pain in your mind, you reflect how suffering affects other people as well: "This phenomenon isn't particular to me. Everyone experiences it, and right now there are many others who are suffering more than I am."

A student of mine told me that at one time he was feeling tremendously depressed. Walking alone in a park one day, he came across a scrap of newspaper. He picked it up and read a story of a man who was walking along, deeply miserable because he had only one shoe. As he limped along, his bare foot cold and sore, the man with one shoe passed a man who had only one leg. Gratitude filled his heart. "Well, at least I still have both legs!" the man said to himself, and his sorrow left him.

Reading this story, my student felt a surge of compassion for those whose troubles are worse than his own, and his depression vanished.

You can use a similar technique anytime thoughts of grief, anger, or mental pain overwhelm you. Just stop and ask yourself: "Why should I complain? My mind is functioning. I have all my senses. I have access to spiritual teachings, and time and a place to meditate. Compared to many people in the world, I live in luxury. Millions of people have no home, no food, no hope. Rather than feeling unhappy, let me cultivate compassion for these people." Compassion calms and soothes our thoughts, so that we can return to the breath with a steadier, more concentrated mind.

This kind of training is not just for formal meditation. What we do in sitting practice, we must carry over to every other moment. We take our training in mindfulness with us into our everyday lives and apply it in all circumstances: on the bus, at work, when we are feeling ill, when we are out shopping. Otherwise, what's the use of so many hours on the cushion? Make every effort to avoid or cut off unwholesome states of mind and to encourage wholesome ones, just as you do on the cushion. It is very challenging to practice in this way outside of meditation, because each day presents us with countless opportunities to get carried away by greedy, angry, or deluded reactions to sense impressions.

Say you are visiting a shopping mall and see some attractive items in the store window. Because of your undisciplined thoughts, you cannot pull your eyes away. You enter the shop and examine the items. You feel you cannot leave without buying one or two. Perhaps you do not have the cash right now, but you have your credit card. You pick something up and buy it.

To practice Skillful Thinking, you must stop yourself during this process, just as you would when recognizing an unwholesome thought while sitting on the cushion. First, sort through and identify your thoughts and feelings. Inquire whether greed or fear or insecurity is driving you to make an unnecessary purchase. Then reason with yourself: "I want to pay off the balance on this card. Do I really want to go deeper into debt?"

Even if you have plenty of money, it is still important to purify greed from your thinking process. Ask yourself, "Is this item necessary, or am

I buying it for some other reason? Do I just want to impress people? Don't I already have some similar things collecting dust in my closet?" You may also ask, "Is there a better use for this money, some way I can use it to help other people?"

If you feel unsure of your motives, perhaps because greed and necessity are mixed together, or because the desire is overwhelming, ask yourself: "Can this purchase wait? Can I walk away for now and come back next week? Can I ask the clerk to hold this while I cool off and think about it?" This kind of reasoning makes skillful use of the good habits that we practice in sitting meditation.

Such training will definitely help us when we encounter more difficult challenges. Once I had to use my practice of Skillful Thinking to overcome fear in a situation of genuine danger.

I had received word of my mother's final illness. On the way to Sri Lanka from Washington, D.C., I changed planes to a jumbo jet in Hawaii. An hour or two after taking off from Hawaii, I looked out my window and noticed flames coming from the plane's engine. Then the pilot's voice came over the intercom. He announced that the engine was on fire and that we were turning back. He told the flight attendants to give instructions on how we should exit the plane if we managed to get back to Hawaii.

The flight attendant told us to sit quietly with our seat belts on. When we landed, floor lights would lead us to the eight emergency doors. The doors would open, and emergency chutes would come out. We were to jump onto the chutes without a moment's hesitation, slide down, and run away from the plane.

I doubt anybody understood much of these instructions. From the moment the pilot had announced that the engine was on fire, everyone in the cabin seemed to be seized with fear of death. Some started crossing themselves, couples clutched each other and kissed, others wept or looked tense and anxious.

I thought, "If this is my time to die, well, I will die anyway, whether I am afraid or not. Let me keep my mind clear." First, I recalled my intellectual understanding of what death is. I considered that death is inevitable, and that this would be a good time for me to die, for I had been doing good deeds, and I had nothing to regret. Then I thought about the likely sequence of events. "If the plane falls quickly from a height of thirty-nine thousand feet, we will be unconscious before the plane hits the ocean." I don't know whether this is scientifically true, but that is what I thought at the time. I exhorted myself, "I have to keep my mind very clear, very pure, before I lose consciousness. This is the time to use my mindfulness to realize the inevitability of death. If I die peacefully with a pure, clear state of mind, my future life will be bright. Perhaps I will attain a stage of enlightenment through seeing the truth of impermanence. I must not block my mind with fear or confusion. No matter how strong my attachment to life, I must let go of that attachment now." Thus I made the effort to prevent any unwholesome state of mind from arising in the face of death and encouraged wholesome states of mind to arise.

Perhaps I was just too stunned to feel afraid, but I felt no fear. I actually enjoyed watching the flames coming out of the engine at thirty-nine feet! The flames were blue, yellow, and red. You seldom see such blue flames. Sometimes they were streaming out; sometimes they were low. They looked like fireworks, or the aurora borealis. While I was enjoying the drama, the three hundred or so other people on the plane were suffering terribly. I looked at the other passengers from time to time and saw the agony they suffered from the very thought of death. They seemed almost to be dead before they died! I noticed, however, that the little children did not seem affected. They kept laughing and playing as they did before the crisis. I thought, "Let me put myself in their place, in a childlike mind."

We did make it back to Hawaii, and the plane made an emergency landing. We went out the emergency doors as instructed, sliding down the chutes. Going down the chute was an entirely new experience for me. Perhaps everyone else on the plane had at least gone down a playground slide in their childhood, but I had never done such a thing in the poor village where I grew up. Thus right up to the end, I enjoyed it all very much.

KEY POINTS FOR MINDFULNESS
OF SKILLFUL THINKING

As we are discovering, walking the Buddha's path to happiness requires practicing each of the eight steps in the real world. We need recipients to accept our generous gifts. We needs friends and enemies to inspire our friendly love. We need suffering beings to develop our compassion. Human society provides a perfect testing ground for these key points of Skillful Thinking:

- When we develop Skillful Understanding, Skillful Thinking flows naturally.

- Thinking can make us happy or miserable.

- The Buddha pointed us toward three skillful thoughts: letting go or generosity in the highest sense, loving-friendliness, and compassion.

- Begin your practice of generosity with giving away material things.

- Clinging to anything—form, feelings, perceptions, volitional formations, or consciousness—makes us unhappy.

- When fear arises, let it grow and watch as it peaks and fades away.

- Loving-friendliness, a sense of interconnectedness with all beings and a sincere wish for them to be happy, has far-reaching effects.

- Your anger will ultimately hurt you more than the person you're angry with; take action to overcome your anger.

- Mindfulness can help you minimize and eventually eliminate your anger.

- Compassion is a spontaneous, wholesome melting of the heart at the suffering of others, coupled with a wish to alleviate their pain.

- Developing compassion for yourself, your parents, your children and your partner will help you relax and soften your heart.

- When negative thoughts arise during meditation, they may go away if you merely pay attention to their passing nature.

- If a negative train of thought persists despite your best efforts, that is the signal to explore it thoroughly—to develop insight into the habits of your life.

- Reflecting on unwholesome thoughts is a critical part of meditation practice.

- Practicing Skillful Thinking on the cushion can help you check your fear, anger, and craving in everyday life.

STEP 3
Skillful Speech

THINK HOW OFTEN you say to yourself, "If only I hadn't said that," or something like "When I saw the look on her face, I knew that what I said had hurt her feelings." Wrong speech causes us many problems. We lie and then get caught in it; we say something nasty about a co-worker and get him into trouble; we speak inconsiderately and offend a client or friend; we spend a whole day in meaningless chatter and get nothing done.

These bad habits of speech are not new. The Buddha considered the practice of Skillful Speech so essential to one's personal and spiritual development that he gave it its own step on the path to happiness. Skillful Speech, the Buddha told us, has four qualities: It is always truthful. It is uplifting, not malicious or unkind. It is gentle, not crude or harsh. It is moderate, not useless or meaningless.

A person who is known for gentle and beautiful speech, the Buddha explained, will quickly be trusted and respected. Such a person enjoys a calm and peaceful state of mind and is able to interact with others lovingly. Have you noticed, for instance, that people tend to speak to us as they have heard us speak? If we are known to exaggerate or to lie, others find it easier to lie to us. If we habitually malign others, people find it easier to speak harshly of us. The converse is also true. If we are known for truthfulness, our words are more readily believed. If we have a reputation for discretion, others find it harder to spread gossip about us. If our speech is always kind and gentle, others feel embarrassed to swear or speak crudely in our presence.

It is clear that speech creates an environment that either contributes to happiness or destroys it. We know this is so because our own experience shows us that how we think and act is heavily influenced by the kind of speech that goes on around us. One of the Buddha's first nuns observed in verse:

> If he resorted to noble friends,
> Even a fool would become wise.
> (Thig 213)

If we wish to be wise, we must not only seek out noble friends but be a noble friend to others. Doing so requires that we make a mindful effort to practice Skillful Speech. A Buddhist folk story illustrates how strongly speech can influence our behavior:

A monk in the Buddha's entourage had a habit of eating sumptuous meals with a group of people misled by the evil monk Devadatta. Tempted by the delicious food these people offered, this monk spent much time in the unwholesome company of this group. The Buddha reprimanded the monk for choosing such companions and warned him of the consequences. To convince him to change his behavior, the Buddha told the monk the story of an incident that had taken place in a former life, in which the monk had been led astray by the harsh, unwholesome speech of those around him.

In a previous birth, the Buddha said, the monk had been a great elephant belonging to a king. This elephant was known for his gentle disposition. Then a group of burglars made a habit of gathering near the elephant's stall each night to discuss their evil plans. They spoke harshly and encouraged each other to commit murder and other cruel acts. The elephant began to believe that their rough words were intended to teach him that he should behave in similar ways. As a result, the formerly noble elephant became murderous, killing anyone who tried to work with him.

The king who owned the elephant sent his minister—the aspiring Buddha—to investigate what was corrupting the gentle elephant. The minister overheard the wicked speech of the burglars and saw how it affected the elephant. He advised the king to send wise sages, known for their gentle speech, to talk together near the elephant's stall every night. The good and wholesome speech soon influenced the elephant to return to his gentle ways, and he was never cruel again. (J 26)

Skillful Speech can improve your life in many ways. Just imagine never having to regret anything you say! That would release many of us from a heavy burden.

Let's look more closely at the four qualities of Skillful Speech and explore how they might help us along on the path to happiness.

SPEAK THE TRUTH

The first quality of Skillful Speech is that it is always truthful. Never lie, the Buddha told us, whether for your own advantage, for someone else's advantage, or for any advantage whatsoever. The Buddha summed up the guidelines for truth-telling this way:

> When [someone is] questioned as a witness thus, "So, good man, tell what you know": knowing, he says, "I know"; not knowing, he says, "I do not know"; not seeing, he says, "I do not see"; or seeing, he says, "I see"; he does not in full awareness speak falsehood for his own ends, or another's ends, or for some trifling worldly end. (M 41)

Occasionally we may be asked a question to which a response of silence indicates a particular answer. If our silence would convey a lie, then we must speak. For example, a police investigator at the scene of a crime asks a crowd of on-lookers whether they saw anything. If everyone remains silent, the investigator will conclude that no one has seen the crime occur. If some of the onlookers are witnesses, then they lie by remaining silent. They may feel that they have good reason to say nothing, such as fear of retaliation, but their silence is a lie nonetheless. We can also lie with our body language. Sometimes a shrug or a raised eyebrow may convey "I don't know." But if you do know, your shrug is a deception.

There are situations, however, where the truth has to be withheld because speaking up might hurt someone. In such cases, we have to wait for the right time to speak the right words to the right person. The Buddha himself frequently resorted to silence when his answering a question would cause someone harm. Once a man asked the Buddha whether there is life after death. The Buddha just sat there, silent, until the man gave up and went away. Later, his attendant, Ananda, asked the Buddha why he had not answered. The Buddha explained that any answer would have caused the man suffering. If he had answered that there is continuation after death, the Buddha knew that the man would have seized on the idea of an eternally existing self, a wrong understanding that leads to suffering. If he had answered negatively, the man would have developed another wrong understanding, thinking, "Then I will be annihilated!" and would have suffered greatly on that account. To avoid causing harm to the man, the Buddha decided not to make any response at all.

The Buddha described the guidelines by which he himself decided whether to speak or to remain silent. If he knew something was untrue, incorrect, or not beneficial, he would not say it. "Such speech [the Buddha] does not utter," he said. If he knew that something was true, correct, and beneficial, then "[the Buddha] knows the time to use such speech." When his words were true, correct, beneficial, and timely, the Buddha spoke regardless of whether his words would be "unwelcome and disagreeable to others" or "welcome and agreeable to others." (M 58) Deeply compassionate and fully focused on people's well-being, the Buddha never spoke only to be a "people pleaser." We can learn much from his example.

When I am tempted to speak words that do not meet the Buddha's guidelines, I remind myself that I gain nothing by speaking, nor does anyone else gain, and nobody loses by my keeping quiet. For example, let's say I am talking with friends, one of whom is monopolizing the conversation. I have something to say and feel impatient to say it. I have reflected on what I want to say and know it is true as to past events, correct as to current facts, and that it would benefit the listeners. If I blurt it out now, however, I may offend the speaker. Thus it is not timely. So I remind myself that I do not gain if I speak in an untimely way, nobody else gains, and furthermore nobody loses by my patient silence. I can say what I want to say some other time.

WORDS ARE NOT WEAPONS

The second aspect of Skillful Speech is avoiding malicious talk. As an old folk saying tells us, "The tongue is a boneless weapon trapped between teeth." When we speak malicious words, our tongue releases verbal daggers. Such words rob people of their good name and their credibility. Even when what we say about someone is true, if its intent is to cause the person harm, it is malicious.

The Buddha defined malicious talk as speech that destroys the friendship between two people. Here's an example: Suppose on a trip I meet one of your good friends who lives far away. I remember that several months before, you had told me an unflattering story about this fellow. I may not remember your exact words, so I add a little flavor when I repeat what you said. I even make it look like I am doing this guy a favor to let him know that you have been talking about him behind his back. Your friend responds in some heat. When I get home, I repeat his words to you, spicing them up a bit to make it a better story. Because it causes disharmony and breaks up a friendship, such speech is malicious.

Sometimes we disguise malicious speech as concern about another's behavior. Or we reveal a secret that someone has confided to us, believing that we are doing so "for his own good." For instance, telling a woman that her husband is being unfaithful because "you don't want her to be the last to know" may cause more suffering for everyone involved. When you are tempted to speak in such a way, ask yourself what you hope to gain. If your goal is to manipulate others or to earn someone's gratitude or appreciation, your speech is self-serving and malicious rather than virtuous.

Public speech can be malicious as well. Tabloid newspapers, talk radio, Internet chat rooms, and even some respectable news media seem to be making their living today using words as weapons. A fresh shot at this week's media target scores points that translate into increased viewers and advertising dollars. Malicious speech knocks someone down to raise someone else up. It tries to make the speaker look incisive, smart, or hip at another's expense.

Not all malicious speech sounds nasty. Sometimes people use words that seem gentle but have a derogatory meaning. Such disguised verbal daggers are even more dangerous than overtly malicious words because they more easily penetrate the listener's mind and heart. In modern terms, we call such speech a "backhanded compliment." We say to someone, "How clever of you to fix up your old house rather than moving to a more fashionable neighborhood," or "Your gray hair is so becoming. Isn't it wonderful that looking older is acceptable in our profession?" Skillful Speech not only means that we pay attention to the words we speak and to their tone but also requires that our words reflect compassion and concern for others and that they help and heal, rather than wound and destroy.

SPEAK SOFTLY

The third kind of wrong speech is harsh language. Verbal abuse, profanity, sarcasm, hypocrisy, and excessively blunt or belittling criticism are all examples of harsh language.

Speech is a powerful tool that can be used for good or for ill. The Buddha compared speech to an ax:

> Every person who is born
> is born with an ax in his mouth.
> A fool who uses abusive language
> cuts himself and others with that ax.
> (Sn 657)

We probably think of an ax merely as a tool for chopping firewood. But in the Buddha's day, the ax was a tool of precision and power. It was used to cut long planks of wood and plane them perfectly smooth and to carve and chisel wood precisely. It could cut down a mighty tree. And it was a deadly weapon, a brutal means to maim or kill. Perhaps a modern parallel to the ax is the computer. Computers can be used to do many wonderful things—to communicate across oceans, make music, or direct a flight to Mars. They can also be used for destruction. Computers help wage wars by controlling missiles and other weapons.

Just as we must choose how we will use the power of an ax or a computer, we must choose how we will use our speech. Will we speak words that awaken, console, and encourage others? Or will we cut them down, injuring ourselves in the process? Slanderous talk, cruel gossip, lies, and crude or profane jokes not only abuse others but make us look like fools who are unable to wield the ax in our mouths without bloodying ourselves.

We are also fools if we think that harsh language ever accomplishes anything positive. Though we may feel very self-satisfied when we have dressed someone down, as we say—given them a piece of our minds— we have won no genuine victory. As the Buddha said:

> The fool thinks he has won a battle,
> when he bullies with harsh speech;
> but knowing how to be forbearing
> alone makes one victorious.
> (S I.7.1 [3])

It is easy to silence people by using harsh, insulting words. A smart adversary will generally withdraw from such an interchange and respond to our harsh words with icy silence. We may congratulate ourselves and think, I really showed him—he shut right up when he heard what I had to say. But our apparent victory is hollow. Our opponent may have pledged never to speak to us again or vowed to thwart us secretly sometime in the future. The ill will and bad feelings we cause will boomerang and strike us when we least anticipate it.

It's easy to think of other examples of the negative effects of harsh language. Perhaps you have a co-worker with enormous talent or technical genius, whose mouth always gets him into trouble. He bullies his associates with words that are harsh, abrasive, arrogant, and obnoxious. Despite the quality of his work, people cannot tolerate him, so his career goes nowhere.

Another particularly sad example of the destructive power of harsh speech is its effect on children. Haven't we all overheard parents telling their children, "You're a disgrace," "You can't do anything right," "You'll never amount to anything." Perhaps we remember being told such things when we were small. Verbal abuse can leave scars on the heart of a child that never completely heal. Of course, parents might sometimes have to speak sharply to a child to stop the child from doing something dangerous, like playing with matches or running into the street. But such strong speech is motivated by love and care, not by the wish to bully or belittle.

Animals also feel the effect of harsh speech. My grandnephew has a great Alaskan husky named Taurus. Taurus is fascinated by the animals on television. He even tries to bite them. Because he is so large, when Taurus is attracted to what he sees on the screen, he blocks the view of the people sitting behind him. One day a member of my grandnephew's family ordered Taurus to get out of the way. Her tone of voice was excessively hard and stern. The dog reacted by going to the basement. For a week Taurus stayed down there, refusing to come out, even to eat. He emerged only occasionally to go outside to relieve himself. Then he went right back downstairs. Finally, the family had to go and plead with him, using sweet words, in affectionate tones, before Taurus rejoined them.

The soft words of my grandnephew's family won back the companionship of their beloved pet. Kind language, as another early Buddhist saying tells us, is always appropriate and welcome:

> Speak kind words, words
> rejoiced at and welcomed,
> words that bear ill will to none;
> always speak kindly to others.
> (Sn 452 [translated by Ven. S. Dhammika])

Telling someone, "I really appreciate the work you did," "You handled that difficult situation beautifully," or "It's such a joy to see you" warms the heart of the speaker and of the person spoken to. Soft words are honey on the tongue. Speaking our praise and appreciation increases the happiness of everyone involved. They help us make and keep friends, for everyone wants to associate with people whose soft and gentle speech makes them feel relaxed, comfortable, and safe. Soft words help children flourish and grow up with a positive feeling of self-worth. Such words can also help people learn and appreciate the Buddha's message. There is no limit to the amount of joy we can spread to those around us if we speak with kindness and skill.

A word of caution: Soft words must also be sincere and motivated by a noble purpose. Speaking gently and kindly while thinking or doing the opposite is hypocrisy, not virtue. We have all heard religious leaders who use soft words to spread fear or manipulate people into sending money to their organization. I remember a man in Sri Lanka who toured the country speaking against the evils of alcohol. This man rose to fame, power, and popularity, drawing large crowds due to the power of his oration. He galvanized the campaign to close the bars, shut down the breweries, and end the sale of liquor. One hot summer day, during one of his powerful speeches, the man carelessly whipped off his jacket. A small bottle of alcohol fell from an inside pocket and hit the floor of the stage. That was the end of the prohibition campaign, and of this man's public career. Even though what the man was saying about the poison of alcohol was true, once people saw the poison of this man's hypocrisy, they could no longer buy his message.

AVOID USELESS CHATTER

The fourth type of wrong speech is gossip, which the Buddha described as foolish or meaningless talk. When we say the word gossip in English, we may be referring to a whole range of negative speech, from malicious invective to merely careless or useless chatter. All such speech is considered wrong according to the Buddha's teachings.

Gossip about other people is a problem regardless of whether what we say about someone else is true. After all, if three people relate a story about a fourth person, each story will be different. Human nature is such that we tend to believe whatever we hear first, even though it is just one person's version. It may be based on truth, but gossip will embellish and exaggerate it.

Gossip leads to quarrels and misunderstandings. It can break up relationships. In the most serious cases, it can lead to lawsuits for libel or defamation. In the Buddha's time, the power of gossip toppled a great confederacy:

> The Licchavi people were a proud, free clan, one of the most powerful and important members of a strong confederacy of eight clans. Their capital city was the capital of the confederacy. An ambitious ruler, King Ajatasattu, the principal supporter of the evil monk Devadatta, planned to invade and defeat the Licchavi people. The king asked the Buddha his opinion of his plan to invade. The Buddha spoke of the harmony in which the Licchavi people lived and told the king, "You cannot invade them so long as they remain unified and harmonious." The king postponed his attack and pondered the Buddha's statement.
>
> Then King Ajatasattu came up with a simple and devious plan. He instructed his prime minister to whisper something into the ear of a Licchavi man. The prime minister went up to one of the Licchavi men and whispered emphatically, "There is rice in a paddy seed." It was a trivial, meaningless statement. Everyone knew that rice can be found in a paddy seed.
>
> But seeing something whispered, another Licchavi man began wondering what King Ajatasattu's prime minister had said to this fellow. When he asked the man what had been said, the man repeated the statement about the paddy seed.
>
> Hearing this, the second Licchavi man thought, "This guy is hiding the truth. He doesn't trust me. He fabricated this silly statement about the paddy seed to deceive me." Filled with suspicion, he told another Licchavi clansman that the man had been whispering with the prime minister. That person told another, and so on, until people believed that the man was a spy and that a secret conspiracy was being hatched in their midst.
>
> Peace was shattered. Accusations and arguments arose among the Licchavi people, and fighting broke out among the leading families. With his enemy in disarray, King Ajatasattu invaded the Licchavi people, and his troops conquered them easily. He then went on to conquer the rest of the confederacy.

I don't need such accounts to convince myself that gossip is harmful. I have experienced myself how damaging gossip can be. It seems that whenever someone tries to do something for the good of society, some people feel opposed to that effort. Maybe they feel insecure or jealous of another's success. Rumors are their weapons. They do not have to come forth and provide any evidence. They can whisper insinuations and rely upon other people's willingness to engage in careless talk to do their dirty work.

When we were first trying to raise funds to build our center, some people spread rumors about the Bhavana Society. People said that I was bilking donors, intending to use the funds we collected to start a shady business for profit. Unsigned letters were sent to key people, telling them not to contribute. The gossip was started maliciously, but it was spread by people who simply did not know the truth. The Buddhist community in the city in which I lived, which had initially been supportive, became divided. Fortunately, those who opposed the building of the Bhavana Society could not find any real faults to magnify, or they would have completely destroyed our efforts.

So long as people are willing to believe whatever they hear and repeat things carelessly, rumors will circulate. Once an American member of the board of directors of the Bhavana Society traveled to Sri Lanka. While there, he joined a group of meditation practitioners from various countries, and they spent an evening talking together about meditation centers in various places. Someone mentioned the Bhavana Society in this gathering, and a woman exclaimed, "Oh! That's the center where they have that tea ceremony in the evenings!" When our board member protested, the lady insisted that she knew her statement to be true. Finally our member said, "Well, I have known Bhante Gunaratana since 1971 and have been involved with the Bhavana Society since its inception. I know there is no tea ceremony there." If someone who knew the truth had not been present, no one would have been able to contradict the woman's statement. Perhaps others would have added further untrue comments and maybe even hurtful things. That is how gossip gets started and how it damages people and institutions. If we hear someone gossip or say something damaging, we have two choices: either we end the conversation or we discourage the person from speaking negatively, as our board member did in this case.

But there's an even more radical and powerful message in the Buddha's teaching that we abstain from gossip. It is that all unnecessary speech is harmful. Many of us spend a great deal of time chattering about the food we ate several days or months ago, or trying to remember the details of some silly movie or TV show that we saw. We waste even more time saying things simply to make others laugh. This kind of talk does not lead to any deepening of wisdom. When we consider how short human life is and how easily it can be snatched away by accident or illness, do we really want to waste our precious time distracting ourselves with idle chitchat? Someone whose hair is on fire must urgently try to put it out; likewise, we must arouse our spiritual urgency to free ourselves from the burning of negative mind states, rather than wasting our time on gossip.

Now, it's true that some seemingly idle or silly talk may actually serve an important purpose. Sometimes we must speak soft meaningless words to comfort someone or to bond lovingly with our children. All mindful speech motivated by love and compassion is an acceptable part of Skillful Speech. The test is to stop and ask ourselves before we speak: "Is it true? Is it kind? Is it beneficial? Does it harm anyone? Is this the right time to say something?"

MINDFULNESS OF SKILLFUL SPEECH

Skillful Speech is not something you practice on the cushion. It happens in dialogue, not silence. During formal meditation, however, you can think about your habits of speech and try to convert the thoughts that arise to skillful thoughts—those motivated by generosity, loving-friendliness, and compassion. You can analyze your past actions and ask yourself: "Did I speak correctly yesterday? Have I spoken only gently, kindly, meaningfully, and truthfully?" If you find that you have erred in some way, you can pledge to improve your mindfulness of Skillful Speech.

The most important resolution you can make is to think before you speak. People say, "Watch your tongue!" But it's more important to watch your mind. The tongue does not wag by itself. The mind controls it. Before you open your mouth, check your mind to see whether your motivation is wholesome. You will come to regret any speech motivated by greed, hatred, or delusion.

Also make a strong determination not to say anything that might hurt another person. This pledge will definitely help you to think carefully before you speak. When you speak mindfully, you automatically speak truthfully, gently, and kindly. Mindfulness will keep you from using verbal daggers that can pierce people to the marrow. If the intent to speak in a harmful way occurs to you, immediately use mindfulness and Skillful Effort to prevent these thoughts from continuing.

The pledge not to wound others with your speech is especially important when talking with someone toward whom you feel resentment, or when discussing a situation about which you have strong feelings. Be careful! Use only gentle, well-selected words. Speaking softly can bring peace and harmony to the situation and help the conversation to continue in a productive, profitable, and friendly way.

If someone approaches you and speaks irritatingly—nagging or gossiping about one of your friends, for instance—and you notice yourself getting upset, simply stop talking. Remind yourself silently, "I must not be reactive. I must not fall into the same lack of mindfulness as this person. This conversation is not going anywhere. I choose to engage only in meaningful conversation." In many cases, the other person will respond to your silence by stopping the irritating talk. You can use the pause that follows to turn the conversation in a better direction.

Actually, as someone following the Buddha's path, the moment you know that a conversation is heading in the wrong direction, you should take responsibility for putting it back on track. It is so easy to get carried away with emotional talk and start shouting. A shouting match causes unhappiness to everyone involved. With mindfulness recall how awful you feel when you are out of control emotionally. Remind yourself that it may take hours or days before you calm down enough to talk to this person again. A lot of good feelings will be lost, perhaps permanently.

In spite of all your good efforts, however, sometimes you still get angry. If another person continually provokes you, assaulting you with verbal daggers, you may become completely confused and bewildered. Then it is very easy for anger to arise. When you see your confusion building up, say "Wait a minute!" to the other person, with the hope of finding a moment to clear your mind. But what if the other person responds with "No, you wait a minute!" and continues to attack—then what?

In these situations, when the conversation spins out of control, your task is to bring mindfulness back quickly and use Skillful Effort to overcome the anger. Even if your feelings of anger cause your heart to beat fast, your body to break into a sweat, and your hands to shake, mindfulness of your resolution to avoid all harsh speech can help you stay in control. Simply refuse to let your anger tell you what to say. Concentrate on your breathing to reestablish mindfulness until your anger has died down.

Calming yourself gives both you and the other person a chance to open your hearts in a more friendly way. As your heart begins to warm, you see the other more clearly, and maybe you will understand why you both got upset. You can also see how confused an angry state of mind makes you. As your feelings of respect and concern grow, you can resolve to use this moment to begin a new and more loving relationship and to strengthen the companionship between you. That is what you should always hope to do.

When you see that you have disciplined your mind and your words and that the situation has become more harmonious, be happy about it! Say to yourself, "This is what I want. I want always to act in ways that allow these good things to happen." Bring up that thought again and again.

Let me tell you a story of a time when I myself had to use mindfulness to practice Skillful Speech. Perhaps my experience will give you some clues about how to apply mindfulness to situations that arise in your life—at your work, at home, and in your personal relationships.

Many years ago, when I was in charge of running a certain temple, a group of people called a meeting for temple supporters. These people opposed some work I had initiated and needed a forum where they could express their frustrations. A bit of character assassination may have been on the agenda, too. Some of these people had very strong feelings about the matters to be discussed. They had been born into Buddhist families, but they had no interest in meditation. In fact, they considered meditation a crazy thing to do. Therefore they did not understand my work. I expected to be on the hot seat during this meeting, but what happened was worse than anyone could have predicted.

About forty people were attending the meeting, including many of my relatives, close friends, and others who hoped to show support for my programs. Before the meeting was properly opened, even before introductions had been made, a very simple man stood up and began to speak. This fellow was uneducated and unskilled, with a tendency toward unrefined speech. He had little to say about the temple business under discussion, but a lot to say about me. In low, vulgar terms, he charged that I had done nothing for the temple for years, that I was damaging support for the temple, and so on. He used socially unacceptable, derogatory, and hurtful language throughout this tirade, which went on for about twenty minutes.

During this shocking verbal assault, I worked with my mind. To prevent anger from arising, I reasoned with myself. I could see that the man was in a disturbed state, and I thought to myself, "I know this man to have a peaceful nature. We have had a good relationship. He must have been poisoned by someone else who feels strongly about these matters to say such things." As the man continued to speak, I reflected that I had had many opportunities for spiritual and cultural development that this man lacked. I recalled that he had only an elementary school education, few skills, and little interest in spiritual training. In this way, I tried to cultivate compassion for him and also gratitude that my training made it unlikely that I would ever speak or act as he was doing.

I also reflected on the context of what was happening. I considered that if I were to say anything to oppose him, my supporters would stand up for me, and the meeting might degenerate into an ugly fight. I watched people's eyes getting bigger and saw them frowning at the man and shifting in their seats. I sensed that my relatives in particular were deeply affected. I am an elder in my family—a brother, uncle, granduncle, and great granduncle—and I am known to be a gentle monk. Naturally, my family respects me and feels protective of me. I knew that if I seemed to be hurt or upset by what this man was saying, my relatives would experience anger and other unwholesome states of mind. They might even physically attack the man. So I told myself: "Here I have to exercise mindfulness, patience, and understanding to bring peace to this meeting."

I established mindfulness by concentrating on my breathing. When challenged like this, it is very important to pause and take some deep breaths before responding—perhaps two minutes of deep breathing, or thirty inhalations and thirty exhalations. This pause gives you time to relax and clear your mind, so you can speak sense, instead of blowing up.

Finally, the man seemed to have exhausted himself and stopped talking. Everybody was tense. They all looked at me. In a quiet voice I said, "This gentleman has been a friend of mine. He has been a very good supporter of this temple and has done many good and helpful things. He also knows what I have done all these years for the temple. But today, somehow, he seems to be upset, disappointed, and maybe not feeling quite himself. Therefore I feel like giving my blessings to him and to everybody."

I asked everyone there to put their hands together in the prayer position and to reverence the Buddha by saying three times, "Homage to the Blissful One, the Noble One, the Fully Enlightened One." This is how we commonly begin formal ceremonies. From the sheer weight of tradition, there was no way anyone could bring up any quarrel or express any negative opinion from that point on. It would have seemed disrespectful to the Buddha. Then I led the group in taking the five precepts, which uplifted their minds and made sure that everyone recalled the Buddha's guidelines for proper, harmless behavior. Finally, I recited a lengthy blessing chant, and when I finished, I said, "Now you can go home. The meeting is over." And that was the end of it. For some years, this man remained cold toward me, but later I had the opportunity to be of service to him when he went through some serious difficulties. Since then and to this day, he remains friendly to me and expresses only his gratitude and respect.

Mindfulness is the key that helped me resolve this difficult situation. The same technique can work for you. I sometimes hear people say that things were happening so fast that "even with mindfulness" they could not control their actions or speech. Saying "even with mindfulness" makes no sense. Perhaps their mindfulness was weak or undermined by greed, hatred, or delusion. But by definition, mindfulness keeps us in control of what we think, how we act, and what we say. It's impossible to shout at someone mindfully, or to abuse alcohol mindfully, or to engage in sexual misconduct mindfully. If you are truly mindful, you simply cannot do these things!

Because our habits are so strong, whenever we open our mouths, things seem just to spill out. We may not be aware of how much energy pours away with our speech. With mindful awareness, we put a stop to this outpouring, and energy collects. We can use this built-up energy to develop insight into the nature of our habits. Using this energy as fuel, we can talk to ourselves mentally in meditation, taking stock of our actions, further training our minds.

However, when we let this bottled-up energy out without mindfulness, it often explodes with a *pop!* like a cork from a bottle. I see this especially at the end of retreats. A few moments before, a perfectly silent group of people were sitting still or moving slowly and quietly. Then the Noble Silence of the retreat ends, and a roar of babbling conversation breaks out. This flood of talk goes on for an hour or two, until all the built-up energy has dissipated. The longer the retreat, the louder and more light-headed people will become, unless they make the effort to remain very mindful of their speech.

The only antidote for wrong speech is a strong dose of mindfulness—not just during retreats, or when you are in a challenging or difficult situation, but for your whole life. Mindfulness of Skillful Speech will contribute to your happiness. I guarantee it.

KEY POINTS FOR MINDFULNESS
OF SKILLFUL SPEECH

Here are the key points for preventing unhappiness by way of Skillful Speech:

- Skillful speech requires that you abstain from lying, malicious words, harsh language, and useless talk.

- Lying by omission is still lying.

- Malicious talk is speech that destroys other people's friendships or damages their reputations.

- Verbal abuse, profanity, sarcasm, hypocrisy, and excessively blunt or belittling criticism are all examples of harsh language.

- Harsh language hurts others and debases you.

- Gossip and idle talk lead to quarrels and misunderstandings, waste your time, and create a confused state of mind.

- All unnecessary speech not motivated by generosity, loving-friendliness, and compassion is harmful.

- The test of Skillful Speech is to stop and ask yourself before you speak: "Is it true? Is it kind? Is it beneficial? Does it harm anyone? Is this the right time to say something?"

- Using mindfulness to strengthen your resolution to say nothing hurtful and to use only soft, well-chosen words can bring harmony to any difficult situation.

STEP 4
Skillful Action

S OME PEOPLE want a simple list of rules to follow so that they can be sure that they are acting in a moral and proper way. Others need rules to feel secure that they will reach their spiritual goal, whether it be heaven or enlightenment. The Buddha did offer a code of conduct that prevents us from adding to our suffering, but truly ethical behavior goes far beyond any list of rules. Rather, it's an interlocking set of principles concerning how our actions cause suffering to ourselves and to others—how each person's moral choices impact the whole.

THE FIVE PRECEPTS

Buddhist morality begins with five moral principles that people are strongly advised to keep if they wish to make spiritual progress. These are:

- abstaining from killing
- abstaining from stealing
- abstaining from speaking falsely
- abstaining from sexual misconduct
- abstaining from misusing alcohol or other intoxicants

Followers of the Buddha are expected to undertake vows to observe these rules, called the five precepts. However, these moral principles are not something created by the Buddha; they are timeless, basic, and universal.

Four of the five precepts are covered directly in the Eightfold Path. Skillful Speech includes abstaining from false speech. Skillful Action is defined as abstaining from killing, stealing, and sexual misconduct. The last of the five precepts, abstaining from intoxicants, is implied in Skillful Action because an intoxicated person cannot guard against engaging in wrong speech and action.

At the initial stage of moral development, we need these five precepts, much as a child needs parents to enforce rules such as "Don't touch a hot stove." When children grow up, they realize that their parents' rules existed to prevent certain kinds of harm. Similarly, when we have perfected our understanding of moral behavior, Skillful Action becomes automatic. It becomes impossible to want to break the five precepts, and we no longer need to refer back to them to keep ourselves on track.

ETHICS IN ACTION

Traditionally we say that the step of Skillful Action consists of abstaining from killing, stealing, and sexual misconduct. Although we use the same words in the five precepts and in the definition of Skillful Action of the Eightfold Path, the meanings are a little different. For the purpose of the precepts, the meaning is very simple and straightforward: Just don't do these three things. Killing, stealing, and sexual misconduct are three of the worst acts you can perform, and if you engage in them you'll find no peace. So, we make a strong, powerful resolution and adhere to it strictly.

However, when the Buddha defined Skillful Action of the Eightfold Path in terms of abstaining from killing, stealing, and sexual misconduct, he was giving only the most gross examples of violations that one may do to others. Thus these abstentions should be understood not only in a limited way, in terms of keeping precepts, but also as broad guides for higher ethical behavior.

For example, in one of the talks in which he urged everyone to act compassionately to all living beings, the Buddha commented,

All living beings are afraid of the stick [violence];
All living beings fear death.
Comparing oneself to others,
Don't hurt or cause another [to hurt].
(Dh 129)

He explained that any physical action that hurts another person—vandalizing property, arson, intimidating someone with a weapon—is wrong, even if no one is killed. I once heard of a young man who disliked his roommates in graduate school. To take revenge, he harassed them by secretly doing things to their personal belongings like dunking their washcloths into the toilet and damaging their computers! Petty meanness and practical jokes that hurt people are also wrong actions.

There is a more refined level of ethical action as well. For example, abstaining from killing reaches its highest meaning when we develop a completely nonharming attitude and continually wish for the well-being of other living beings.

We practice Skillful Action not because we want to avoid breaking the Buddha's rules or because we fear that someone will punish us if we do. We avoid cruel and hurtful behavior because we see the consequences of such actions—that they lead to profound unhappiness for us and for everyone around us, now and in the future. We practice Skillful Action because we want our lives to be helpful and harmonious, not destructive and contentious, and because we want a calm and happy mind, untroubled by regret or remorse.

Our mind plays many tricks on us when it comes to observing moral principles. Some people tell themselves that moral rules do not apply to the young. "I can have a good time now," they say, "and do whatever I want. When I get older, I'll clean up my act." Unfortunately, observing moral principles at the end of life is like winning the lottery on your deathbed. If you wait too long, you won't be able to enjoy the benefits that a moral life brings—freedom from addictions, healthy relationships, a clear conscience, and an untroubled mind. It's best to enjoy the wholesome effects of morality while you're young, healthy, and strong. In old age, you won't need moral principles to keep you from misbehaving!

Another trick we play is saying to ourselves, "What good are these moral principles to me? My life is fine just the way it is." If this is your response, you'd best look at your reasoning carefully. If your life is so fine, why do you lie, steal, drink, or kill? Breaking moral principles quickly becomes a habit that is hard to break. Moreover, these behaviors inevitably lead to negative consequences. There's no running away from the law of cause and effect. Break moral principles, and you risk losing your health, your property, the affection of your loved ones, and many other things you value. Moreover, you'll face worry, guilt, and even more dissatisfaction. Remember, we observe moral principles to make us happy, not miserable.

Even small, seemingly trivial immoral acts have some impact. I heard of a man who lost a bid for partnership in a multimillion-dollar business—just by killing a bug. He was a very savvy, talented businessman, who had set up a meeting with a potential partner to discuss a deal. As they talked, an insect landed on the edge of the businessman's beer glass. He pushed it down into the beer with a little stirring stick. When the bug crawled back up the glass the man pushed it down again. While discussing business worth millions of dollars, he toyed with the bug, repeatedly pushing it down until it drowned.

The potential partner told me later that after seeing this, he thought, "This man is most cruel. Perhaps he'll do something wicked just to make money. I don't want to do business with him." So he backed out of the deal.

You might wonder why the principles of Skillful Action are expressed in negative terms—not killing, not stealing, and the like. The reason for this is very simple. We cannot find the joy of good behavior until we let go of the wrong. We tend to act with a mind filled with attachment, which leads us to all kinds of depravity. First we must oppose this natural tendency. Then we can see how comfortable, relaxed, free, and peaceful we feel when we act ethically. It's impossible to cook a delicious meal in a pot caked with dirt, or to grow a beautiful garden on land choked with weeds. Abstaining from the negative, we create the proper conditions for the positive to flourish. For instance, refraining from killing or other acts of active hostility creates the right atmosphere for loving-friendliness and compassion to enter our dealings with others. Similarly, abstaining from stealing—taking what is not given, whether it is someone else's possessions or credit for someone else's work or ideas—gives rise to its opposite, generosity.

Ethical action shifts our focus from what we personally want to what will most benefit us and others. When we are obsessed with our own desires, we are motivated primarily by hatred, greed, envy, lust, and other selfish preoccupations. Then we have neither the self-control nor the wisdom to act rightly. But when we abstain from negativity, our mental fog clears a bit, and we begin to see that loving-friendliness, compassion, and generosity genuinely make us happy. This clarity of mind helps us to make ethical choices and to progress on the Buddha's path.

Not Killing

The inclination to harm or hurt other living beings generally arises out of hatred or fear. When we purposely kill living beings, even small creatures like insects, we diminish our respect for all life—and thus for ourselves. Mindfulness helps us to recognize our own aversions and to take responsibility for them. As we examine our mental states, we see that hatred and fear lead to a cycle of cruelty and violence, actions that damage others and destroy our own peace of mind. Abstaining from killing makes the mind peaceful and free from hatred. This clarity helps us to refrain from destructive actions and to embrace actions motivated by generosity and compassion.

One of my students told me that she used to feel fear and revulsion toward certain small creatures, like mice, fleas, and ticks. Because of these feelings, she was willing to kill them. As her mindfulness practice helped her to become more gentle, she resolved not to kill these creatures. As a result, her feelings of fear and revulsion diminished. Not long ago, she even managed to scoop up a large cockroach in her bare hands and carry it outdoors to safety.

When we abstain from killing, our respect for life grows, and we begin to act with compassion toward all living beings. This same student told me of visiting a friend who lived at a certain meditation center. When she arrived, she noticed an insect trap hung up on the porch of the center's staff housing. Dozens of yellow jackets were in the trap, drawn by the sweet smell of apple juice. Once they entered the small opening in the trap, they could not get out. When they became exhausted by flying in the small space, they fell into the apple juice at the bottom of the trap and slowly drowned. The visiting student asked her friend about the trap. He agreed that such a device was a shameful thing to have at a meditation center, but he said that the higher-ups had put the trap there and that there was nothing he could do about it.

Though she tried to ignore the buzzing coming from the trap, the woman could not get the suffering of the yellow jackets out of her mind. Soon she felt she had to do something to give a few of them a chance to escape. She took a knife, poked a tiny hole at the top of the trap, and inserted the knife to hold it open. A few yellow jackets crawled up the knife blade and escaped to safety. Then she enlarged the hole a bit more, and a few more got out. Finally, she realized that she could not bear to leave even one to die in the trap. Though she was nervous about interfering, she took the trap to a nearby field and cut it completely open, releasing all the yellow jackets that remained alive. As she did so, she made the wish, "May I be released from my negative attitudes and behaviors even as these insects are released from the trap."

The student told me that since that time, she has had no fear of yellow jackets. Last spring, a nest of yellow jackets appeared under the main doorway of the Bhavana Society. People using that doorway got stung, and the area was roped off. However, this one woman continued to use that doorway, stepping over the nest without harm until it was removed. "I'll be very surprised if I'm ever stung by yellow jackets again," she said. "But if I do get stung, I'll be more worried about the poor yellow jacket who gets upset and may get injured by stinging me."

As you can see from this student's experience, refraining from killing creates the right atmosphere for compassionate action to grow in our lives. This is wonderful and a great aid to progress on the Buddha's path. But we shouldn't become militant in our support of nonharming! Skillful Action asks us to make our own decisions about moral behavior, not to insist adamantly that everyone follow our example.

Take the issue of eating meat. Though I do not eat meat myself, I do not insist that everyone become a vegetarian. Looking at the bigger picture, I see that even vegetarians contribute indirectly to killing. Suppose there is a village where a thousand vegetarians live, and in the next village, there is a farmer who cultivates vegetables, fruit, and grain to feed the thousand villagers. When he tills the land or controls the insects that might damage the vegetables, the farmer kills many small beings. Many other animals and insects are killed by his farm machinery as he harvests the crop. The vegetarians in the next village feel very comfortable. Even though creatures did die, the vegetarians have a clear conscience when eating, because they lack the intent to kill. You can see from this example that eating vegetables and killing beings in the process of growing vegetables are two separate things. The same logic applies to eating meat. Eating meat and killing beings for their meat are two separate things. The Buddha himself sometimes ate meat that was offered to him. Those who are merely eating meat also lack the intent to kill.

For the purpose of keeping the precept against killing, the Buddha defined killing very specifically as the act of purposely taking life. In the rules he set down for monks, the Buddha further clarifies the conditions necessary for an act of killing:

- There must be a being.

- You must know that there is a being.

- You must intend to kill.

- You must plan to use a method to kill the being.

- You must kill the being, using only the planned method.

Meat-eaters do not fulfill any of these conditions. They know that what they are eating is meat and that the meat came from some animal. Yet they had no intention of killing the animal, nor did they participate in killing it.

If meat is not available, people should not go out and hunt or kill animals in order to eat. They should eat something else. But they should also not become neurotic trying to avoid everything that contributes indirectly to killing. When we think about it, a certain amount of indirect contribution to killing can be found in most contemporary lives. Even driving a car or walking across the lawn kills beings. Various types of medicines we use have been tested on animals—killing them, maiming them, or making them sick. Benefiting from these medicines is not killing. The Buddha said very clearly that your intention is what really counts.

As far as spiritual progress is concerned, there is no difference between vegetarians and nonvegetarians. When vegetarians get angry or become greedy or confused, they behave the same way that people who eat meat do. If you want to be a vegetarian, by all means do so. Vegetarian meals are very healthy. I personally remain vegetarian out of compassion to animals. However, do not feel obligated to avoid eating meat in order to reach your goal of highest happiness.

Many laypeople ask me how to deal with insect pests in their homes and gardens. They want to be good Buddhists and not kill, but their flowers will wither or their homes deteriorate if they ignore the insects. I tell them that killing insects, even for a good reason, is still killing. However, not all killing has the same kammic (karmic) consequences. Killing an insect generally does not hinder one's progress as much as killing an animal, such as a dog. Killing a dog causes less impact to the mind than killing a human being. No act of killing causes more harm to oneself than killing one's parents or killing an enlightened being. This kind of killing would prevent the killer from attaining enlightenment in this life and lead to the worst kind of rebirth. Killing insects is not so grave a matter as this. Understanding that there are differing levels of impact, we make our choices and accept the consequences.

Not Stealing

Stealing is an expression of our greed or envy. Taking what does not belong to us is a bad habit that is hard to break. Some people are so undisciplined in this area that even when they attend a meditation training course to try to gain some peace and happiness, they continue their stealing habit. At the Bhavana Society, we know of incidents of people stealing meditation cushions. I doubt anyone has ever attained enlightenment by practicing meditation on a stolen meditation cushion! Our library has a similar problem. Because the Bhavana Society is located in a forest without quick access to any major collection of Buddhist books, we maintain our own collection. Over time, some books have disappeared. Isn't it ironic that people who come to the center to meditate and study the Buddha's teachings can't see that taking things that do not belong to them can never help them toward an untroubled mind?

Practicing the Skillful Action of not stealing means making an effort to be honest and to respect the property of others. It means pointing out the error to a clerk in a store who has forgotten to charge you for something that you have bought or who has given you too much change. It means going out of your way to return what is not yours, with no expectation of being rewarded for your actions.

Of course, sometimes honesty does lead to material rewards. I remember a news account of two boys who found a bag full of money in the bathroom of a Sears store. They took the bag home and discovered that it contained more than thirty-six thousand dollars! With their parents' support, the boys decided to turn the money over to the police.

It turned out that the money belonged to a man who had stopped at the store to use the rest room on his way to depositing the money in a bank. When he was able to identify the bag and the amount of money it contained, the man's property was returned to him. Imagine how he suffered when he discovered that the money was missing and how grateful he felt when it was returned. His belief in justice and in human goodness must have risen. He expressed his gratitude by giving the boys a generous reward, and the community honored them for their honesty.

It's easy to see that taking someone's property or money is stealing, but we are often confronted with more subtle occasions to steal. Taking credit for someone else's ideas is also stealing. So is lifting small items from the office, such as pens, notebooks, or computer disks, and taking them home for your personal use. Often we justify such actions by telling ourselves, "I could have thought of that idea myself," or "The company owes me this stuff. I've been underpaid for years." Cheating on your income taxes, writing bad checks, taking bribes, and engaging in fraudulent business practices are also stealing. Even shoplifting groceries when you are hungry constitutes theft. Remember, it is never good to feed the body at the expense of the mind.

Our purpose in practicing the moral guidelines of Skillful Action is to make our lives happy. If we break them, misery is sure to follow, in this life or in the future. Happiness requires peace of mind and a clear conscience. Do not think that you are refraining from stealing to please the world. You are doing so for your own contentment, now and in the future.

As we go beyond the coarse level of struggling against any form of stealing, we begin to refine our consideration for others' needs and become less self-centered in the way we regard material things. Using the rule against stealing as a guide, we become less envious of other people's possessions or good fortune. Instead we discover appreciative joy and rejoice in other peoples' happiness.

Not Engaging in Sexual Misconduct

The Buddha's words usually translated as abstaining from "sexual misconduct" actually apply to more than just sexual behavior. The words that he used literally mean that one should abstain from "abuse of the senses"—all the senses. Sexual misconduct is one particularly damaging form of sensual abuse.

For the purpose of keeping precepts, it is traditionally assumed that by "abuse of the senses" the Buddha specifically meant abstention from sexual misconduct. Sexual misconduct includes rape and manipulating someone into having sex against their wishes. The prohibition also refers to having sex with minors, animals, someone else's spouse or partner, or someone protected by parents or guardians. If one of the partners in a committed unmarried couple betrays the other, that can also be considered sexual misconduct. Having sex with an appropriate and consenting adult partner is not considered misconduct.

These definitions aside, people get into lot of trouble because of their sexual desires. The irony is that lust can never be completely satisfied. No matter how many risks people take or how much pain and suffering people go though to try to fulfill their desires, the wish to fulfill desires does not go away. Some people turn to meditation out of the pain and suffering caused by their sexual desires. Unfortunately, all too often, even during their efforts to gain some concentration and peace of mind, lust keeps bothering them.

The only solution to this problem is to begin with disciplining your sexual activity. If you are incapable of a bit of self-discipline, the path to happiness will forever remain elusive. Some very sincere meditators have made great strides in cleaning up bad habits such as drinking or lying, yet fail to see why they should rein in their sexual behavior. They say, "I don't see what's wrong with having a little fun." The traditional list of inappropriate partners seems to provide a loophole for them. They notice right away that nothing is said against having relations with many partners so long as they are appropriate and unmarried, or against seeking cheap thrills. But cheap thrills cheapen you and degrade your self-worth. Casual sex hurts you and can injure others.

What is the point of this kind of fun? To give you pleasure? To fulfill your desires? Yet, we've been saying all along that craving—desire—is the very root of our misery. The Buddha's second truth tells us that all suffering stems from desire. Confused sexual behavior is one of the easiest ways to trap the mind into a cycle of craving and aversion. Sexual pleasures are so alluring, and their downsides—rejection, embarrassment, frustration, jealousy, insecurity, remorse, loneliness, and craving for more—are so unbearable that they keep people running on an endless treadmill.

The problem is that lust cannot be eased by fulfilling it physically. Doing so is like scratching a poison ivy rash. Though scratching may bring a brief sense of relief, it spreads the poison and makes the underlying problem worse. Curing your condition requires restraint, holding back from doing things that will intensify your discomfort later.

The Buddha used a powerful metaphor to illustrate the common mistakes people make in thinking about sexuality. In his day, lepers could be seen gathered around fires, burning their wounds. Their disease gave them the most unbearable itching. Applying fire to their sores gave them some relief. But the fire did not heal their wounds or cure their disease. Instead, they burned themselves. Once the feeling of temporary ease left them, the sores swelled and festered from the burns. The poor sufferers were left with even more discomfort and itching than before. So, the lepers went back to the fire and burned themselves again.

People do the same thing when they seek relief from their lust, the Buddha said. When they go to the fire of sexual indulgence, they get a temporary sense of release from the pain and dissatisfaction of their sexual desire. But there is no healing power in indulgence. They only burn themselves. Then how much more maddening is the craving, the itching?

Now imagine, the Buddha continued, that a great physician comes along and brings healing medicine to a leper. The leper applies the medicine and is fully cured. Now what does the leper think of the fire? No power on earth can make him want to burn himself again. His former companions call to him to join them around the fire and to burn himself again. The healed leper remembers what that was like—the insanity of the craving and the short-lived release of the fire. Nothing can make him go back to it. He feels great compassion for his former companions and for his own previous suffering. (M 75)

The Buddha often referred to himself as a physician and to his teaching, the Dhamma, as medicine. He is quoted as saying,

> Of all the medicines in the world,
> Manifold and various,
> There is none like the medicine of Dhamma.
> Therefore, O monks, drink of this.
>
> Having drunk this Dhamma medicine,
> You will be ageless and beyond death.
> Having developed and seen the truth,
> You will be quenched, free from craving.
>   (Miln 335 [V] [translated by Ven. S. Dhammika])

Hearing this, you may wonder, "Must I choose between my partner and the path?" This misunderstanding causes concern for many people. But loving sexual behavior between committed partners is no obstacle to one's practice. In fact, a supportive relationship can be a great asset to progress through the Buddha's eight steps to happiness.

Abstention from sexual misconduct can be kept in a more and more refined way, far beyond the technical abstention of the precept. At its highest level, you view all women as your sisters, all men as your brothers, older people as your parents, and younger people as your children. Lust disappears. You simply do not see people in that way anymore. Any predatory attitude is gone, and even subtle lust disappears into openhearted compassion and concern for others' well-being.

Moreover, to perfect the step of Skillful Action, the Buddha urged us to stop abusing any of our senses. Aside from sexual misconduct, what does this mean? When one indulges one's cravings by stimulating any senses to the point of weariness, it is sense abuse.

What areas of your behavior have you left unexamined, areas in which you push your mind or body beyond a reasonable point just for pleasure or escape? Ask yourself: "Am I indulging in hours of watching television or doing nonessential paperwork late into the night? Eating more than what is necessary to sustain my life? Going to clubs where the music is so loud that my ears ring when I leave? Using my body for pleasure in ways that make it tired, sore, and unfit for work the next day? Do I make use of the Internet in ways that benefit my life and my community or am I simply entertaining myself until my eyes are bleary and my mind is numb?"

These kinds of activities are not right for the body and not right for a spiritual path. What would it be like to abandon them? Self-respect can grow in their place. The self-centeredness rooted in these activities can melt away, leaving room for a spirited, generous heart, no longer a slave to craving's call.

Not Using Intoxicants

The last of the five precepts says to avoid alcohol, drugs, or other intoxicants, and the same principle is implied in Skillful Action. In giving this precept, the Buddha used conditional wording. He did not tell lay followers to avoid all intoxicants, but only those that cause "negligence, infatuation, and heedlessness." In other words, the careful use of painkilling drugs and other narcotics prescribed by a doctor does not violate the prohibition. Nor does occasional, light use of alcohol, such as a glass of wine. We must use common sense.

Though light use of alcohol may be allowed, it is inadvisable. One drink tends to lead to another. Some people with sensitivity to alcohol may lose control and drink to excess after just one drink. Thus, the most effective time to exercise control is before that first drink, not after. Others develop an addictive habit more slowly, drinking a little more each time, unaware that their casual use of alcohol is becoming a serious problem. Moreover, the presence of alcohol in the house may tempt people to get drunk impulsively during a time of stress or sorrow. We can live quite healthily without alcohol, and it is better not to give it a chance to ruin our lives.

Over the years I have heard many stories of how alcohol leads to unhappiness. For instance, a resident at the Bhavana Society told me that many years ago she was indifferent to alcohol and drank only a little when others insisted. At parties where alcohol was served, she never finished even one beer. She just carried the bottle around all evening to fit in with those who were drinking. After graduating from college, she moved to another community. Her new friends drank frequently, and she developed a casual social drinking habit, which increased slowly. She told me that one night, when she was in a very bad mood, she drank one kind of hard drink and then another. When her friends expressed surprise at her having more than one drink, she swore at them, telling them to mind their own business. Suddenly, a strange feeling went through her body. Later she realized that it must have been a chemical change. From that moment on, she craved alcohol. Within two years she was drinking every day and getting drunk several times a week. Her personality changed in negative ways, and she suffered a great deal of unhappiness. Eventually, she sought help through an alcohol recovery program and now has been sober for many years.

People use intoxicants for many reasons. Young people want to feel more grown-up or sophisticated; shy or nervous people want to relax or feel more sociable; troubled people want to forget their problems. All of these motivations arise from dissatisfaction—from wanting to escape the reality of what is happening in the present moment.

Yet, when we think about it, running away never solved any problem or relieved any kind of suffering. Addiction to alcohol or drugs only makes your suffering worse. It can cause you to lose your sense of decency, your moral principles, your inhibitions. You may lie, commit sexual misconduct, steal, or worse. You may ruin your health, wealth, marriage, family, job, business. You may lose the respect of others and your respect for yourself. In the end you are left wallowing in misery and wondering why all these bad things happen to you. All in all, the best cure for addiction to intoxicants is not to use them in the first place!

For the purpose of the Eightfold Path, we can look beyond the words of the fifth precept to see what higher level of meaning we can find in abstaining from intoxicants. In what other ways do we drug ourselves, and why? Using this aspect of Skillful Action as a general guideline, question your motivations, ask whether you are trying to avoid being mindful. What are your escapes? Reading the newspaper? Engaging in unnecessary chatter? Mindfulness can help you identify the tricks you use to avoid continuous awareness of reality.

HIGHER PRECEPTS FOR LAYPEOPLE

Everyone should follow the five precepts every day. But people who want to progress more quickly on the Buddhist path may commit to a more comprehensive set of training rules for a period of time. These rules include the five basic precepts and a few more rigorous restrictions. Some meditators observe these rules on special occasions, such as while they attend a retreat. Others observe them while they live at a meditation center or monastery.

There are eight traditional training precepts:

- not killing
- not stealing
- not engaging in sexual activity
- not lying
- not using intoxicants
- not eating after midday
- not dancing, singing, indulging in music, or watching shows, and not using perfumes, cosmetics, or adornments
- not using high and large (that is, luxurious) beds or seats

Observing the eight precepts from time to time can help improve your meditation practice. When your conscience is clear and you have no reason for remorse, your concentration grows stronger.

In ancient times, people in Buddhist countries observed these eight training precepts for a day four times a month, on every quarter phase of the moon. They spent the day meditating in a monastery or temple, reading Buddhist books, and listening to the Buddha's message and discussing it. Sometimes they made a pilgrimage from one temple or religious site to another. Wherever they assembled, they meditated or listened to a talk by a learned layperson or monk. The next day they resumed their regular activities.

Nowadays very few people practice this religious observance. Most of us spend the time when we're not earning a living or tending to children, doing household chores, watching television, and going to parties, movies, restaurants, or bars. When we get tired of all these activities, we take a vacation. We may have worked very hard to save money for this vacation, which often consists of another frantic round of pleasure-seeking activities. When we get home, we sometimes feel that we need a vacation to recuperate from our vacation! Then it's back to work, for there is no vacation without money, and no money without very hard work. Perhaps you recognize this trap of suffering.

The eight precepts of Buddhist training offer an alternative. Taking the eight training precepts for a day, a weekend, or longer can give you a genuine break from your ordinary routine and leave you refreshed and clear-headed, not hungover, tired, and crabby. You don't have to go to a temple to take the eight precepts. You can undertake them privately in your home. In a house with children, opportunities for some free and quiet time may be rare. It is all the more important, then, to spend such precious hours in a way that will cultivate your inner peace. The immediate benefits of observing the temporary precepts are a sense of peace, contentment, and relaxation, as well as improved health and the prospect of an unconfused death. Occasional discipline soothes and comforts both body and mind.

For instance, people who generally eat three or four meals a day may find that fasting one day a week is a very good practice. They can start by eating only two meals and fasting for the rest of the day. These two meals should be a good breakfast and a light lunch. They should skip the evening meal. Since there are not too many activities after a heavy meal in the evening, the digestive process is very slow, and food stays in the stomach until the next morning. When you do not eat anything at night, you feel quite hungry the next morning. Then you can eat a good breakfast. Perhaps on most days, your family's needs and your work schedule do not allow you to eat well early in the day and lightly (or nothing) at night. Taking a special day to keep the eight precepts gives you a chance to try this style of eating.

The time you save in the evening when you don't have to cook, eat, and clean up from a big meal can be used to do many beneficial things, like meditating or reading a book on the Buddha's message. Though this practice is not very easy at first, it is a wonderful habit to cultivate. Remember, nothing is very easy at first. After you get used to not eating so much, you can also try fasting for a full day. Do not eat any solid food, but do drink plenty of water and fruit juice. Spend the day by yourself, reading and meditating. This mini-vacation is a wonderful break for the body and mind.

Taking the eight precepts in a formal way reminds you to be mindful. When you start to do something that would violate one of the precepts, your mind will say, "Just a minute, remember...!" and you will recall, "Oh, I'm not supposed to ..." The precept operates like the light touch of a whip that a buggy driver uses to remind the horse to stay on course, or the beep of a car's horn that reminds a driver to stay in his lane.

Laypeople can also make a commitment to a set of training rules called the eight lifetime precepts. This set of principles is made up of the five basic precepts plus three additional rules regarding Skillful Speech: not engaging in malicious speech, not speaking harshly, and not speaking frivolously. In 1998, for the ten-year anniversary of the opening of the Bhavana Society, members were invited to participate in a ceremony to take these eight lifetime precepts. The suggestion came from one of our board members who wanted take these precepts herself. Candidates were asked to attend a two-day retreat just prior to the ceremony to focus on the meaning of the vows. The response to this invitation was heartening. Thirty-six people attended the retreat, took lifetime refuge in the Buddha, and received the eight lifetime precepts. We have offered this opportunity each year since then.

Preparing for the vow ceremony was very difficult for some of the candidates. Many expressed some fear, and some experienced a lot of resistance. How difficult it is for us to make a commitment! The vow ceremony itself was very simple. The candidates recited the verses together as a group. Then each received a new name in the ancient language of Pali. This simple ceremony had a beautiful effect on peoples' lives, especially on the way they spoke. After taking the vows, they found that if harsh or frivolous words slipped out, they would notice immediately how silly it is to speak in such a way. The precept made them stop, like a sudden tug in the mind. The next time, they found, the words would not even slip out. This simple shift helped them to see how precepts work to create happiness.

Many of these people have written to thank me for these precepts. They say it was a turning point in their lives. But why should they thank me? I did not ask them to take these precepts. They volunteered. They did not take these vows for me, or for other people, or for their spouses or kids, or because of a law, or for the world. They made the vow to observe these training rules for themselves, for their own lives, and for their present and future happiness.

You should not be afraid to make the commitment to practice the principles of Skillful Action or to take either the eight training precepts or the eight lifetime precepts. You should rejoice that you have determined to take steps to make your life happy. People who are addicted to alcohol, drugs, gambling, or some other unwholesome activity have a very hard time deciding to stop. They drag their feet and come up with many excuses. But once they have made the commitment to change and have maintained that discipline for a period of time, they find they are thinking clearly, eating well, saving money, and developing good relations with their families and other people. Then they are grateful and congratulate themselves for taking this positive step.

In the same way, we may have difficulty making the commitment to abandon unwholesome behavior. But once we have done so and have worked at it consistently, we will be happy, very glad to have made a decision that brings such improvement to our lives.

MINDFULNESS OF SKILLFUL ACTION

The Buddha said, "All wholesome words, deeds, and thoughts have mindfulness as their root." In other words, Skillful Action grows naturally out of mindfulness.

Let's look more closely at why this is so. Every intentional action of body, speech, or mind impacts us strongly. When we hurt someone or commit some other negative action, we often suffer physical stress and develop a confused, unhappy state of mind. Mindfulness helps us to see this harmful impact clearly. We see that an unwholesome action leads to feelings of remorse, which leads to worry, which prevents the mind from becoming calm. When the mind is agitated, we lose the ability to concentrate. The more negative our action, the more upset and worried we feel. A vicious cycle begins, in which negative states of mind influence us to engage in other unwholesome actions.

The converse is also true. With mindfulness, we see that when we act with loving-friendliness, our mind becomes peaceful and relaxed. A peaceful mind enhances our joy and helps us concentrate more deeply. Realizing this, we feel encouraged to pursue wholesome actions. We become healthier physically and mentally. This positive feedback keeps us moving in a good direction.

I even go so far as to say that mindfulness of observing the precepts—whether the five, eight, or lifetime precepts—makes you look more beautiful! When you speak or act while keeping the precepts in mind, you feel peaceful and happy. An unclouded mind makes your face bright and radiant. When you think of your good actions, you feel delighted. This delight shines in your eyes and your expressions. People feel drawn to someone who looks this way.

When we are mindful of Skillful Action, our unclouded mind also helps us focus on every passing moment, but not in a dull, passive way. We bring all of our skills and intelligence to the task of knowing both what is going on in our minds and how well we are interacting with the world around us. In this way we develop a comprehensive awareness of our actions.

Such mindfulness is especially crucial when others test our patience.

It's relatively easy to observe the precepts and act harmoniously so long as no one provokes you. But if someone says something that angers or hurts you, your mind may be sent spinning for a moment. If you are mindful, you'll have enough presence of mind to think, "I must be careful now. Let me pause for a moment until my mind is clear. I better not say or do anything I'll regret."

If you stay mindfully aware of the whole context of every interaction, you will also remember to be extra careful when you are vulnerable. If you are grieving the loss of someone or something you love, for instance, it may take less provocation to make you angry. You know, then, to be especially careful around other people, like a man without shoes walking softly where there may be glass. This is important, too, when you are ill, tired, hungry, lonely, in pain, or just plain grouchy. When you are under stress, moment-to-moment mindfulness helps you remember your vulnerability and avoid regrettable actions.

Another time when you must be especially mindful is when you find yourself in a situation in which your past habits may tempt you to violate a moral principle. A person who once found it easy to steal must immediately become mindful when someone's wallet lies within easy reach. A former drinker must snap to attention when free beer is being passed around. When a married man who has struggled with lust is handed a business card by a woman who flirts with him, he must say to himself, "If I take this phone number, it will result in temptation. My peace of mind will be affected. I love my wife and don't want to jeopardize my family. I've taken other people's cards today, but I had better pass on this one or throw it away immediately."

Until you are enlightened and your mind is fully trained, many other kinds of wrong actions will occasionally occur to you. Before doing anything you know to be wrong, you should step back and reflect mindfully on how this action might hurt you. For example, if you feel tempted to steal money from your employer, you can examine the consequences: You will live in fear of being caught. If you are caught, you will certainly lose your job, your reputation, and perhaps your freedom as well. Even if you are not caught by the law, your conscience will catch you immediately. The very thought of doing such a thing disturbs the mind. How much more will your mind be disturbed if you follow through on the action? When an unwholesome intention remains a passing thought, you can live with it. But once you put it into action, you will never live in peace.

You should also weigh the brief pleasure a wrongful action may yield against the lasting suffering it brings. Say you feel tempted to hit someone. This intent may come with the belief that you will feel satisfied afterward: "I've done my job," you'll be able to say, "and this guy won't try that again!" But you can't predict results so precisely. The man may become furious and hit back harder. He may develop a grudge and plan secretly to attack you. One wrong deed can lead to a long and bitter quarrel.

I knew a man in Sri Lanka who had a long-standing quarrel with his neighbors. To get back at them, he built a primitive outhouse close to the property line, right beside his neighbors' well. The neighbors complained, asking him to remove the privy, but he refused. One by one the neighbors fell sick. The fighting between the two families escalated, until someone committed a murder. The police became involved, and I think that this man ended up in jail. Both families were devastated. They will hate each other for generations! Quarreling between neighbors goes on everywhere. There are a billion such quarrels. If we find ourselves in such a dispute, we must cease immediately and try to smooth things over. Quarrels that get out of hand hurt everyone involved.

Skillful Action is not something invented by the Buddha. It is universally true that wrong actions cause suffering and perpetuate hatred. As the Buddha expressed this idea:

> Hatred is never overcome by hatred.
> Only through loving-friendliness does hatred cease.
> This is an eternal law.
>   (Dh 5)

The Buddha did not claim credit for this law. It does not belong to Buddhists only or to anyone else. In his enlightened state, the Buddha could see clearly the negative consequences that inevitably arise from wrong action. If you "act or speak with a defiled state of mind," he said, "suffering will follow you as surely as the cart wheel follows the foot of the ox." If you act or speak with a pure state of mind, he continued, "happiness will follow as your shadow follows without departing from you." (Dh 1–2)

Skillful Action not only soothes your mind but has a positive effect on everyone around you. I once heard a story of a monk who demonstrated how mindfulness of Skillful Action helps others. The temple where the monk lived had a jackfruit tree that was bearing fruit. Jackfruit is very useful for a monastery. Each fruit is very large, with a big seed that is full of protein and a thick flesh that can be cooked in many ways. Poor families who lack other food can live on jackfruit. Though jackfruit does not cost much at the market, stealing jackfruit from trees in a poor area has been known to provoke murder.

One night the monk noticed a thief in the temple's jackfruit tree. The thief was high up in the branches of the tree, lowering each fruit by means of a string so that it would not clunk on the ground and draw attention. The thief looped the string around the fruit in such a way that when the fruit touched the ground, the string would loosen. Then the thief would pull the string up for the next fruit. The monk went to stand quietly beneath the tree. As each fruit touched the ground, he helped to loosen the string.

Eventually the thief came down as well. He nearly fainted at the sight of the cheerful monk standing there. The monk spoke to him gently, not like the victim of a theft, but more like a concerned grandparent, asking earnestly, "Have you gotten enough fruit? Do you need more?" There was no need to raise a great hue and cry and risk the man being hurt in a struggle with the temple's supporters. The monk's peaceful and generous response made the thief so ashamed that he left quickly and never returned to steal from the temple.

What should you do when you have violated one of the moral principles of Skillful Action? The answer is simple: Apply mindfulness. First, notice what you have done. Then, if possible, make amends. Finally, make a strong determination to observe the principles of Skillful Action in the future. If you have broken a precept, renew your precept vows. Then let your faulty actions go. Feeling guilty or worrying about consequences beyond your control cannot help you. Regard your past transgressions with the same generous and compassionate attitude that the monk showed to the jackfruit thief. When you react in this way, you will redouble your efforts to practice Skillful Action.

KEY POINTS FOR MINDFULNESS OF SKILLFUL ACTION

- Anyone interested in spiritual progress should follow five precepts of abstention from killing, stealing, false speech, sexual misconduct, and using drugs or alcohol.

- Eating meat does not fit the definition of killing.

- Killing requires intent, knowledge, planning, and carrying out that plan.

- When we don't kill, we can become truly harmless and practice loving-friendliness.

- Stealing means taking anything not given, including others' ideas.

- When we don't steal, we can develop respect for the needs of others and practice appreciative joy.

- The precept against sexual misconduct includes rape, manipulating someone into having sex against their wishes, and sex with minors, animals, someone's spouse, or someone protected by parents or guardians; it also includes breaking trust in a relationship.

- When we avoid sexual misconduct, troublesome lust can be abated.

- A sexual relationship with your spouse or partner is not considered misconduct.

- We should avoid all deliberate abuse of our senses. This helps us let go of our greed, and in this way, we develop a generous spirit toward others.

- Addiction to alcohol or drugs may come on quickly or may be a gradually conditioned behavior; it causes great harm, and it is best to avoid getting started.

- When we abstain from intoxicants we can maintain a clear mind and work to remove our delusions. We can develop mindfulness and learn to act in accordance with reality.

- Taking additional precepts, either the eight training precepts or the eight lifetime precepts, can be a great aid to concentration and to furthering progress on the Buddha's path.

- Mindfulness can help us to overcome temptation, avoid quarrels, and respond compassionately to others' moral failings as well as our own.

Step 5
Skillful Livelihood

A STUDENT OF MINE told me about a shrewd businesswoman who practices Buddhist principles. Once when she was looking to make a new investment, some liquor stores came up for sale. She knew that if she bought them, she could expect an excellent profit. Yet something prevented her. As she reflected on the business of selling liquor, she realized that some of the customers at the stores might be harmed. They might drink and do something hurtful; they might become alcoholic or worsen their addiction. To protect her spiritual growth, she backed out of the deal.

This little story illustrates a powerful truth: Our means of sustenance should not interfere with our spiritual development. We cannot come up with a complete list of occupations that constitute Skillful Livelihood, but the Buddha did give us a basic guideline: Any job can be Skillful Livelihood so long as it does not cause harm to the person doing the job or to someone else. Of course, until we are enlightened, no job will be perfect. The only truly perfect livelihood is a job performed by a person who is perfected—someone who has eradicated completely all greed, hatred, and delusion. But those of us on the path toward perfection can still do much to harmonize our working life and our spiritual life.

As with most questions of Buddhist ethics, the rationale behind Skillful Livelihood is twofold. Working at a job that harms others is wrong in itself because it violates moral principles. But such a job is also wrong because it harms us. Since we are not enlightened, we cannot completely avoid agitation and suffering. Things happen at work that cause us to struggle with greed and aversion. But we can avoid jobs that obstruct our spiritual progress. If our job causes excessive agitation, our mind cannot calm down enough to meditate.

Let's look at an obvious example. Say a man's job requires him to kill animals. He might be a researcher who tests new drugs on laboratory mice. Or he might be a commercial fisherman or a hog butcher. When the man comes to meditate, his mind may be troubled. Daily he sees living creatures suffering because of what he does. He sees the fear in their eyes and their struggles to escape; he hears their squeals and their bleats of pain. These images stay with him when he goes home. In order to do his job, he must pretend to himself that animals do not have feelings, that they are not really living beings like himself. In his heart, he knows that these thoughts are untrue, but he continues to kill because that is his job. This inner struggle causes disturbing thoughts and images to arise during his meditation. He cannot practice loving-friendliness; he cannot even relax. Clearly this man's job cannot be Skillful Livelihood.

It's easy to see that some occupations, like killing animals, are inherently disturbing. But for most of us, the task of assessing whether a particular job qualifies as Skillful Livelihood is much more complicated. Some jobs might be acceptable in some workplaces and not in others depending on circumstances, such as whether the boss asks employees to act immorally. A three-tiered inquiry will help us decide whether a job qualifies as Skillful Livelihood.

QUESTIONS FOR ASSESSING SKILLFUL LIVELIHOOD

You can determine whether a job is suitable to be Skillful Livelihood by asking yourself three interrelated questions.

First, is my job an inherently wrong occupation?

That is, does it cause harm by definition? Does it involve manufacturing, buying, selling, promoting, or using guns or other weapons? Does it involve intoxicants or poisons? Does it entail harming or killing living beings? The Buddha himself mentioned that jobs involving weapons, poisons, or killing are definitely wrong livelihood.

Many jobs clearly fall into this category. For example, research and development of chemical and biological weapons, manufacturing or selling insecticides, designing computer guidance systems for missiles, and profiting from sweatshop labor are clearly wrong. I would add that writing for a tabloid newspaper that harms the reputations of public figures or working for a radio talk show that broadcasts hateful speech should be considered among the "poisons" the Buddha mentioned as wrong livelihood.

We also have to extend the Buddha's guidance beyond its traditional applications. Making a living from certain violent sports in which people are hurt, such as boxing, is wrong livelihood. So is owning or working for a casino or other gambling establishment. Like alcohol, gambling can be addictive. It is motivated by greed and often leads to crime or hurts the innocent. Needless to say, criminal activity of any kind is also wrong livelihood, including black-market or other illegal transactions, fraud, extortion, and white-collar crime. Damaging your own health on the job is also wrong livelihood.

Selling drugs falls under the category of dealing in "poisons." Drug traffickers are notorious for violent and corrupt actions to protect territories, enforce deals, and avoid prosecution. Moreover, the weak and vulnerable people who buy and use the drugs are undoubtedly harmed by them. Drug users commit crimes to get money. Innocent family members also suffer: from domestic abuse, from lack of food money, and from grief when the drug user is jailed or hurt.

However, because our economic system has become so complex, sometimes the determination of what constitutes wrong livelihood is not so clear-cut. For instance, is working for the military always inherently wrong? It depends. If the job puts the person in a position to use weapons, including using a computer to launch missiles, it is probably wrong livelihood. But being a medic or a cook might not be inherently wrong. I doubt that the cook in the mess hall ever thinks, "I want to feed these soldiers so they can go and kill!"

Many other job situations come to mind. Building nuclear warheads clearly fits the Buddha's list of forbidden occupations, but what about mining the uranium used in nuclear weapons? Is it inherently wrong to work for a general merchandise chain store that makes substantial profits from selling guns? What about working for the minimum wage flipping burgers at a fast food outlet? You can imagine many ways in which a job might indirectly cause harm to others. A university professor might feel uncomfortable doing basic scientific research because the results could be used by the military. Or, a steelworker might manufacture the raw material used to make hunting rifles.

In such cases, you should ask yourself, "Am I directly involved in dealing with poisons, weapons, or killing? Am I intentionally causing harm to others or to myself?" As a general rule, the more distance there is between your on-the-job activities and the harm that might befall others as a result, the less likely it is that the job fits the category of inherently wrong occupations.

Second, does my job lead me to break the five moral precepts?

If an occupation passes the first level of inquiry, then consider whether working in the job encourages you to break any of the five precepts of Skillful Action. The ethics of a particular workplace can make an otherwise acceptable job into wrong livelihood. For instance, in one law firm, attorneys may be urged to maintain the highest standards of ethical conduct. In another, attorneys may feel pressured to destroy evidence, deceive juries, or bill excessive hours to clients. Committing such immoral actions on the job causes the mind to become agitated and hinders a person's spiritual progress. I remember an attorney who used to come to the Bhavana Society. He would cry and cry when he tried to meditate. I always wondered whether he was so troubled because he did wrong things to win his cases in court.

It is also the case that an otherwise excellent job situation can become wrong livelihood for an individual who chooses to act in a corrupt way. For example, someone who gives behind-the-wheel road tests before issuing drivers' licenses may work with integrity, refusing bribes. Another person with the same job in the same office may be blatantly corrupt. The corrupt worker does not have Skillful Livelihood, but the honest one may. Any good job or profession can be made corrupt. I knew a doctor in Malaysia who issued sick leave certificates for workers to give to their employers; he charged about five dollars for a day off. The doctor was so in the habit of doing this that when a patient entered his office, the first question he would ask was, "How many days?"

A famous story about the Buddha and his evil-minded cousin, the powerful monk Devadatta, tells of two people working in the same profession, only one of whom follows Skillful Livelihood:

> According to folklore, the future Devadatta first conceived a grudge against the Buddha in a past life, when the honest business practices of the Bodhisatta—the future Buddha—caused the unscrupulous Devadatta to lose out in a business deal.
>
> In that past life, the future Devadatta and the Bodhisatta were rival peddlers traveling together selling pots and pans. At each town, they would divide the streets between them to decide who would approach each house first. Then they would go their separate ways, calling out, "Pots for sale! Pans for sale!" At the home of a formerly wealthy widow and her daughter, who were now desperately poor, there was a great golden bowl covered with grime. The women did not guess its value. When Devadatta appeared at their door, the daughter asked her mother to trade the bowl for a trinket. The greedy Devadatta quickly saw that the bowl was worth a fortune but decided to deceive the poor women. He declared that the bowl was worthless, tossed it on the floor, and left, intending to return later and offer them virtually nothing for it.
>
> Sometime later, when the Bodhisatta appeared at the same door, the women asked him with some hesitation to trade the bowl for a trinket. The honest Bodhisatta told them the bowl's worth and said that he was unable to pay them even a small fraction of its value. The women were delighted and greatly respected the Bodhisatta for his honesty. They asked him please just to give them what he could. So he gave them all his money and all his pots and pans. Taking the golden bowl, the Bodhisatta hastened to the river crossing, for he guessed what Devadatta intended to do.
>
> Soon after the Bodhisatta left, Devadatta returned to the women's house. As he approached, the elder woman rushed at him, crying out that he had tried to deceive them. She told him

that the other peddler had been honest with them and had paid them well. Realizing his loss, Devadatta cried out and became like one deranged. He ripped his clothes, threw aside all his goods, and chased after the Bodhisatta, crying out that the Bodhisatta had stolen his golden bowl. When he reached the river, he saw the Bodhisatta halfway across, being rowed by the boatsman. He yelled at him to stop, but the Bodhisatta quietly instructed the boatman to pay no attention, and they went on. As he gazed at the Bodhisatta's receding figure, Devadatta was filled with hatred and sorrow. Hot blood gushed from his mouth. His heart split, and he fell down dead.

Thus was Devadatta ruined by his own dishonest business practices. The Bodhisatta became wealthy from the sale of the golden bowl for which he had bartered honestly. He spent his life in charity and good deeds. When he died, his honesty sent him onward to good future lives, until he eventually attained Buddhahood. Devadatta's deeds also propelled him into appropriate future lives. He continued to be the Buddha's rival. In the Buddha's final lifetime, after the Buddha's enlightenment, Devadatta even tried to assassinate the Buddha. It is said that the earth opened up and he fell into hell. (J 3)

Finally, are there other aspects of my job that disturb me and keep my mind from settling down?

If an occupation passes the first two levels of inquiry, then you need to consider what other factors might impede your spiritual progress. This can be complicated. Since no work situation is perfect, we each have to decide for ourselves what constitutes an insurmountable problem. Dishonest coworkers? Rude clients? Chemical solvents that might injure the lungs? Products with a harmful impact on the environment? Indirect connections with companies employing sweatshop workers?

In my opinion, the best way to determine whether a job qualifies as Skillful Livelihood is to gauge its effect on the mind. Imagine that a company dumps toxins into a river and causes great harm to fish and other wildlife. Later the employees learn about the dumping. Two of these employees are interested in practicing Skillful Livelihood. Must they quit working for the company?

One employee is filled with loathing over what happened. In his mind, he goes over and over the images from a television news report about the incident. He thinks about the unwholesome qualities of the people who made the decision and mentally argues his side of the story with imaginary accusers. The other employee goes about her job with a feeling of compassion for all those affected, including the people responsible for the decision. She continues to hope that company officials will come to see that such actions are wrong and take steps to prevent similar occurrences in the future. These thoughts do not disturb her mind. Some people might argue that both employees must quit because they work for an immoral company. Others might say only the employee who is filled with unwholesome thoughts must quit, due to the negative influence of these working conditions on his mind.

We must use our common sense and our understanding of the Buddha's teachings to figure out what's right. Moral principals do count. We don't want to take part in or support actions that are unethical. We know that indifference to moral outrage is also immoral. If we say to ourselves, "What I do makes no difference, and besides, what happened does not really affect me personally," we cut us ourselves off from the world. The Buddha's teachings on loving-friendliness tell us that we must care not only about ourselves and our immediate family but about our extended family, our neighbors, our community—everyone! Each of us is only a small individual cell, but joined with trillions of others we are the body of the world. So we have a responsibility to stand up for what is right. But—and this is a very important point—when we do so, we must be careful that we do not revile other people or accuse them hatefully. Any action that we contemplate, even an action intended to right a terrible wrong, must be motivated by loving, friendly feelings for others and for all beings. With this in mind, and filled with great compassion, then we act.

Returning to our question of whether the two employees of the polluting company must quit, we cannot jump to a quick decision. Depending on our mental attitude, quitting may or may not be the right thing to do. Only one thing is certain: the right thing to do is always to protect and nourish the wholesomeness of one's own mind. Indifference to harm is not wholesome. Yet becoming upset, furious, or hateful is also unwholesome. Even if we decide that we must leave a job in order to achieve Skillful Livelihood, quitting in a rage does not help us on the path. Our mind must remain calm, loving, and mindful. We must always remember that our highest goal is to free our mind from all greed, all hatred, all confusion. The greatest impact we can have on the world is to face every circumstance with a mind of clarity, compassion, and love. From a place of calm and equanimity, we act or decline to act, doing whatever most skillfully cultivates and expresses our loving-friendliness and our compassion.

Given this, the best thing for the employees of the polluting company to do is to work with their own minds to find peace. Then from a clear, peaceful state of mind and taking personal and social factors into consideration, they must decide whether continued association with this company is the most loving and compassionate thing to do. They might consider how serious the incident was, whether it was an isolated occurrence or part of a pattern, how personally involved they were in the incident, and whether they can continue on the job without feeling excessively disturbed. A sensitive employee only remotely connected to management may feel more upset than a hardened top executive. If the company's immoral behavior disturbs an employee and causes restlessness and an inability to concentrate, then the employee surely must take action.

Quitting the job is one option, but there are others as well. For instance, an employee might take action within the company to stop the wrongdoing, or report the company's activities to a regulatory authority, or assist the victims, or write probing articles about how companies can prevent such mistakes, or transfer to a more ethical branch of the business. If the employee does choose to quit, he or she should move slowly, perhaps beginning with discreet inquiries about possible new jobs. At every stage the employee must ask, "What actions can I take with equanimity, loving-friendliness, compassion, and concern for all beings? What actions support my wholesomeness of mind?"

Disturbances to the mind other than concern about the company's ethics might also jeopardize Skillful Livelihood. Perhaps an otherwise ideal situation goes sour for you when a new employee begins to harass you sexually. Perhaps you are transferred to a department where the boss is continually angry, or where your co-workers habitually drink alcohol at lunch or have "closed-door parties," taking drugs in the offices after work.

Assuming that you can maintain your own integrity in those kinds of difficult environments, you must decide for yourself whether the behavior of your co-workers disturbs your mind and hinders your spiritual progress. Assessing Skillful Livelihood is an individual thing. The same situation that locks one person in unwholesome thoughts may provide another person with an opportunity to practice patience and compassion.

FINDING SKILLFUL LIVELIHOOD

Some of you may by now be experiencing a sinking feeling if you recognize that your job does not fulfill Skillful Livelihood. "What should I do now?" you may wonder. You have many options, including ways to improve the situation without having to leave your job or profession. As I mentioned, you might first try to encourage your company to clean up its act.

If your uncomfortable feeling is due to the behavior of other people in your workplace, do not forget the Buddha's tool of *metta*, loving-friendliness. The hardest hearts can be won with loving-friendliness. It is said that nothing can harm a person who is pouring out loving-friendliness—not even bullets or fire, much less harassment at the office! If you cultivate strong loving-friendliness as you begin each workday, who knows how many things may change? Even habitual wrongdoers sometimes reform their behavior when someone, somewhere, sends them strong, pure loving-friendliness each day. It may be worth trying this approach before you give up on a difficult job site. Even if your co-workers do not change, your own heart will definitely soften. Perhaps you will begin to feel kindness and compassion toward people when they do things that previously made you very upset.

Some occupations or situations cannot be salvaged, and we may have to leave. Sometimes we have to make sacrifices in order to follow the Buddha's path. The Buddha himself said that we should not seek prosperity through wrong means:

> When, neither for one's own sake nor for the sake of another,
> One wishes not for children, wealth, a kingdom,
> Or for prosperity gained by unjust means,
> Only then is one virtuous, wise, and righteous.
>
> (Dh 84)

For those who have valuable skills or good connections, leaving a job or changing professions may be an easy decision, without much sacrifice involved. Those who have fewer options may feel terrified at the idea of giving up a steady paycheck, especially people who have children to support. Yet, when it comes to matters of personal integrity, we have to take action. I am not talking about some dramatic, impulsive action. First, plan everything the best you can. Then, when you've planned all you can, simply make a leap of faith. It is said, "Those who protect the Dhamma are protected by the Dhamma." (Thag 303) That means that when you rely upon what you know in your heart to be true, things work out for your highest happiness. I have tested this in my own life and always found it to be accurate. Here is my own story about making a leap of faith into Skillful Livelihood.

Prior to founding the Bhavana Society, I ran a small, well-known temple in Washington, D.C., for about twenty years. I was established in the community, with a secure position, a strong board of directors, and surrounded by family and friends. Yet in my heart I had a dream of establishing a residential meditation center, where people could come to learn the Dhamma and practice meditation. The Buddha repeatedly spoke of learning Dhamma and practicing meditation as being of the utmost importance, yet I saw that many people had nowhere to go where they could stay for a period of time in order to learn to meditate. My intentions were good and my faith was strong.

My friends and my family said to me, "You are in a prestigious position, at the first Theravada temple in the United States, right here in the nation's capital. You should not give all that up." In a way, they were right, of course. Leaving Washington to found a rural retreat center was leaping from a very comfortable position into the unknown.

The land my friend Matthew Flickstein and I found to build our center was deep in the backwoods of West Virginia. The isolated forest, so calm and peaceful, seemed an ideal environment for teaching Dhamma and meditation. The land was beautiful, far away from the busy-ness of Washington, but also in a very conservative Christian area and far from our supporters. The place was completely strange to me, and we began work there not knowing even one person. Our new society did not have members. We did not know how we would survive. My family and my friends worried about how I would eat. Some also worried for my safety, but I thought that with my good intentions, no matter how conservative the people in the area might be, since I would not be harming them, and I am not against their religion, they would not harm me. Soon after buying the place, we put up a sign near the road saying, ambitiously, "Dhamma Village." When I returned one time to show the place to a friend, someone had covered the letters to read, "Dam Village." The next time I came back, the sign was gone.

Despite these kinds of omens and all the obstacles, I plunged further into the project. Almost everyone I knew urged me not to do this. I think fewer than five people encouraged me. There would be no one to come help in an emergency. My relatives and friends would be in Washington, a hundred miles away.

I cannot tell you how difficult it was in the beginning. Even my friend who helped me start the center seemed to have his doubts during one very low period. What protected me was trust in the Dhamma. My dream was to spread the Dhamma through teaching and writing, without charging people anything. Even when I was a child and a novice monk, when people offered me gifts in exchange for Dhamma teachings, I would refuse to take them. When I grew up, I learned that the Buddha prohibited the selling of Dhamma. "Don't be a merchant of the Dhamma," he said. (Ud VI.2) Slowly, over time, things came together, and we carved a meditation center out of the woods. Amazing things happened—help arrived from unanticipated sources just when we needed it most, and unexpected connections yielded breakthroughs. Somehow, we managed to make progress and to grow.

My own experience has taught me that when we follow our heart's yearning for peace and happiness, and make sacrifices out of integrity and a love for truth, the rewards of Skillful Livelihood will come to us.

I also know, however, that economic conditions can create very difficult choices, especially for those whose education and skills are limited or highly specialized. What if there is only one source of jobs in the area? What if you have many children, ailing parents, or a chronically sick child to support, and the only job you can get to easily is working at a nearby liquor store? What if you live in an area where hunting and fishing are necessary to get by? What is Skillful Livelihood for people who live in extreme economic deprivation or who are coerced by those in power to engage in illegal activities, such as growing plants to produce illegal drugs? If you are in such a situation, comfort yourself with the knowledge that so long as you have no intention to harm, you are not responsible for harmful consequences that you do not personally and directly cause. A story from the time of the Buddha illustrates this point.

A rich merchant's daughter who had heard the Dhamma had reached the first stage of enlightenment. One day, a handsome hunter came through the town selling venison, and the young woman fell in love with him. Without saying good-bye to her family, she followed the hunter home, and they became husband and wife. As a hunter's wife, the woman had to clean and prepare his arrows and the nets and traps that he used for hunting. She performed these duties obediently. The couple had seven children, and in time they all were married.

One day as the Buddha surveyed the world with his psychic vision, he saw that this entire family could become enlightened, so he paid them a visit. The Buddha went first to an empty trap set by the hunter. He placed his footprint beside the trap, then waited in the bushes. When the hunter came and saw the trap empty, with the footprint beside it, he thought that someone had stolen from his trap. On spying the Buddha in the bushes, he aimed his bow and arrow at him and then became immobilized in that position. The seven children came looking for their father, and finding him standing there, bow drawn, not moving, they also aimed their bows and arrows at the Buddha and also became immobile.

Finally, the wife went looking for her family. She found them pointing arrows at the Buddha. Throwing up her hands, she shouted, "Don't kill my father!" When her family heard these words, they thought that the man must be her father, whom they had never met. The husband thought, "This is my father-in-law!" The children thought, "This is our grandfather!" Their hearts filled with love for the man, and so they put down their weapons and bowed. Then the Buddha gave them a Dhamma talk, and they all reached the first stage of enlightenment.

Later, when he had returned to his monastery, the Buddha's monks became curious and asked the Buddha a question. "How was it," they wondered, "that this woman could prepare the arrows and traps to help kill animals after having understood the Dhamma?" The Buddha explained that the woman did not participate in the killing of the animals. Moreover, she had no wish for the animals to be hurt. She was merely doing her duties as the wife of a hunter. (DhA 124)

Then the Buddha explained further:

> The palm without wounds
> Can hold poison safely;
> Just as without a wound, poison does not enter,
> So evil does not penetrate
> The innocent mind. (Dh 124)

Just as you can hold poison in your hand so long as your palm has no wound through which the poison can enter, so, too, harmful actions cannot hurt you if you lack the intention to harm. Although the hunter's wife prepared instruments for killing animals, she did so only to obey her husband, for in that culture in those times, a wife did not have much choice about such things. The woman's lack of intention to harm shielded her mind from the negative consequences of her actions. Since she did not wish any harm to the animals, her actions were innocent.

If you feel your livelihood is harmful, but you know for certain that nothing else is available that would allow you and your family to survive, you can gradually try to find a better situation. In the meantime, send loving-friendliness to everyone affected by your work, and calm your mind by remaining focused on your wholesome intentions.

If we adopt Skillful Livelihood as our goal, we can gradually move toward it as our spiritual practice matures. Ultimately, your job should actively promote the spiritual well-being of everyone involved, because your behavior influences others. I know of a couple who created a family business making delightful wooden toys designed to be especially safe for children. Eventually, they expanded their business into a poor community, providing livelihood for many people. Rather than requiring workers to do their work in the factory, they provided materials and training and allowed workers to build the toys at home, paying by the piece for their finished work. This approach allowed employees to center their lives around their families, and to work or relax as they felt the need to do.

Sometimes people ask me, "How can I find a skillful form of livelihood?" Since I have had basically the same profession since I was twelve years old, I may not be the best person to tell others how to choose a new career or conduct a job search. I can tell you this much, however: The way to find your Skillful Livelihood is the same way that you begin any great new undertaking. Don't make a big fuss about it. Just do the next right thing.

MINDFULNESS OF SKILLFUL LIVELIHOOD

Accepting that our job situation is an aspect of our spiritual practice is not easy. Many people box off their work from their spiritual life. When we sit down to meditate and review our past actions, however, we must acknowledge that the things we do at our jobs are our own actions, even if they were instigated by the boss or required as part of the job. Lying is still lying, even if we get paid to do it. We must bear the current and future results of whatever we say and do. Thus we should hold our job-related activities to the same ethical standards we hold for our other actions. As with Skillful Speech and Action, Skillful Livelihood requires that we continually purify our behavior, whether at home or on the job.

When we work in a job that fulfills Skillful Livelihood, throughout each workday we should remain sensitive to issues of morality as they arise. We must be very clear about the five precepts and take care never to violate them. Moral issues not directly involving the five precepts call for us to reflect upon whether we can live with the consequences of our actions.

As our practice of mindfulness meditation deepens, we may develop so much calm and patience that a previously unacceptable situation becomes no problem, and just about any honest job becomes perfect for us. The most important consideration is that a job does not interfere with our ability to make spiritual progress. So long as we are not hurting ourselves by breaking precepts or becoming involved in other worrisome ethical situations, our mind can become calm and peaceful. With a calm and peaceful mind, we can grow. Once we clear away the obstacles, the rest takes care of itself.

The situation is comparable to the way we stay alive. When we are hungry, we eat. When we are thirsty, we drink. We put on a sweater when we are cold. We do things to avoid illness. We avoid harmful and dangerous activities and situations. But we do not go around saying, "I must live, I must live!" If we just take care of our basic needs, the body maintains itself in life. Similarly, in Skillful Livelihood, our only responsibility is to avoid causing harm to ourselves or others, so that we remain calm and peaceful. So long as our mind is calm and peaceful, we can meditate and progress on the Buddha's path to happiness.

If we wish to progress more quickly, we can seek employment that nurtures our practice and propels us along more quickly. Such a job presents situations that challenge our weak areas in a way that strengthens them without being overwhelming, and avoids presenting us with problems we are not currently prepared to deal with. For example, someone trying to cultivate refined, sublime states of concentration may be best served by a job that provides easy, routine work that does not overly excite the mind. Someone who is deliberately cultivating patience may flourish in a job that requires working with challenging situations and difficult people.

In your meditation period, take some time to use the three-tiered inquiry to assess to what extent your current job constitutes Skillful

Livelihood. You may decide that your current job has aspects that need improvement. Ask yourself what you can do today to make your job situation more actively helpful to yourself and to others.

KEY POINTS FOR MINDFULNESS OF SKILLFUL LIVELIHOOD

Here are the key points to remember concerning mindfulness of Skillful Livelihood:

- Our means of sustenance should not interfere with our spiritual development.

- We can assess whether a job qualifies as Skillful Livelihood by means of a three-tiered inquiry.

- At the first level of inquiry, we examine whether a job is inherently harmful to others or to oneself.

- At the second level, we consider whether a job causes us to break any of the five moral precepts.

- Finally, we ask whether other factors related to the job make it difficult for the mind to settle down.

- Loving-friendliness may improve a difficult job situation.

- If you lack harmful intentions, your mind will not be harmed by a job's adverse consequences.

- Skillful Livelihood is a goal to be sought gradually as our spiritual practice matures.

STEP 6
Skillful Effort

AT EVERY MOMENT we choose whether to embrace wholesomeness or unwholesomeness. We are not helpless, passive victims of fate. We are not pawns moved about by greater forces, nor do our experiences happen due to predetermination. In this moment we choose, and then in the next moment we experience the results of that choice, along with any continuing effects of past choices. A wholesome choice in this moment sets up a good mental environment for happiness in the next moment. If the previous moment was relatively pure and clean, the current one will be, too. With billions of fairly pure moments, we experience a second of happiness. With good mental habits developing, second by second, these seconds eventually add up to make longer moments of happiness. Our lives are created out of these tiny little choices, billions of them happening in just seconds.

But these subtleties of mind are not the place to begin the practice. You must start where you can see clearly, with your outward behavior. First, observe the five precepts and stop behavior deadly to spiritual progress. Once the mind no longer is shaken by the effects of unskillful behavior, it becomes easier to see what is going on inside. We can then slow down enough to see our train of thought. Later, as we refine our ability to see how the mind moves, we may see individual mind moments arise, peak, and pass away. To begin, however, it is enough just to become aware of general trends of thought as they occur.

With that awareness, we can use Skillful Effort to make new choices. The Buddha urged everyone to choose wholesome mental states over unwholesome ones and to cultivate wholesome mental states moment by moment, until the unwholesome ones stop returning. We do this, the Buddha said, by continually rousing ourselves, "making effort, stirring up energy, and exerting mind." (D 22)

In the sixth step of the path, Skillful Effort, the Buddha explained more precisely how to direct our efforts, breaking the process down for us into four parts. First, with strong determination and energy, we do whatever we can to prevent the arising of painful, unwholesome states of mind, such as resentment, jealousy, or greed. Since we are not yet enlightened, however, some negative mind states are going to sneak in, despite our best efforts. We then make the second effort, rousing ourselves to overcome whatever unwholesome states have taken hold. Third, we replace those states with wholesome ones, such as loving thoughts, ideas of generosity, or feelings of compassion. Finally, we exert effort to cultivate further these pleasing, wholesome mental states. The more we make these efforts, the more clear and free of pain our minds become, and the more happiness we experience as the natural result.

Accomplishing anything requires effort. This is true in everyday activities such as painting a house or making a sales presentation, and even more so in our spiritual endeavors. Skillful Effort is woven into every step of the path. When we study the Buddha's message with the four kinds of effort, making the mind wholesome, clear, and able to comprehend, we can achieve Skillful Understanding of the path. Then we apply the fourfold effort to our thoughts, words, and deeds, resulting in Skillful Thinking, Skillful Speech, and Skillful Action. When we make the same fourfold effort to apply moral principles to our work life, we achieve Skillful Livelihood. Applying this effort to our meditation practice leads to Skillful Mindfulness and Skillful Concentration. We might rightly conclude that Skillful Effort is the fuel needed to power our accomplishment of each of the steps on the Buddha's path. In fact, making a strong effort to discipline ourselves is about half the battle. Without a powerful effort to achieve wholesome states of mind, we won't get far toward reaching the happiness we seek.

We may like to believe that all we have to do to progress on the

Buddha's path is pay attention. Paying attention certainly sounds easier than making strong effort. But the hard truth is that simple, ordinary attention is not enough. We must learn to pay mindful attention—both when we are engaging in meditation or other spiritual practice and when we are going about the activities of our everyday lives. The Buddha knew that unless we make the mindful effort to eliminate negative states of mind and cultivate positive ones in every aspect of our lives, our minds will never settle down enough to allow us to progress.

About now, you might be thinking, "I knew there was a catch! This sounds like a lot of hard work." Of course, you'd be right. It's certainly easier to bury our negative qualities deep in the unconscious mind than to let them go. Greed, anger, hatred, sloppiness, arrogance, snobbishness, spitefulness, vindictiveness, and fear may have become our familiar, everyday habits. We'd rather not make the effort to give them up. Yet, at the same time, we want to be happy and to move toward our spiritual goals.

Skillful Effort is the stick-to-it quality that makes the whole path possible. It is the gumption to say, "These unwholesome habits of thought and behavior must go, now!" and the wisdom to see that only by cultivating positive and wholesome ways of thinking, acting, and speaking can we hope to achieve happiness.

THE TEN FETTERS

In order to let go of our unwholesome mind habits, we need to recognize them. In general terms, what we want to eliminate are any states of mind that block us from experiencing happiness. If you want to weed a garden, you have to be able to distinguish the weeds from the flowers. The same is true here. At the beginning, we find our mental gardens choked with weeds. We identify and remove unwholesome qualities, such as anger, and replace them with useful, skillful qualities such as loving-friendliness.

If you think about it for a moment, you'll be able to come up with your own list of mental weeds. You'll know that when you're experiencing rage, jealousy, lust, or vengefulness, you can't simultaneously be happy. Underneath these negative states, no matter how they manifest, are the same basic roots: greed (desire), hatred (the flip side of greed), and delusion (or ignorance).

You can think of greed, in combination with ignorance, as the root of all mental weeds. Greed manifests as ten deep, powerful psychic irritants called "the fetters." These are distortions of understanding that affect your thoughts the way canals affect the flow of water. Fetters cause your thoughts to flow directly into suffering. A difficult childhood or other bad experiences in this life do not cause the fetters. They come down to you from many lifetimes past. They are the cause of each lifetime and its suffering. The presence of fetters prevents enlightenment and guarantees future lives. The fetters caused this life, too.

We usually group these ten fetters to reflect the stages by which they must be overcome on the way to enlightenment.

Fetters overcome to reach the first stage of enlightenment:

- belief in the existence of a permanent self or soul

- doubt in the message of the Buddha

- belief that one can end suffering merely by following rules and rituals

Fetters overcome to reach the second and third stages:

- greed for sensual pleasures (gross greed)

- hatred

Fetters overcome to reach the fourth stage:

- subtle desire to exist in fine material form

- subtle desire to exist in immaterial form

- conceit, or the underlying perception of self-identity

- restlessness and worry

- ignorance

All ten fetters remain in the mind of an unenlightened person, at least in a dormant way, all the time. Sometimes one of these fetters will come to the forefront of the mind, causing the person to profoundly misunderstand reality and to suffer. Every mind moment contains at least the fetters of subtle desire and ignorance, but other fetters sometimes join with them.

As we gain wisdom bit by bit, we weaken these fetters, finally breaking through and destroying them in stages. After each breakthrough we reach a higher level of enlightenment. When we break the first three fetters, we attain the first stage of enlightenment. When we weaken the next two, we achieve the second stage. The small amount of greed and hatred that remains is far more subtle than what has been removed. When we break through the remaining greed and hatred, we reach the third stage. The five last fetters are very subtle. With their destruction comes the fourth and final stage of enlightenment.

Belief in a Permanent Self

The first fetter, belief in a permanent self or soul, causes a conviction that the aggregates of existence have some sort of relationship with a self or soul. This fetter may manifest as a belief that physical form, feelings, perceptions, thoughts, and consciousness are one and the same thing as the soul, that they are *identical*. At other times this fetter may cause a conviction that these aggregates *possess* a soul (or that the soul is in possession of these aggregates). We may have the belief that the soul *caused* the combination of aggregates (or that the aggregates caused the soul). Finally, it may manifest as a belief that our soul or self is one thing, and the body, feelings, perceptions, thoughts, and consciousness are a totally *separate* thing, unrelated to the soul.

The most common way that this fetter manifests is in the idea that we possessed a soul in a previous life, that this soul came into this life and currently possesses our aggregates, and that it will leave our body and go to another existence after our death. In essence, this belief rests on the idea that the soul is permanent, eternal, and never changing.

Doubt

The second fetter, doubt, refers specifically to doubt that the Buddha's practice of cultivating morality, concentration, and wisdom will bring lasting happiness. Doubt may become active when you stray from what you truly know in the present moment and reflect unwisely upon matters that tend to stimulate uncertainty. Certain "imponderables" are well known for their power to stimulate and strengthen the fetter of doubt. These are speculative questions such as how and when the universe came into existence, and other such things.

One set of doubt-inspiring topics involves questions about the past and future: "Did I exist before birth? What kinds of past lives did I have, and what were they like? Is there life after death? Will I be annihilated? Is there a heaven or a hell? Will I be reborn? What kinds of lives will I have?"

The present can also fill us with doubt: "Do I exist? Do I not exist? Am I okay? Who am I? How did I arrive at my present state?"

Another set of related considerations comes to our mind from time to time and stirs up the fetter of doubt: "Do I have a self or not? Am I perceiving the self by means of the self, or by means of something that is not the self? Or am I perceiving that which is not the self by means of the self? Isn't this surely my self which thinks and feels, and which now and then experiences the fruits of good and evil deeds? And isn't this self something that is permanent, stable, eternal, and not subject to change?" (M 2)

All these questions and considerations lead us down blind alleys and into the thickets of doubt and confusion. Engaging in them keeps us from paying mindful attention to what is really important. These kinds of questions can never be answered satisfactorily and just distract us. But until we attain the first stage of enlightenment, they will linger in the mind. The Buddha advised people simply to watch such questions arise and pass away. Do not follow them or worry about them. Proceed with your attempts to understand and reflect upon what you can know by personal experience, not merely by reasoning, in this moment.

Have faith in the Buddha's path to happiness that so many people have followed to enlightenment. Faith, in Buddhist terms, means confidence—confidence based on what you have seen so far, and confidence in what you can project to be true based on what you have seen. For example, you have personally observed that whenever you were full of negative mental states, you suffered. You recall that whenever you were full of positive states of mind, you felt happy. When all these states changed you saw their impermanence. These are facts. You can have confidence in this. This kind of confidence keeps you on course until a deep realization of truth leaves no more room for doubt.

Belief in Rites and Rituals

The third fetter is an instinctive movement of the mind to find some source of assistance from outside, rather than from internal purification. It manifests as clinging to belief in the efficacy of rules and rituals to bring enlightenment. You may think that the highest happiness can be attained by performing ceremonies, engaging in celebrations, organizing processions, making offerings to the Buddha or to deities, chanting, praying, and saying mantras rather than meditating and applying the Buddha's message to your daily life. This clinging wastes your time and blocks your ability to see the truth. Thus you impede your progress along the path.

Gross Greed

The fetter of greed is the desire for any sensual pleasure. It includes desire for any pleasant sights, sounds, smells, tastes, and tangibles, even the physical material body itself. It also includes all thoughts, ideas, beliefs, and opinions.

Hatred

The fetter of hatred is aversion to anything unpleasant, anything you don't like.

Subtle Desire for Existence

The subtle desire to exist in material or immaterial form, conceit, and the fetters of restlessness and ignorance are the most refined forms of greed. These five fetters form the last obstacles to full enlightenment.

The subtle desire for existence in fine material or immaterial forms refers to the general will to live, to exist in some form, any form.

The desire to exist "in" this physical body disappears with the removal of the grosser level of greed. However, the desire to exist in a more refined, "fine material" form still remains, such as the desire for existence in some kind of ethereal body. This is said to be the form of some of the higher gods. Or if not in an ethereal body, one desires to exist even with no body at all. This is said to be the future existence of those who have accomplished the highest level of concentration; they become the highest gods.

Conceit

Conceit refers to the experiential quality of seeming to exist as someone. This fetter is the moment-to-moment sense of "I" from which so much misunderstanding and confusion flows. The mind thinks "I..., I..., I...," most of the time, never understanding that the sense of "I" is yet another impermanent and impersonal experience of the mental processes. For example, the mind may say, "I heard a sound," but with wisdom comes the truth, the knowing that there was only a sound.

Restlessness and Worry

The fetter of restlessness and worry is very subtle, unlike the hindrance of the same name. Worry is a kind of fretting due to the expected future impact of having even the most subtle unwholesomeness remaining in the mind. Worry causes restlessness, in which the mind cannot settle on anything. The fetter of restlessness and worry keeps the mind fluttering like a banner in the wind, so that it cannot stop and understand the truth of its own impermanence. It is as if the mind were startled again and again by fear of its nonexistence. Experienced meditators sometimes feel frustrated that restlessness comes up again and again. This fetter never goes away completely until full enlightenment.

Ignorance

Ignorance as a fetter refers to a persistent blindness to the nature of suffering, its source, its possible extinction, and the way to end suffering. In other words, ignorance of the Four Noble Truths.

The ten fetters are incredibly powerful. When they arise in our awareness, hot as a boiling pot of water, it takes great effort to cool them down. Why are they called fetters? Because like strong iron chains they keep us bound to suffering in this lifetime and to future repeated deaths and rebirths.

The functioning of these chains is subtle and insidious, but with mindfulness, we can discern how it happens. Let's examine gross greed, the fourth fetter. We know that we have senses—eyes, ears, nose, tongue, body, and mind. We can notice that these senses are in touch with the external world. Because of the constant interaction between the senses and the objects of this world, pleasant feelings may arise, and then the desire for enjoying sensual pleasure arises in us. With mindfulness, we can notice the arising of desire. If, for some reason, desire does not arise, we can notice this lack of desire as well.

Desire makes us want this thing or that thing, prefer this time or that time, like this person or that person—or situation, sight, sound, smell, taste, touch, thought. Because of all this liking or disliking, our mind is always either clinging or rejecting. Most significantly, we like life and cling to it, or we reject it. Thus gross greed for sensual pleasures strengthens the chain that binds us to repeated existence in this world.

Any fetter may arise at the instant of contact. Let us look at the belief in a permanent self. With contact, a feeling arises that may be pleasant, unpleasant, or neutral. At that instant the notion of permanent selfhood arises: "This is 'I' that is making 'me' feel. And this 'I' is in 'me' in a solid, unchanging, permanent way." This fetter of belief in a permanent, eternal "I" binds us to seeking pleasant objects and rejecting unpleasant objects. This "I" isn't happy. It does not get exposed only to pleasant objects all the time, the way it wants to. Objects surround us, and not all of them are pleasant.

If, however, we could really see that a feeling that arises is impermanent—if we could be aware of its appearance and disappearance—we wouldn't hang onto it. We would move on. If we could recognize that the nature of anything is to pass away, and let it go when it has passed, the mind would be relieved of the tension of seeking pleasant objects all the time. If we could remain mindful of whatever comes up, knowing that it must pass away, the fetter of belief in a permanent self would not appear.

Let's look at another fetter, the belief in rites and rituals. Perhaps you have a ritual of lighting a candle every morning and praying for relief from suffering. As you get up in the morning, you think, "Ah, I must do my ritual." You do not try to reduce your psychic irritants by cultivating wisdom, concentration, or wholesome states such as loving-friendliness. Instead, you cling to the belief that performing this ritual in the morning will bring happiness. Years later, even if you never miss a day, you will not have moved an inch toward enlightenment.

When you watch your mind with attention, you can see the fetters arising when the senses make contact with the world. Until you reach enlightenment, each time any of the six senses contact their objects, fetters will arise. Mindfulness can help you discriminate between the senses, sensory objects, and the fetters as they arise. When the fetters come up, you should use mindful effort to overcome them. When they disappear, you should be mindful of that state, and when they do not appear, you should be aware of that state as well.

THE FIVE HINDRANCES

Out of the ten fetters come certain crude, extremely unwholesome mind states that prevent you from making any progress in your meditation or from doing things skillfully in your life. We call these mind states hindrances. If a fetter is like wind, a hindrance would be like a tornado. The hindrances create havoc for new meditators.

The five hindrances are greed, ill will, dullness and drowsiness, restlessness and worry, and doubt. They arise out of the fetters according to circumstances, flaring up like flames from searing-hot coals. But, like flames, hindrances can be doused with Skillful Effort, rightly applied.

The hindrances can be prevented by concentration or by steady mindfulness. Mindfulness or concentration cool the hindrances down and overcome them when they have arisen. When the mind lacks any hindrances, it automatically becomes bright, luminous, and clear. Such a mind is receptive to the development of wholesome states, to concentration, and to the ability to see clearly into the impermanent nature of things. Any of us can be rid of all these hindrances, at least temporarily. So long as the underlying ten fetters continue to exist, the hindrances may return to visit the mind, again and again. But with application of the four kinds of Skillful Effort, you can reduce and shorten their visits. When you become skillful in applying effort, the hindrances cause little or no problem to your meditation or to your daily life.

Greed

The hindrance of greed or covetousness is the desire to obtain things. In meditation, this hindrance comes as greedy thoughts about food or things you want to possess, or as lust. Such thoughts can waste much of the meditation session, and indulging in them can become a difficult habit to break.

This trap of greed is not unlike the way monkeys are trapped in some cultures. A trapper slices a small hole across the top of a coconut and empties out the liquid. He cuts some chunks of coconut flesh and leaves them in the bottom of the shell, then ties the shell tightly to a tree. The monkey slips his hand into the hole and grabs the loose chunks of coconut. He tries to pull out the coconut chunks, but his fist cannot come through the small hole. When the trapper returns, the greedy monkey is so attached to the bits of coconut he holds in his fist that he will not let go and withdraw his hand. While the monkey is struggling, the trapper captures him. It's easy to feel sorry for the monkey. We have all been trapped by greed.

Ill Will

The hindrance of ill will, including hatred, anger, and resentment, springs from the desire to avoid things we do not like. Ill will is compared to boiling water. When water is boiling, you cannot touch it without being scalded. Nor can you see the bottom of the pot. In other words, ill will burns you more than it hurts someone else, and you'll never find the true cause or "get to the bottom" of your hostile feelings while anger is boiling inside you. Ill will also distorts our perceptions and sours our joys. It is like a sickness that makes delicious food so tasteless that we cannot enjoy it. Similarly, when our mind is filled with hatred, we cannot appreciate the fine qualities of the people around us.

Dullness and Drowsiness

During meditation it often happens that people struggle with greed and then with ill will. Once these are overcome, there is a moment of peace, but then the mind falls asleep! Dullness and drowsiness come out of the fetter of ignorance. Dullness is sluggishness of mind, while drowsiness is physical languor. When we are feeling slothful or sleepy, it's impossible to concentrate or to get any work done. It's also impossible to practice mindfulness or to meditate. The hindrance of dullness and drowsiness is compared to being in prison. When you are locked up, you do not know what's happening outside the prison walls. In the same way, when you allow your mind to sink into dullness or your body into drowsiness, you do not know what is happening around you or within you.

Restlessness and Worry

Worrying causes restlessness, so these two mental states go together. Neither is conducive to clear thinking, clear understanding, or clear knowing. This hindrance is compared to slavery. The slave works very hard to please his or her cruel master, always worrying and nervous in fear of punishment. The more nervous and restless the slave gets, the more he or she will worry. The slave never enjoys peace of mind.

Doubt

The hindrance of doubt is perplexity, not knowing the right direction or where to turn. Doubt is sparked by thinking about things other than what you can observe happening in the present moment. Doubt is like going into the desert without a map or a set of directions. When you walk through the desert, it's easy to get confused because the landscape markings are hard to distinguish. A given direction could be the right one or the wrong. Just so, when doubt arises about the truth of the Buddha's teachings, you become perplexed and have a hard time deciding what to do.

You sit there thinking, "Do people really become enlightened? Is this practice really going to help? Am I doing it right? Those other people seem to be doing it better. Maybe I should be doing it differently, or trying another teacher, or exploring something altogether different." These doubts sap your energy, create confusion, and make it impossible to see anything clearly.

FOUR STEPS TO SKILLFUL EFFORT

Now we can discuss just how we deal with the mental weeds of hindrances and fetters and cultivate better states of mind. The Buddha taught a four-step approach to working with the mind. You should apply Skillful Effort to:

- prevent negative states of mind

- overcome negative states of mind

- cultivate positive states of mind

- maintain positive states of mind

Preventing Negative States of Mind

Your first line of defense is to prevent negative or unwholesome states of mind from arising in the first place. How? By maintaining unremitting mindfulness. Just that.

Mindfulness requires training, and training requires effort. There are five points to mindfulness training: morality, mindfulness, wisdom, patience, and effort. Effort is used with each of the other points. You start with good morality, which takes effort, as we saw in discussions of previous steps of the path. With morality as a stable base, you make the effort to exercise whatever mindfulness you can already remember to practice. One aspect of mindfulness is "remembering," and this should be kept alive all the time. Again and again, you remember to reapply the mind to the present moment. You bring together more and more moments in which you are successfully mindful. I've heard it said, "A moment of mindfulness is never wasted."

You then apply your insights, bringing increasing wisdom to your efforts. You stop and think, "How did this go last time?" Feeling the impact of your mistakes gives you great incentive to avoid them in the future. You recall what you have learned and stop repeating mistakes. This way, you mold your behavior very quickly. As your wisdom about reality deepens, you remind yourself repeatedly about your new priorities and become unwilling to let a moment go by without bringing up mindfulness and wisdom. If you fail, you apply patience: you suffer the consequences and then patiently make the effort to be mindful again.

Developing steady mindfulness can be a lengthy process, so the Buddha gave his disciples some tips on how to protect their minds. He advised them to exercise "wise attention" and to avoid "unwise attention." (M 2) He explained that you should stick to what you know to be true right now through the five senses. That is your own domain, your true home. Thinking carries you away from that safe place. For instance, on hearing a sound during meditation, just know "sound," instead of speculating about who made that sound and what it might mean. On noticing unpleasant sensations of coolness while at work, just observe this sensation without forming an opinion about the air-conditioning system of the building. As you wait at a bus stop, observe your thoughts as just passing phenomena, like the passing cars, without hitching a ride with them.

The Buddha urged his monks to put up with the small uncomfortable realities of life without automatically trying to fix things. If you keep choosing to change things to get comfortable all the time, the mind gets fussy, and unwholesome states arise more quickly. Let's say you notice that the meditation room is too warm. Instead of getting up to adjust the thermostat or open the window, just notice the feeling of warmth. Notice the changes in your physical discomfort and your mind's changing reactions to it. Learn to endure the small things. Of course, some people may carry this kind of advice too far. If urgent things arise, you should mindfully take care of them!

The Buddha also encouraged avoidance of foolish, unmindful people, since we all tend to pick up each other's behaviors. Associate with people who have qualities you want to emulate. Find a good spiritual friend who is upright, mindful, well restrained, and moderate in behavior. Stick close and seek the advice of this person when needed.

The Buddha further advised his disciples not to notice the "signs and features" of any external stimulus that might give rise to unwholesome mind states. "Sign" refers to the hook, the thing that catches your eye and makes you want to observe something more closely in order to rouse up some unwholesome state. "Feature" refers to specific qualities of the object of your attention that may further stir up the unwholesome state. For instance, a married man might be advised not to note or linger upon the coy behavior or the specific attractive features of a woman to whom he might become attracted. Similarly, a married woman might be well advised not to note whether a nice-looking man wears a wedding ring or allow herself to pause to admire his smile. A story from the time of the Buddha illustrates this point.

There was a monk whose vow of celibacy was threatened by recurring sexual fantasies. He practiced meditating on the body as a skeleton to rid himself of these troubling thoughts. One day he was walking on a forest path. A beautiful woman came along this same path, headed alone toward her parents' house after a fight with her husband. When she saw the monk, she smiled at him as she passed.

A little while later, the woman's husband came walking along the same path looking for his wife. When he saw the monk, he asked him, "Sir, did you see a beautiful young woman passing this way?"

"I don't know whether it was a man or a woman," the monk replied, "but I saw a skeleton passing this way." (Vsm 1 [55])

The monk had prevented lustful thoughts from arising by applying Skillful Effort to his meditation practice. He had thus protected his mind from unwholesome states.

If you are able to maintain continuous mindfulness, nothing will upset you. You will not become angry or agitated. You can be patient no matter what anyone says or does. You can stay peaceful and happy. An unwholesome or negative state of mind cannot arise at the same moment as a moment of mindfulness.

Perhaps you find that preventing negative mind states is easy so long as you do not encounter unpleasant people or situations. When everything is going smoothly, it's easy to keep your mindfulness intact. You might even congratulate yourself for being able to remain patient and accept praise for your self-control and forbearance from your family, friends, and colleagues. But when things start to go wrong, your patience and mindfulness may start to break down. A story told by the Buddha describes how easily this can happen.

Once there was a rich lady who had a dutiful and skillful servant woman. The servant got up very early and started her work before anybody in the house woke up. She worked all day until very late in the evening. Her only rest was a few hours of sleep each night.

Often, she heard the neighbors speaking very highly of her mistress. They said, "This rich lady is very kind to her servant woman. She is very patient. We never see her lose her temper. We wonder how she became such a wonderful person."

The servant woman thought, "These people speak very highly of my mistress. They do not know how hard I work to keep this house neat. I must test for myself how kind and patient this lady is."

The next day, the servant woke up a little late. When the rich lady woke up, she noticed that the servant woman was still sleeping. She scolded her, "You foolish woman! You slept until the sun came up. Get up this very minute and go back to work."

The servant woman got up. She had not been asleep. She was simply pretending to sleep. When she got up, she apologized to her mistress and started her work.

The next day, the servant woke up later than the previous day. The rich lady was furious. She scolded the servant woman, using harsh words, and threatened that if the servant woman woke up late again, she would beat her.

On the third day, the servant woman woke up later still. The rich lady was so enraged that she took a broom and struck the servant woman until her head was bleeding. The servant woman ran out of the house with her bloody head and cried very loudly, "Look, friends! My mistress beat me up for getting up a little late today. Last night I worked until midnight, and I had a headache. Therefore, I slept a little later today."

The neighbors who had praised the rich lady for her patience and compassion quickly changed their views. (M 21)

You may have experienced this same kind of breakdown after a long and relaxing vacation or when you return from a spiritual retreat. While you were away, your anger, impatience, jealousy, and fear were inactive, and you felt peaceful and happy. But the moment you came home, you got an upsetting phone message, or you saw a bill you forgot to pay, or someone stepped on your toe, and all your anger rushed back. In an instant, your peace of mind was gone. Then you wondered, "How can I maintain this happy vacation feeling or retreat feeling in everyday life?"

The everyday answer is mindfulness. You must remember that it is not some other person or some difficult situation that is causing your problems. It is your own past conditioning. In addition to trying to maintain continuous awareness, learning to recognize the particular weaknesses in your mental habits can help you prevent unwholesome responses from arising.

For example, suppose you go to buy a pair of gloves in an expensive store, and the salesperson is very rude. From past experience, you know that rude salespeople make you angry. So, you take care to be especially mindful and head off any angry thoughts. You reason with yourself by thinking: "Well, this salesperson is also a human being. Perhaps he did not get a good night's sleep. Or he may have financial worries or family problems. Maybe he suffers from insecurities about people of my race or nationality. Or maybe he's not feeling very well today. That may be why he is unable to speak politely to his customers."

This technique may sound easy, but it's not. Our minds have not been trained to prevent negative patterns of thinking. Getting angry is very easy, criticizing others is very easy, worrying about tomorrow is very easy, desiring things is very easy. These habits of mind are like junk food. Once you start eating a bag of potato chips, it's hard to stop. Preventing negative thoughts from arising is hard, too. Once you are hooked, it is difficult to let go. As the Buddha said:

Easy it is for the good to do good.
Difficult it is for the evil to do good.
Easy it is for the evil to do evil.
Difficult it is for the good to do evil.
(Ud V.8)

It is very easy to do things that are harmful to oneself.
It is very difficult to do things that are beneficial to oneself.
(Dh 163)

Nevertheless, you should hold firmly to the knowledge that prevention is always easier than cure. Mindfulness practiced with Skillful Effort can prevent negative thoughts and actions from arising in the future. Preventing harmful habits of body, speech, and mind is not impossible, if you train yourself in mindfulness. When negative thoughts and actions do arise in spite of your sincere effort to prevent them, you should not be depressed or disappointed. It doesn't mean that you are a bad person, it just means you have more work to do. Be happy in realizing that you have a helper to assist you: the effort to overcome negative states of mind.

Overcoming Negative States of Mind

Prior to full enlightenment, we cannot choose what thoughts will arise, so there's no need to be ashamed or to react with aversion to whatever comes up. We do choose, however, what thoughts we allow to proliferate. Positive and wholesome thoughts help the mind. They should be cultivated. Negative and unwholesome thoughts, such as the five hindrances and the ten fetters, harm the mind. They should be opposed immediately with Skillful Effort and overcome. This is the Buddha's own advice.

Overcoming the Hindrances

How you respond to a hindrance depends upon how entrenched it is. Hindrances do not arrive full-blown. They start as a single negative mind moment and then proliferate. The sooner you catch this train of thought, the easier it is to stop it. Any time hindrances are present, you cannot make progress with mindfulness or concentration.

At first it is very simple. A hindrance arises, and you simply notice it. You notice, for instance, that you are having greedy, angry, confused, or worried thoughts or that your mind has become trapped in a restless, dull, or depressed state. At this first level, the hindrances are very weak, so the method of overcoming them is mild as well. You simply notice the presence of the negative mind state. By mere attention, the negative thought fades away, and you notice its absence and how this absence gives rise to thoughts of generosity, loving-friendliness, and wise clarity.

If a hindrance has developed beyond that initial stage, you have to take stronger measures. First, look at the negative thought with complete mindfulness. Pay it total attention. Notice its impact on your mind and body. Notice how it blocks your mental development. Look at its impermanent nature. Look at the impermanent nature of the circumstances, appearances, moods, tastes, interests, and numerous other conditions that caused the thought to arise. Reflect on the harm you might cause yourself by entertaining this negative thought and the worse harm that might come from acting upon it.

Now, reason with yourself. Remind yourself that everything is impermanent and that the situation that caused this thought or mind state to arise will certainly change. For example, if someone has said something that angers you, remind yourself of the problems you face in your life—concerns about money or health, worries about your job or family. Tell yourself that this person may be experiencing similar problems. You do not really know what is going on in someone's mind at any given moment. Frankly speaking, you do not know even what is happening in your mind at any given moment. Your state of mind depends on numerous conditions. In fact, everything that happens depends on many different causes and conditions. Reflecting in this way may cause your negative mind state to fade.

Say you wake up in the morning in a bad mood. You do not know any specific reason why you feel upset, angry, depressed, edgy, or grouchy. But if you think very carefully, you may remember that you ate some spicy food for dinner or watched TV for several hours before going to bed. Yet eating spicy food or watching TV are not themselves the causes for your bad mood this morning. These actions are themselves the results of other causes. Maybe you had an argument earlier in the day with your son or your husband and watched TV longer than usual because you were upset or anxious. Then you might remember that your argument was triggered by a bad situation at the office, which was itself the result of other causes and conditions. Thus everything we experience has causes and circumstances behind it—many more than we can analyze or even know. All of these causes are related to each other. No single event can cause anything else. Therefore there is no need to make your negative mind state worse by blaming yourself for it—or by blaming anyone else!

Moreover, you can remind yourself that, fortunately, all events and situations change. Nothing ever remains the same. When you feel utterly desperate, you may believe that nothing will ever change. However, when you look more closely, you can see that this belief is mistaken. People do change. Situations change. You change. There is nothing that does not change. Therefore, as time passes, that depressing mood or angry state of mind also changes. Your feeling about an unpleasant person or situation changes. Your attitude changes. Other people's attitudes change. Sometimes when you are in a bad mood, or in a good one, you think that your mood will never change. This very thought of "this will never change" is also changing. When you come to this realization, you relax a little, and your negative thoughts start to fade.

The most difficult kind of negative thought to overcome is one that you do not notice until it is deeply entrenched. Such thoughts block the mind and prevent it from developing. You may notice the existence of such thoughts when you sit down to meditate and work with your practice of mindfulness or concentration. You cannot focus your mind on the breath because some negative thought whirls round and round in your head. In such cases, you need to use stronger effort.

This may be the time to develop insight by examining the problematic thought. If so, you temporarily put aside your plan to work on concentration or to observe the rising, peaking, and falling away of sensations and mental states, and set your mind to examining thoroughly what is going on. The method to use for this examination is given in step two in the section on Mindfulness of Skillful Thinking. If you would prefer to get on with your intended practice, however, there are several remedies you can use. They are listed in order of increasing forcefulness. If one fails, try the next.

- Ignore it.

- Divert the mind to something else.

- Replace the hindrance by its opposite.

- Reflect on fact that every hindrance arises from a great number of causes and conditions and is in flux.

- With clenched teeth, pressing the tongue against the upper palate, apply all your energy to overcome it.

Let's say, for example, that you keep thinking angrily about a dispute with your friend. Simply paying attention to the thoughts has not brought you relief. Reasoning with yourself has also failed. You have also tried ignoring the thoughts. (As the Buddha said: "All things arise in [your] mind only when you pay attention to them." (A IV (Eights) IX.3) When you do not pay attention to any kind of thought, it wastes away.) Yet this method, too, has failed to overcome your angry state of mind. When you sit down to meditate, the conversation you had with your friend keeps replaying in your mind. These thoughts fuel your anger and make it impossible for your mind to settle down.

What can you do? You can try diverting your mind to something else. Switch your attention to something completely different, such as the pleasant activities you have planned for tomorrow. If that fails, divert your mind to the opposite of anger, loving-friendliness. Recall times of peace and harmony you have had with your friend. Allow these good memories to fill your mind. Then try to send loving thoughts to your friend. If this seems too difficult, send loving thoughts to your child or stir up loving feelings by reflecting on the qualities of your teacher or someone else whom you love. When you are radiating loving thoughts, there is no room in your mind for anger.

If the angry thoughts still persist, take a hard look at them. Notice how they change, arising and passing, appearing and disappearing. Consider the loss you suffer to your own peace of mind and to your spiritual development from entertaining unwholesome mind states.

If all else fails, you must crush the negative thought with all your might—according to the Buddha's own words, "like a strong man might crush a weaker man." In other words, you must never let the unwholesome thought win. You may be thinking that this method of gritting your teeth and crushing a negative thought seems so harsh, so unlike any other instructions you may have heard for dealing with the mind. You might even think that it seems out of character with the gentle nature of Buddhism.

But forceful effort is quite consistent with the Buddha's life and teaching. He taught us to strive with diligence. As we have noted, Skillful Effort is the fuel that powers our accomplishment of every step on the path to happiness. With Skillful Effort we take precautions to prevent harmful thoughts, words, and deeds. With Skillful Effort we overcome tension, anxiety, worry, fear, and resentment. With Skillful Effort we practice mindfulness to cultivate those wonderful qualities within us that we are not yet aware we have.

Arouse your wonderful qualities and bring them to the surface of your mind. With Skillful Effort, maintain them and do not forget them. Practice them repeatedly over and over. As the Buddha said: "Let my blood dry up! Let the flesh of my body wither away! Let my body be reduced to a skeleton! I will not get up from this meditation seat without attaining enlightenment." (M 70) From the day he attained enlightenment until he passed away, the Buddha reminded people to be similarly diligent in their spiritual efforts.

In spite of this teaching, sometimes people say that spiritual growth takes "effortless effort." I'm sorry to disillusion you, friends, but there is no effortless effort. Effort must be balanced. Too much effort or unskillful effort can cause more stress for the mind and lead to a downward spiral into unwholesome states. Yet if effort is too slack, you will become bored or tired or lose interest. Then you must make unrelenting effort to bring effort back into balance with other wholesome mental factors.

The truth is that you can never achieve anything great without effort. Every great invention took effort. The electric light, the automobile, and the computer did not happen because someone just sat back and relaxed. The inventors worked very hard on their projects. If you undertake a big project like meditation, you must be willing to make a great effort to achieve your goal. You must also be willing to discipline yourself, if necessary. A story about the Buddha makes this point clear:

A horse trainer asked the Buddha, "How do you train disciples?"

Buddha asked him, "How do you train horses?"

The trainer answered, "I apply gentle ways. If that does not work, I apply harsh methods. If I cannot train them by harsh methods, I kill the horses."

Buddha said, "I do the same thing. I use a gentle method. If by using that method, I cannot train my disciples, I use harsh methods. If I cannot train them by using harsh methods, I kill them."

Then the horse trainer said, "You are supposed to be teaching nonviolence! How can you kill?"

Then the Buddha explained his killing method. He "killed" an offending person by boycotting or ignoring the person totally, who was then cut off from the community of monks. (A II (Fours) XII.1)

The suttas tell of a famous incident in which the Buddha used this method:

The Buddha had an old friend named Channa. He had been the Buddha's charioteer and playmate when they were children, and he was the charioteer who drove Siddhattha out of the palace to live an ascetic life. Channa went forth as a monk when he was advanced in age. Because of the role he had played in the Buddha's life, Channa took all the credit for the accomplishments of the Buddha and became very proud. From the time of his ordination he showed disrespect for the Sangha. For example, when senior monks visited him, he did not perform the customary duties such as getting up and offering them a seat or bringing them water to wash their feet and faces.

The Buddha told Channa that his behavior was very arrogant. He said to him, "You must respect these monks." But Channa never obeyed the Buddha.

Finally, when Buddha was going to pass away, Venerable Ananda asked the Buddha what to do with Channa. The Buddha asked the community to boycott him. Ananda was assigned the task of pronouncing the boycott.

When the Buddha passed away, Channa was so shocked and grief-stricken that he began to think, "All my reputation, power, and courage came from the Buddha. Now that he is gone, I have no support from anybody. Now the whole world is empty. I have offended many monks, and they are no longer my friends."

When Ananda pronounced the boycott on Channa, Channa was shocked a second time, and he passed out. When he regained consciousness, he became very humble. The Buddha knew that Channa would respond this way. Channa practiced meditation obediently and diligently. Eventually, he became enlightened. Harsh methods are sometimes necessary. Harshness sometimes works. (D 16; V ii 292)

You can use the same technique on your own hindrances. Begin with a gentle method, but be willing to use a harsh method if you have to.

When you are tempted to buy another pretty sweater although your closet is full of them, discipline the mind as we have described. Ignore the thought; divert the mind to something else; replace the greedy thought with a generous one; reflect mindfully on the impermanent nature of sweaters and all material things. If the mind is still whining and crying for that sweater, you may need to get harsh with yourself. Tell yourself to stop, or there will be no new sweaters this season. If that doesn't work, decide there will be no new sweaters this year. As a last resort, threaten that you will buy all your sweaters from the Salvation Army resale shop for the next five years! Then carry out your threat. The mind learns to let go.

There is a special situation that calls for a very strict method. Occasionally when you sit in meditation, the mind is completely chaotic. This may be due to something that happened prior to the meditation session, such as excessive stimulation during the day or something that caused overwhelming anxiety. The mind is so agitated, with images and emotions coming so quickly, that you have hardly dealt with one negative thought before you face the next. You may experience what I have heard students call a "multiple hindrance attack." That is when several hindrances arise and take over the mind, one after another. If you accept the mind running around in this way, it can become a difficult habit to overcome. It is better to use everything you've got to calm the mind.

If all of the usual methods fail in such a case, there is another method: try counting your breaths. This is a trick to get the mind focused on one thing. First count the breaths from 1 to 10; then from 10 to 1. Next, count from 1 to 9 and from 9 to 1. Continue counting to 8, to 7, and so forth, until you reach 1 to 2 and from 2 to 1. Here's the stern part: If the mind wanders even the tiniest bit while you are counting, you must start over. You continue this counting until you can complete the entire cycle of counting without distraction; then you can return to your usual method of meditation. This is a challenge. Starting over again with each distraction causes the mind to get tired of running around.

Even though this method is strong, some people may suffer too much chaos even to do the counting. In that case, make the chaos itself the object of meditation. Watch as the chaos changes.

OVERCOMING THE FETTERS
Using the techniques we just discussed, you can train yourself to recognize the fetters when they arise and take steps to overcome them.

With mindful attention and active opposition, the fetter that is trou-bling you—doubt, greed, hatred, restlessness—slowly weakens and fades from the mind. That particular fetter may not arise again for some time. The mind knows it is gone and becomes clear. But then, depend-ing on your temperament and life circumstances, another fetter will surface.

As you pay mindful attention to this cycle of the fetters arising, fad-ing away, and then reappearing in some other form, you start to realize just how powerful these fetters are, just how strongly they bind you to suffering and unhappiness. No matter how often you temporarily over-come the fetters, the tendencies of mind that appeared as fetters continue to exist within you, binding or trapping you again and again. You see that you carry a prison within yourself. As your mindfulness develops, you realize that these negative states of mind—greed, hatred, and delu-sion—not only distort your thoughts but make every aspect of your life more miserable, more painful. The mind keeps returning to the same negative patterns. You feel that you are trapped—fettered—to a never-ending cycle of birth and death.

The truth is that mindfulness can help you suppress the fetters only temporarily. It takes high attainment on the Buddha's path to enlight-enment to destroy them. As we mentioned before, the fetters are destroyed in four stages. How? You abandon them through five appli-cations of effort, known as suppressing, substituting, destroying, sub-siding, and escaping.

"Suppressing" refers to pushing all unwholesome states back, hold-ing them at bay through mindfulness or concentration. Whenever you remain mindful or whenever you go into deep concentration, the fetters remain dormant. When you make a habit of pushing the fetters down, the suppressed fetters are weakened. Weakened fetters cause less trou-ble, moment to moment, and have less impact on your thinking processes. The hindrances also calm down a bit. This respite creates more opportunity for insight to happen and makes it more likely that some fetters will be destroyed when wisdom arises.

"Substituting" is the effort to oppose an individual unwholesome state by cultivating its opposite. You substitute for anger by cultivating loving-friendliness. The belief in things being eternal is opposed by examining impermanence. You counter the instinctive belief in a self by analyzing the fluctuating elements that make up your body and mind.

When suppression and substitution are well developed, it becomes possible to break through some weakened fetters. "Destroying" is the moment when any fetter gives way, like a palm tree splitting apart when it is hit by lightening. "Subsiding" refers to the disappearance of those fetters immediately after they are destroyed. "Escaping" refers to the release of mind that follows the destruction of any group of fetters. The most dramatic escape occurs at the first of the four stages of enlightenment when one transcends ordinary life and becomes partially awakened.

Let's assume that you have targeted the first three fetters—belief in permanent self, doubt, and belief in the power of rites and rituals—and have deeply studied their opposites. As you sit in meditation, observing with strong concentration the characteristics of the breath, insight may arise. Your examination of the impermanence, dissatisfaction, and self-lessness of the breath allows you, in one great insight, to penetrate the fact that all reality shares these three characteristics. Seeing the impermanence of all things so clearly, you get it on the intuitive level that there cannot be anything permanent called "self" or "soul." Thus you break through the first fetter. You also realize that there must have been a great person who figured all this out while practicing this path, which thus must truly work to uproot all negative states of mind. Thus you lose the second fetter, doubt. You now know that nothing can free your mind except the cultivation of wisdom through a path that emphasizes morality, concentration, and insight. Knowing this, you cease to believe that mere rituals have the power to save you, and so, you shake off the third fetter.

Once you break away from these three fetters, you attain the first stage of enlightenment. Now, there is no falling back. You will never again doubt your potential for full enlightenment or wonder how you can achieve it. You are guaranteed to reach your goal. You become a "stream-enterer," because the pull of the spiritual current will carry you to enlightenment, just as a twig is carried along by the current of a stream.

From this point on, there is a new buoyancy to the mind, a sense that, no matter how difficult life's circumstances may seem, underneath it all everything is okay. You know, for certain, that everything is impermanent, and this brings comfort to your heart. You are no longer able to commit any seriously unwholesome acts, because you know too well the law of cause and effect. With such good behavior, there is no reason for heavy remorse to arise; thus you are freed from that burden. If you do slip up and, say, tell a small lie, you cannot rest until you have set things right. You may still fall into explosions of anger, grief, or greed, but these episodes do not take you down so far as before, and they pass quickly. The whole path makes perfect sense to you, and you have keen, vigorous interest in continuing your training. You become generally more confident, less self-centered, more generous and kind, better able to concentrate, and more competent at anything you undertake. Your co-workers and friends notice a change in you, how much sweeter, more lighthearted, and relaxed you have become. The sparkle in your eyes opens other people's hearts, and they begin to ask you about the source of your well-being.

To show the significance of attaining stream-entry the Buddha took a little bit of dirt onto his fingernail and said, "Which is more, monks, this little bit of dirt, or all the dirt in the entire world?" Of course the monks answered that the dirt in the rest of the world was much, much more than the little bit upon his fingernail. Then the Buddha said, "Similarly, monks, the amount of defilement that one destroys by the attainment of stream-entry is as much as the dirt in the rest of the world. And what the stream-enterer has left to destroy is like the dirt on my fingernail." (S V.56.6 [1]) For this reason, he said, attaining stream-entry is greater than becoming a "universal monarch" ruling all other kingdoms. It is greater than going to heaven to be like an angel; it is even greater than becoming a god.

Having accomplished this breakthrough, you begin to tackle the next hurdle: the fetters of gross greed and hatred. When you broke through the first three fetters, you also lightened the weight of the remaining fetters. Thus the greed and hatred you now face are much less than what you experienced as an ordinary person.

You watch for greed and hatred and use Skillful Effort to beat back these enemies again and again. You develop generosity and loving-friendliness. You become thoroughly fed up with your mind's clinging, whining, and grouching. As you cultivate deeper awareness of impermanence, seeing more clearly the changing nature of all pleasant, unpleasant, and neutral feelings, you see the futility of trying to have things your own way. You let go more and more.

Finally the day comes when gross greed and hatred are greatly reduced. Some less obvious greed and hatred remain, holding your personality in place, but much of the job is done. You become a "once-returner," meaning that you can be reborn in the physical world only one more time before becoming fully enlightened.

The peace that comes over the mind is indescribable. All your cares, duties, and burdens fall away, forever. No harsh words or personal misfortune rattles you. You are done with being rattled. People may notice your purity and your unending kindness and begin to think of you as a saint. Yet, to start out with, you were no better than anyone else. It is an impersonal process, a natural shift in the mind, that you have achieved thus far by following the Buddha's directions. Although you no longer have any clinging or grief for your own losses, your heart is so great, and enough clinging remains, that you can still become overly involved in and saddened by the losses of others. There is more work to be done. The remains of greed and hatred have yet to be mopped up.

When the fetters of gross greed and hatred are finally broken, you achieve the third stage of enlightenment. A person at this stage is known as a "nonreturner," someone who will never be born again into this world, though one rebirth in a nonmaterial plane of existence is possible.

Once the work of removing gross greed and hatred is done, then the final group, the most subtle of psychic irritants—the last five fetters—must be tackled. These problems in the mind are so subtle that no ordinary person can notice them, much less feel inspired to try to remove them. The nonreturner continues to experience, for example, restlessness caused by the worry of anticipating one more future rebirth. Yet for someone at this level of refinement, these remaining fetters are like a little spot of food staining a perfectly pure, white shirt.

Continuing the training, the nonreturner removes the remaining, subtle desires for any kind of existence. He or she gets rid of "conceit," the experiential quality of seeming to have a self. Restlessness is removed, as is the last remaining bit of ignorance. In one great moment, all these last fetters are ripped away, and there stands the perfected enlightened one, the arahant. This one can never again do any acts based upon greed, hatred, or delusion, because these things are forever banished from the mind. As the Buddha said many times, an arahant is one who has "laid down the burden."

It may occur to you that perhaps the arahant can fall down to a lower level and be tempted into sexual intercourse, theft, or some other worldly behavior. If you recall the nature of fetters—how fetters misguide our behaviors and how they are vanquished—you will not entertain such thoughts about the perfectly enlightened ones. Arahants find even indulgence in sense pleasure unthinkable—much less any immoral actions. Arahants can never again do wrong. They continuously taste ultimate happiness, and they remain fully at peace.

At enlightenment, we come to see clearly that everything we need to know is contained within the Four Noble Truths. We become free from any speculative views or theories about reality, about the past, present, and future, about the existence of the self, and about the universe. We understand what physical reality is and how it arises and passes away. We understand what feeling is and how it arises and passes away. And we understand perception, mental formations, and consciousness in the same way.

We have won complete deliverance from all opinions and conjectures, from all inclinations to claiming or feeling the personal identification of "I" and "mine." All of the theories, views, and beliefs that boost the ego have disappeared. Being totally free from all ten fetters is the stage of full enlightenment.

Cultivating Positive States of Mind

Most people have a tremendous amount of work to do before they can hope to achieve enlightenment. Overcoming the hindrances and suppressing the fetters is a necessary first step. But even when your efforts at temporarily overcoming negative states of mind have been successful, the mind remains vulnerable. It may sink back down into painful, obstructive states, like an airplane descending into clouds. Once you have temporarily cleared the mind of all unwholesome states, you must use Skillful Effort to gladden, uplift, and energize the mind in order to make progress.

When an unwholesome state has been overcome, the mind goes into a neutral state. But it does not stay neutral for long. It's much like the transmission on a car. You've got reverse gear, neutral, and drive. You cannot go directly from reverse to drive without passing through neutral. From the neutral position, the gears can shift in either direction. Similarly, the mind cannot shift directly from wholesome to unwholesome states or back; it must go through a neutral state in between.

You can use this interval of neutrality to cultivate positive states of mind. Let's say you are sitting in meditation, and a negative state of mind arises. Your mindfulness clicks in, and you recognize the unwholesome state. You overcome it, perhaps by seeing the danger in it, and return to the breath. Since the breath is a neutral object, your mind remains neutral as you watch it. But soon your mindfulness lapses, and another painful state of mind arises. Again, mindfulness snaps to attention. You overcome the unwholesome state of mind and return to the breath with a neutral state of mind. This sequence happens again and again.

Finally you say to yourself, "This is ridiculous!" Mindfulness makes you aware that you need to stop this pattern of repetitive negativity. As you pay attention, you begin to see the sequence of your mental activity. You realize that rather than allowing negativity an opening in which it can take hold, you must take advantage of the time when the mind is neutral to arouse a wholesome state of mind. You go back to the breath and relax. You take a few deep breaths and then begin to cultivate a wholesome state of mind.

There are countless ways to bring up wholesome states of mind. One of the most powerful methods to use during meditation is to remember any skillful act that you have done in the past and the pleasant states of mind that went with that action. For example, perhaps you once helped an elderly woman who was trying to cross a busy street. She was struggling with a bag of groceries, and the cars were going by too quickly for her to cross. You did not know her, and you had no interest in any reward or even any thanks. With a mind free of desire for anything, with no attachment, you stepped into the road and carefully signaled the cars to stop. The lady crossed safely. At that time, your mind felt light, free, relaxed, and happy. When you think of this incident now, how do you feel? Again you feel light, free, relaxed, and happy. Having brought these feelings to mind, you reflect, "This is the state of mind I should cultivate." So you use that memory to encourage positive feelings to arise and grow strong.

You can use the memory of any good deed you've done, so long as there's no attachment involved. These kinds of acts brought you happy feelings when you did them, and you can let the same good feelings fill the mind when you think back on them. Perhaps you helped a child who got separated from his mother at the grocery store, or you assisted an injured animal along the road. Maybe you saw two people in a bitter argument over some tiny matter, and you helped them resolve it. Perhaps in your job you have caused young people to become enthusiastic about learning. Another option is to recall with gratitude the good deeds that others have done for you, or to reflect on famous accounts of good deeds. On recalling these things, your mind fills with wholesome states and you become relaxed, happy, and contented.

Another method for cultivating wholesome states of mind is to recall your past successes in battling greed, hatred, or delusion. For instance, you remember a time when your child really upset you and you felt like smacking him. Then mindfulness came up, you recalled that acting out of anger is not what you are supposed to be doing. Your fury abated and you calmed down and became peaceful. You remember this great change from seething anger to pleasant calm, and you reflect on how good it felt. You say to yourself, "This good feeling is something I want to cultivate." This recollection helps you relax and fills you with quiet joy.

You can assemble your own toolbox of reliable methods to raise up wholesome states. Perhaps you notice that whenever you recall the time that your child took his or her first steps, you get a rush of loving emotion. Tuck that memory into the box. In the future, you can use that feeling as a springboard for cultivating wholesome states of mind.

This technique of mindful effort to cultivate positive states of mind is useful not only for meditation. You can use it while eating, walking, working, talking.

You no longer have to merely hope that life will give you reasons to feel happy. Strategize. Apply your mind to figure out what actions create the mental states that make your life more pleasant. Recall what worked in the past—and what failed. Uncover the cause and effect of these simple mental processes. Then cultivate these pleasant wholesome mental states in everything you do.

For example, while washing dishes you can cultivate thoughts of loving-friendliness for those who will use the dishes. When starting a conversation you can stay on your toes by being mindful of possible results of positive or negative speech. This is called a "well-started" conversation. By relaxing and bringing every ounce of patience, loving-friendliness, compassion, and insight into the conversation, you make it go more smoothly, benefiting yourself as well as others.

Heading off possible problems by knowing one's own shortcomings is part of the process. If you have a bad temper, for example, and you recognize it, that recognition is wholesome. Then you can cultivate pleasant states that will keep your temper from arising. When a challenging situation arises, such as a visit from an irritating executive of your company, you can remind yourself of possible pleasant or unpleasant outcomes of your actions. Then you make a determination to remain relaxed and filled with loving-friendliness. If the executive says or does something annoying, you get to enjoy your pleasant state of mind instead of engaging in a painful display of anger.

Likewise, if you know you tend to fret, prepare yourself. Before your grandchild takes her first airplane flight, do whatever has worked in the past to overcome fretting and bring up good feelings. Then you need not suffer as result of her flight. You can enjoy pleasant states instead.

It's a self-taught skill. The more we deliberately bring up enjoyable states of mind, the more interesting it becomes, and the better we get at it. Every day, every moment, we can cultivate unbounded loving-friendliness, sympathetic joy, deep compassion, and profound equanimity. These four wholesome qualities bring the mind into such a wonderful, high feeling that they are called "divine abidings." Someone who knows how to bring them up can enjoy heaven on earth anytime.

Maintaining Positive States of Mind

Ideally, once you arouse a wholesome, skillful state of mind, you will maintain it and not let it disappear. You know that if you let it slip away, your mind will go back into neutral and then maybe fall into some unwholesome state. So, you do whatever you can to keep that pleasant state of mind going continuously. This moment's wholesomeness should be the wholesomeness of the next moment, and the next hour, day, week. You try to keep your positive state of mind alive, like someone trying to keep a special candle burning.

This is not easy.

How often have you made wonderful promises to yourself? Remember the New Year's resolutions or the wedding vows you made in front of the priest or friends? Remember how many times you made hopeful wishes on your birthday? How many of them did you keep? You may have promised yourself: "I will never touch another cigarette, never take another drink, never lie, never speak harshly or insult anyone. I will never gamble again, never steal, never kill any living being." Or after one good meditation session or an inspiring spiritual retreat, you may have thought, "This retreat was wonderful. I never thought meditation was so easy. Oh, how calm and peaceful I have been during this retreat! This is what I will do in the future."

All these are positive thoughts. But how many of them do you continuously put into action every day? These thoughts arise in your mind like the bubbles in a glass of soda water. After a few hours, the water goes flat. You lose your enthusiasm and return to your old habits. In order to maintain your initial effort, you must develop strong mindfulness.

Remember that nothing important can be perfected by doing it only once. You have to repeat a positive thought or action again and again until your practice becomes perfect. We marvel at the skills of Olympic athletes—did they perfect these abilities in a day? How many times did you fall from your bicycle when you first tried to ride? Perfecting good thoughts is just like that. You have to practice very diligently. Whenever your effort slackens, recall occasions when you applied continuous effort until you achieved your goal.

Of course, there are some practical things you can do to support your practice of Skillful Effort. You can associate with good friends and avoid foolish people. You can live in a suitable location, read inspiring books, keep in touch with Buddhist discussions. You can also practice mindfulness diligently. These actions can help maintain your good thoughts.

Let me tell you a story of a monk who made a great commitment and great effort.

In ancient India, there was an elderly monk who was a great master. A monk slightly junior to him failed in a duty. The great master decided to discipline the junior monk by asking him to go to a certain house to collect alms food. He wanted the junior monk to make a good connection with that household, for they had a newborn child that the monks expected to become a great Buddhist leader. The owner of this house was well known for his stinginess and hostility toward mendicants. When this monk appeared at his house for the first time, the owner got very upset. He gave a standing order to his wife, children, and servants not to give the monk anything—and not to talk to him or even look at him. The monk returned to the monastery without receiving any alms from that house.

When the monk returned to the house on the second day, the same thing happened. No one gave him any food. No one spoke to him or even looked at him. But this monk did not get discouraged. He returned to that house day after day, week after week, month after month, and year after year for seven long years.

Then the owner of the house hired a new servant woman. She did not know anything about the standing order not to give alms to this monk. One day in the seventh year, when the monk went to this house, the new servant woman spoke to the monk, saying, "Go away. We don't have anything to give you."

The monk was very pleased to have been acknowledged at last. On his way back to the monastery, the monk passed the stingy owner of the house riding home on his horse. In a contemptuous voice, the man asked the monk, "Did you receive anything from my house?"

"Yes, sir, thank you," the monk replied. "I received something today."

The stingy man became very angry. He galloped to the house, leapt from his horse, ran into the house, and shouted at the top of his lungs, "What did you give to that wretched bald-headed man?

Who is it that gave him anything?"

Everyone in the house denied having given the monk alms. But the owner was still not satisfied. He went around to each person individually asking the same question. When he came to the new servant woman, he asked her, "Did you give anything to that monk?"

"No, sir," she replied.

"Are you sure?"

"Yes, sir, I am sure. I did not give him anything."

"Did you speak to him?"

"Yes, sir."

"What did you say to him?"

"I said, 'Go away. We don't have anything to give you.'"

The stingy man thought that the monk had deceived him. This thought made him even more angry. He said, "Let this liar come tomorrow. I will scold him for playing a trick on me."

The next day, the monk appeared at the house as usual. The stingy owner came out and spoke to the monk in anger, "Yesterday you said that you received something from my house. I checked with everybody and found that no one gave you anything. You lied to me, you miserable trickster. Tell me what you received from my house."

"Sir, I came to your beautiful house for seven years and received nothing. But yesterday, one kind lady came out and said, 'Go away. We have nothing to give you.' That was what I received from your house."

The stingy man felt so embarrassed. In that instant, he saw the spark within himself of loving-friendliness and generosity. This monk must be a saint, he thought. He is so grateful for receiving our servant's words of rejection, how much more grateful would he be if he received a little food from my house?

The owner immediately changed his order and asked the people in his house to give the monk some food. After that, the monk continued to receive alms from that house. His determination, his Skillful Effort to maintain his patience, and his positive state of mind paid off in the end. The newborn child in that house later became an arahant and one of the most important Buddhist leaders of that time. (Mhvs V)

You may wonder why we make so much effort in our practice and in our lives, when everything is impermanent anyway, and even the highest mental states eventually fall away. You're right, of course. Everything is impermanent. Moreover, there is no permanently existing "you" to experience things. Yet suffering and happiness do happen. If you step on a wasp and are stung, you don't think "I" am hurting. It's *owww!* Even without the awareness of "I" in that moment, suffering nonetheless exists.

Some people get confused when they hear the doctrine of no-self. They tend to believe that for suffering to happen there must be "someone" who suffers. Yet this assumption is mistaken. So long as there are aggregates of body and mind, suffering inevitably exists—until enlightenment is reached. It is said,

> It is only suffering that arises,
> Suffering that persists, and suffering that passes away.
> Nothing but suffering comes to be,
> And nothing but suffering ceases.
> (S I.5.10)

Another misconception is the idea that since there is no one to feel the suffering, suffering does not matter. When people raise this point I try to bring them out of their intellectual concepts and back to reality. I say, "Whether there is a self or not, you suffer. Do you enjoy suffering? Is that the purpose of living? Whether there is self or not, this is what you don't want: suffering! Therefore of course it matters, very much, whether you suffer." After all, suffering is why, after his enlightenment, the Buddha devoted himself to teaching others for the rest of his life. Out of great compassion, he showed others the mental training that removes all suffering states.

It is true, too, that even the higher, more pleasant and refined mental states fall away at some point. That is why once we cultivate skillful states, we must put them to work while we've got them. Skillful states

of mind are the necessary means for uprooting suffering, and maintaining skillful states yields benefits lasting long beyond any temporary relief and joy. Clear, wholesome states of mind are the basis for
developing insight into impermanence, so that we can uproot craving
and ignorance once and for all.

REMEMBER THE BIG PICTURE

Using Skillful Effort to pull the mind out of unwholesome states and to
cultivate wholesome states is a critical part of the Eightfold Path—no
less important than mindfulness. However, people often overlook the
skillful part of Skillful Effort. They forget the big picture and get caught
up in interesting details of the Buddha's teaching. Many times such people understand the path only partially. They take some idea they have
heard and run with it, to the point of absurdity, and then do self-defeating, unskillful things. Instead of becoming happier, they increase their
suffering.

I know a young woman who became uncomfortably aware of the
craving underlying most of her actions, particularly around eating.
Instead of becoming mindful, she tried to oppose her feelings directly.
At meal times she tried not to feel greediness. She even tried to eat less
than she needed and supplemented her diet with protein drinks. So
instead of ordinary greed, she developed a neurotic aversion and became
despondent. A good friend reminded her that she should remember the
big picture and cultivate wholesome states of mind. The friend suggested
ways to break out of the despondency: reading a good book, taking hikes,
doing good deeds, or keeping busy with work. This young lady
responded fiercely, "But I don't want to escape reality!" Doing what is
needed to break the grip of unwholesome states is not escaping reality.
It is escaping a worsening of suffering.

If you just end up with more unwholesome states that bring suffering,
what is the point of all the work you have been doing to follow the Buddha's path? You must reflect repeatedly on your actions and on the
results your actions bring. You must continually ask yourself, "What, in
this moment, am I cultivating?"

One time the Buddha's aunt, the nun Maha Pajapati Gotami, asked the Buddha for brief advice to guide her practice. The Buddha told her to do whatever she knew from her own experience and common sense to lead to good qualities in herself. The things you do, he said, should lead to:

- dispassion, not passion

- disentangling, not entanglement

- dispersion (of causes of suffering), not accumulation

- wanting little, not much

- contentment, not discontent

- peaceful solitude, not gregariousness

- effort, not laziness

- being easily supportable, not fussy and demanding
  (A IV (Eights) VI.3)

This list offers us a good guide for making sure that our efforts are useful according to the big picture.

Here is another rule of thumb we can use to judge our efforts. As the Buddha told us, the basic teaching of all Buddhas has always been, "Do good, do no evil, and purify the mind." (Dh 183)

MINDFULNESS OF SKILLFUL EFFORT

When the mind is plagued by negative thoughts, meditation practice is very difficult. When some certain people sit down to meditate, they are restless and agitated, wiggling, coughing, scratching, twisting, turning here and there, looking at other meditators, changing their postures very often. Other people tend to yawn and feel that they can't stay awake. Those in the habit of anger may feel resentment or nagging hatred while they try to meditate. Others may be overwhelmed by sensual desires. Still others are besieged by doubts.

Over years of practice, meditators have developed strategies known to have special power for overcoming particular blocks to mindfulness meditation practice.

- When desire for sensual pleasure troubles your mind, mentally dissect the object to which you are attracted. If your desire is for a piece of chocolate cream pie, remind yourself that the pie is composed of elements and that it will decay. Think of how the pie will look after it has been digested. Reflect on these things over and over again until your desire fades. The same technique can be effective if your desire is for a person. Consider the compound nature of the body—its bones, intestines and other organs, phlegm and other body fluids. Keep reflecting on these parts, or consider how this person will look as a corpse, until lust has faded. But if this technique somehow inflames your desire, stop immediately and concentrate upon the breath.

- When anger arises, apply the antidotes we have discussed, such as becoming aware of your anger, recognizing the impermanent nature of all emotions, contemplating the benefits of patience, reasoning with yourself to see a different perspective, and cultivating feelings of loving-friendliness.

- When dullness or sleepiness arises, visualize a bright light. If that doesn't work, try these remedies: Pinch your earlobes with your thumb and index finger (not using the fingernails). Open your eyes, roll your eyeballs for a few seconds, and then close your eyes again. Take a deep breath and hold it as long as you can, then slowly breathe out; repeat several times if necessary until your heart pounds and you break into a sweat. Meditate with your eyes slightly open. Get up and practice standing meditation, or do walking meditation. Go wash your face with cold water. If nothing works, go have a short nap.

- When restlessness or worry arises, reflect on tranquillity, calmness, or peace. Bring your mind back to the breath and anchor it there. Take a few deep breaths and feel the breath at your nose and in your body. Take another. Direct your attention to your buttocks or the bottoms of your feet and feel the weight of your body.

- When doubt arises, reflect on the Buddha's enlightenment, the timeless nature of his teachings, and the attainment of enlightenment by his disciples. If you have been engaged in speculative thinking, drop the useless topic and reflect upon some aspect of the Buddha's teaching. Focus on what you know to be true about impermanence, about suffering, about your lack of control of anything. Keep your attention on the present moment.

When your greed fades away, you feel as though you have paid off a debt. When your hatred fades away, you feel as though you have recovered from an illness. When your sleepiness and drowsiness fade away, you feel as though you have been released from prison. When your restlessness and worry fade away, you feel as though you have been freed from slavery. And when your doubt fades away, you feel as though you are no longer lost in a desert and have arrived at a safe and secure place.

You feel happy at the moment when your negative mind states disappear, and you feel happy later on whenever you think about their disappearance. When you remember how much pain and suffering your hindrances and fetters caused you in the past, you feel happy to see that they no longer make you feel uncomfortable. Your mind is peaceful and calm. You looked forward to this state of mind. Now you have achieved it, and you are very happy.

When negative thoughts fade away, the mind is ready to cultivate positive thoughts. When wholesome thoughts arise during meditation, watch them mindfully without getting attached to them. Thoughts that should be encouraged during meditation include friendliness, compassion, generosity, appreciative joy, understanding, peace, tolerance, determination, patience, and service to all living beings. When such thoughts fade, renew your effort to cultivate them, remembering why they arose in the first place. The roots of all these good thoughts are in your mind. They have simply been suppressed by negative conditioning.

Using Skillful Effort to prevent and overcome negative states of mind and to cultivate and maintain positive states is like climbing a mountain. Before you begin your climb, you take precautions to prevent problems from arising on the way. You make sure that you are fit physically and psychologically. You pack some medicine in case of sudden illness. You put on sturdy hiking boots. You take a rope, a walking stick, food, water, and suitable clothing. These measures are like the Skillful Effort of preventing negative states of mind from arising.

Despite your precautions, however, problems will arise. You get hungry, so you eat. When you get thirsty, you stop to drink. When you need to answer the call of nature, you do so. When you are tired, you rest. If you get a high fever, you take the medicine that you have brought along. These actions are like overcoming unwholesome states of mind as they arise.

You keep your energy up by resting, eating right, drinking plenty of water, and avoiding overexertion. These positive activities are like cultivating wholesome mental states.

When, after great difficulty, you reach the summit, you feel great relief, satisfaction, and joy. You rejoice that you have, with effort, managed to achieve your goal. You may say, "I am glad that is over," or, "I am glad that I was able to overcome all difficulties." Similarly, when you cultivate wholesome mental states and maintain them, you rejoice that your struggle is over and that you will never have to struggle with unwholesome states again. This is how Skillful Effort leads to joy.

Happiness is right there when you make the effort to achieve it. Remember your goal, and do not abandon your efforts until you become totally happy. Say to yourself:

> Happy, indeed, we live, friendly amidst the hateful.
> Amidst hostile men, we dwell free from hatred.
>
> Happy, indeed, we live, in good [mental] health amidst
>   the ailing.
> Amidst ailing men, we dwell free from ill.
>
> Happy, indeed, we live, free from greed amidst the greedy.
> Amidst greedy men, we dwell free from greed.
>   (Dh 197–199 [translated by Bhikkhu Buddharakkhita])

KEY POINTS FOR MINDFULNESS
OF SKILLFUL EFFORT

- Although rarely emphasized, Skillful Effort is essential to your spiritual progress.

- Skillful Effort has four parts: preventing negative states of mind, overcoming negative states of mind, cultivating positive states of mind, and maintaining positive states of mind.

- Fetters are deeply entrenched unwholesome tendencies of mind that arise out of greed and keep beings fettered to suffering states. The ten fetters are belief in a permanent self/soul, doubt, belief in the efficacy of rules and rituals, greed, hatred, desire for rebirth in material form, desire for rebirth in immaterial form, conceit, restlessness and worry, and ignorance.

- Hindrances are intense, gross manifestations of fetters. You should use Skillful Effort to prevent and overcome the five hindrances: greed, ill will, dullness and drowsiness, restlessness and worry, and doubt.

- The ways to overcome a hindrance are: to ignore it, to divert your attention, to replace the hindrance with its opposite quality, to reason with yourself, and, if all else fails, to crush it with all your might.

- Until they are destroyed, the fetters can only be suppressed. Fetters are weakened by mindfulness and concentration; development of their opposites weakens them more. When fetters are finally broken, this brings about the stages of enlightenment.

- To prevent negative thoughts from arising, maintain mindfulness. Mindfulness is developed through morality, the practice of mindfulness, wisdom, patience, and effort.

- To overcome arisen negative thoughts, just notice them.

- If you fail to notice negative thoughts quickly, they gather strength, and you must drop everything and pay total attention to them. Try reflecting on the harm they cause and the impermanence of whatever triggered them, or replace them with positive thoughts.

- When negative thoughts have faded away, cultivate wholesome thoughts by recalling how helpful such thoughts are and by deliberately creating thoughts of friendliness, determination, patience, and so forth. Use whatever methods you know to develop wholesome states of mind.

- Don't get lost in the details of practice and forget the big picture. Always make sure your efforts actually bring more wholesome states.

- Adjust your lifestyle to support maintaining wholesome thoughts, being sure to do such things as gathering with like-minded friends and reading Buddhist texts.

- Without strong mindfulness, your mind quickly reverts to its old habits; thus you must diligently repeat your efforts to maintain the wholesome thinking that will make you happy.

STEP 7
Skillful Mindfulness

MINDFULNESS is paying attention from moment to moment to what is. Because we unknowingly perceive ourselves and the world around us through thought patterns that are limited, habitual, and conditioned by delusions, our perception and subsequent mental conceptualization of reality is scattered and confused. Mindfulness teaches us to suspend temporarily all concepts, images, value judgments, mental comments, opinions, and interpretations. A mindful mind is precise, penetrating, balanced, and uncluttered. It is like a mirror that reflects without distortion whatever stands before it.

The Buddha often told his disciples to "keep mindfulness in front." By "in front" he meant in the present moment. This means more than just staying clear about what the mind is doing while we are sitting in meditation; it means clearly understanding every single physical and mental movement we make throughout every waking hour of every day. It means, in other words, being here, now.

The present moment is changing so fast that we often do not notice its existence at all. Every moment of mind is like a series of pictures passing though a projector. Some of the pictures come from sense impressions. Others come from memories of past experiences or from fantasies of the future. Mindfulness helps us freeze the frame so that we can become aware of our sensations and experiences as they are, without the distorting coloration of socially conditioned responses or habitual reactions.

Once we learn to notice without comment exactly what is happening, we can observe our feelings and thoughts without being caught up in them, without being carried away by our typical patterns of reacting. Thus mindfulness gives us the time we need to prevent and overcome negative patterns of thought and behavior and to cultivate and maintain positive patterns. It gets us off automatic pilot and helps us take charge of our thoughts, words, and deeds.

Moreover, mindfulness leads to insight, clear and undistorted "inner seeing" of the way things really are. With regular practice, both in formal meditation sessions and as we go about the activities of our daily lives, mindfulness teaches us to see the world and ourselves with the inner eye of wisdom. Wisdom is the crown of insight. Opening the wisdom eye is the real purpose of mindfulness, for insight into the true nature of reality is the ultimate secret of lasting peace and happiness. We need not search for it outside ourselves; each of us has the innate ability to cultivate wisdom. A traditional story underscores this point:

> Once there was a divine being who wanted to hide an important secret—the secret of happiness. He thought first of hiding the secret at the bottom of the sea. But then he said to himself, "No, I cannot hide my secret there. Human beings are very clever. One day they will find it."
>
> Next, he thought of hiding the secret in a cave. But he rejected this idea as well. "Many people visit caves. No, no, people will find the secret there as well."
>
> Then he thought of hiding the secret on the highest mountain. But then he thought, "People are so curious these days. One day someone will climb the mountain and discover it."
>
> At last he devised the perfect solution. "Ah! I know the place where no one will ever look. I'll hide my secret in the human mind."

This deity hid the truth in the human mind. Now let us find it! Mindfulness is not aimed at learning something external. Its goal is to find the truth hidden within us—at our very heart and core.

According to the Buddha our minds are naturally luminous. In each moment, as consciousness first arises, its spark is bright. In the unenlightened mind, however, that spark gets covered up by the impurities of greed, hatred, and delusion. These impurities obstruct the mind's brightness, leaving the mind dark and miserable.

We cannot say that the mind is already pure. We must do the work to make it that way. We have to cleanse this luminous mind to let it shine without any impurities blocking its brightness. Wisdom cultivated through mindfulness burns away the obstructions of greed, hatred, and delusion. The more we remove them, the more the mind becomes comfortable, happy, and radiant. Mindfulness also keeps impurities from arising. Therefore the deeply hidden secret of happiness is this truth: Happiness comes from within our own minds through the use of mindfulness to clear away greed, hatred, and delusion. This secret of happiness is revealed as the layers of impurities are peeled off through wisdom.

How does mindfulness bring wisdom, and how does wisdom cause us to let go of the obstructions? As we search within ourselves, seeking to understand the truth of happiness, we become aware of and observe the five aggregates of body and mind. As we mindfully observe, we begin to see how each of these aggregates comes into being, grows, matures, decays, and dies.

For instance, this beautiful body whose health we guard so carefully is changing at every moment. While we are reading this page, every cell, molecule, and subatomic particle of our physical being is changing— growing, decaying, or dying. The heart is beating; the lungs, kidneys, liver, and brain are performing their functions. While these physical components are changing, feelings, perceptions, consciousness, and mental objects are also arising and passing away. Mindfulness of the present moment grants us insight into these changes—into the pervasive impermanence of all that exists.

Noticing the impermanence of all phenomena gives us the opportunity to see the dissatisfaction that change engenders. For instance, bring to mind some wonderful feeling that you had in the past. Can you experience this feeling now, exactly as before? Even if you could recreate the conditions that gave rise to this wonderful feeling, would you experience the feeling again in the identical way? The realization that the wonderful experiences of the past are gone forever makes us feel sad. As we see how everything is slipping away—body, feelings, the people and things we love—not just every moment but many times every moment, we gain insight into the cause of our dissatisfaction and unhappiness: attachment to things that are constantly in flux.

Finally, mindfulness grants us insight into the way beings, including ourselves, really exist. Insight into impermanence and dissatisfaction helps us see that reality is not something "out there," separate from us. Rather, reality is our ever changing experience of the ever changing world—the world within us and the world we perceive through our senses.

Practicing mindfulness makes quarreling with the world seem ridiculous. We do not cut off our hand when it does something wrong. Similarly, it is silly to cut ourselves off from people who do things differently from us, for all of us partake of the same ever changing, ever suffering nature. Quarreling with the world is like one arm fighting with the other, or the right eye battling the left.

Life, we discover, is not a static entity. It is a dynamic flow of incessant change. When we look for the meaning of life, all we can find is this change. As we return to this dynamic aspect over and over again, we find no permanent or eternal entity in it—no permanent or eternal self or soul within us to cling to, and no permanent or eternal self or soul within others to quarrel with.

Thus mindfulness grants us insight into the three characteristics of all things: impermanence, dissatisfaction, and the nonexistence of an eternal or unchanging self or soul. Looking within ourselves, we see how quickly our physical form is changing, and we see how dissatisfaction is brought about by these changes. We see how fervently we wish not to have any more births, not to grow older or fall ill, not to experience sorrow, despair, or disappointment. We see how dissatisfying it is to want to be associated with things or persons we like and how dissatisfying it is to want not to be associated with things or persons we do not like. We see that any desire, no matter how subtle or how noble, causes pain. We see that even the desire connected with the wish to overcome desire—although wholesome and necessary for progress—is painful. Ultimately, we see that our sense of self, the personal identity we protect so fervently, is an illusion, for we are a process, a constant flow of physical, emotional, and mental events new each moment.

Hindus express this truth vividly when they speak of three deities—Brahma the Creator, Vishnu the Preserver, and Shiva the Destroyer. The creator is the arising moment; the preserver is the peak moment; and the destroyer is the passing-away moment. Every moment something is created; every moment something exists; and every moment something is passing away. There is no static moment, because nothing, even for a fraction of a second, stays the same. This cycle goes on incessantly.

When we come to this realization, we allow sensations, feelings, and thoughts to pass through the mind without holding on to any particular thing, no matter how pleasant or beautiful. When unpleasant, painful, or unbearable states surface, we let them pass without becoming upset. We just let things happen without trying to stop them, without succumbing to them or trying to get away. We just notice things as they are.

We see, not only with the eye of wisdom but even with our everyday awareness, that all things and beings depend for their existence on constantly changing causes and conditions. Since there is nothing permanent to attach to and nothing permanent to push away, we relax into perfect peace of mind, perfect happiness.

THE FOUR FOUNDATIONS OF MINDFULNESS

Skillful Mindfulness is the incorporation of our whole life into meditation practice. The mindfulness techniques that follow are based on a discourse given by the Buddha to his disciples on the Four Foundations of Mindfulness. (*Maha-Satipatthana Sutta*, D 22) In it, the Buddha taught many methods of meditation. He began the explanation of each method with the words "Again, monks..." By this he meant that these ideas were supposed to be put into practice. He made clear that whoever practiced mindfulness in these ways would be sure to attain the lasting happiness of enlightenment. Yet he taught so very many methods. How can we practice all of them?

The variety of techniques the Buddha taught are daunting only to those who do not understand the Buddha's system. Actually, the practices are geared toward the kinds of activities we encounter every day. Moreover, the Buddha's system is based on his profound understanding of the way the human mind operates.

Consider a little baby. It is cute and wonderful but also very demanding. The baby demands food, clean diapers, fresh air, naps, and many other things. A baby's attention span is short. A good parent keeps the baby occupied and stimulated by making sure the baby has a selection of interesting toys and a variety of things to do. Our minds are similarly demanding, and our attention span sometimes seems as short as a baby's. The Buddha understood this. He gave us a whole list of things to do. We start with any one object of meditation: the breath, a feeling, a mind state, one of the hindrances or fetters—it doesn't matter. Whatever we focus on will soon change. When the mind moves to something unwholesome, we quickly give it something better, the way a skillful parent gives a toddler a ball while taking away the scissors the child has picked up. When the mind moves to a wholesome subject, we encourage it.

Anything that comes up in the mind becomes the object of mindfulness meditation. We can use any subject to further our insight into the three characteristics of everything that exists: impermanence, dissatisfaction, and the nonexistence of an eternal self or soul. When whatever we are thinking of naturally fades away, we turn our mind back to the original object of meditation.

You may wonder, "What if my mind doesn't stay with the original object? What if I chose to work with the meditation on the thirty-two parts of the body, but in an hour I barely manage to reflect on the first five parts?" Well, if other objects came into your mind and you used them to reflect on the three characteristics of reality, what's the problem? Any meditation that helps you to see the truth is a good meditation. Do not expect the mind to stick to this or that thing. The mind is naturally fickle. It goes from object to object.

But do not shift from object to object deliberately. Begin with your focus on a chosen object of meditation, such as the breath, and turn to another object only if something else comes up spontaneously. Let's say you are focusing on the breath, and then a thought arises about the healthiness of your skin. As that thought passes, the mind will catch the next breath. If the mind remains focused on your skin, you engage in thinking about the impermanence of skin—how fragile it is, how it is always changing and will become full of wrinkles. You also think about how useless and painful it is to cling to your skin, since it will change no matter what, and the more you cling, the more you suffer. You also consider the selflessness of the skin—that there is no "you" in it or controlling it. Then you watch as these thoughts disappear. You also notice that the observing function that is mindfully aware of these thoughts is itself impermanent. When all thoughts have subsided and nothing else jumps to mind, you let the mind return to the breath. Whatever new ideas arise, you examine them in the same way. Practicing in this manner, eventually the thoughts cease, and the mind gains concentration.

The Buddha's many meditation techniques are like a fully stocked medicine cabinet. You cannot swallow all the medications at once, nor can you practice everything in the Four Foundations of Mindfulness all at once. You start with whatever technique you feel comfortable using. Then you use whatever comes up in the process of working with that object of observation or reflection. Your mind may seem chaotic now, but it will settle down. When your mindfulness becomes strong and sharp, the mind will naturally begin investigating the more profound aspects of Buddha's teachings.

The Four Foundations of Mindfulness are:

- mindfulness of the body

- mindfulness of feelings

- mindfulness of the mind

- mindfulness of mental objects

We begin with mindfulness of the body, particularly of the breath. Meditating on the breath gives your mind and body a little time to settle down. Then, as other foundations of mindfulness arise, we become aware of them. No matter what subject arises, make sure that you pay attention to the impermanence, dissatisfaction, and selflessness of your experiences, whether they are physical or psychological.

MINDFULNESS OF THE BODY

Thus far, we have spoken only of the breath as an object of meditation—and indeed it can take you all the way to perfect freedom. But other objects can also be used. Traditionally we speak of forty kinds of primary objects of meditation, including the body and its parts. Three of the most useful ways of cultivating mindfulness of the body are: mindfulness of the breath, mindfulness of posture, and mindfulness of the parts of the body.

Mindfulness of the Breath

The Buddha always recommended that one start insight meditation with mindfulness of breathing. The breath is the one object that is both consistently present and yet also changing in a way that naturally draws the mind's attention. When the mind is united with the breath, you are naturally able to focus the mind on the present moment. You can notice the feeling arising from the contact of the breath with the rim of the nostrils. You can notice the long inhaling and long exhaling of breath. You can notice when the length of the breath changes, and air flows in and out a little more rapidly than before. You can notice when a series of short breaths is interrupted by a deep breath. You can notice the expansion and contraction of the lungs, abdomen, and lower abdomen. Noticing these aspects of breathing keeps the mind continuously engaged in the present moment.

Observing your breathing with mindfulness can also teach you many things about how your mind works. As you breathe in, you experience a small degree of calmness, and as you breathe out, you experience a small degree of calmness. The calmness you get as a result of inhaling is interrupted by exhaling, and the calmness you get as a result of exhaling is interrupted by inhaling. Yet, if you hold the inhaled breath a little longer than usual to prolong that feeling of calmness, you experience tension, and if you wait a little longer than usual before inhaling again to prolong that feeling of calmness, you experience tension. Waiting even longer before inhaling or exhaling might even cause pain.

Observing this, you see that you desire calmness and the release of tension and want to avoid the discomfort of waiting too long before inhaling and exhaling. You see that you wish that the calmness you experience as part of the cycle of breathing would stay longer and that the tension would disappear more quickly. Because the tension does not go away as fast as you would like, nor the calmness stay as long as you would like, you get irritated. Thus just by observing the breath, you see how even a small desire for permanency in an impermanent world causes unhappiness. Moreover, since there is no self-entity to control this situation, your wishes for calmness and a lack of tension will be forever frustrated. However, if you relax your mind and watch your breathing without desiring calmness and without resenting the tension that arises, experiencing only the impermanence, dissatisfaction, and selflessness of the breath, the mind becomes peaceful and calm.

While you are practicing mindfulness of the breath, the mind does not stay with the sensation of breathing. It goes to sense objects such as sounds, and mental objects such as memories, emotions, and perceptions. When you experience these other objects, you should forget about the breath for a while and focus your attention on them—one at a time. As each fades away, allow your mind to return to the breath, the home base for the mind after quick or lengthy journeys to various states of mind and body.

Every time the mind returns to the breath, it comes back with deeper insight into impermanence, dissatisfaction, and selflessness. So, the mind learns from impartial and unbiased watching of these occurrences that these aggregates—this physical form, these feelings and perceptions, these various states of volitional activities, and consciousness—exist only for the purpose of gaining deeper insight into the reality of the mind and body. They are not here for you to get attached to them.

Mindfulness of Posture

Mindfulness of posture means sitting, standing, walking, and lying down with mindful attention. You might wonder, "What is there to be mindful of? When I walk, I walk. When I sit, I sit. When I lie down, I lie down. I know what I'm doing. What special knowledge or insight can I gain by focusing my mind on sitting, standing, walking, or lying down?" As you pay mindful attention to the postures of the body you see that your physical movements are always changing, even if you seem to be holding still. Your heart pulses, heat radiates from your body, your lungs expand and contract. Cultivate awareness of their impermanence. You may notice that you have only limited control over the outward movements of your body, and that there is no control at all over the subtle, internal bodily movements. Lack of control is frustrating. Seeing this, you cultivate insight into the suffering and selfless nature of the movements of the body.

Also notice the physical elements that make up the body and the things that you contact—for example, the heaviness and solidity of the earth element. See how all these physical elements change constantly. Notice how everything in your physical experience is impermanent. However, just as in mindfulness of breathing, do not focus only on physical change. When any mental factors become prominent, turn your attention to them. The feelings and perceptions created by your physical movements are changing; notice their impermanence. If, while sitting, standing, walking or lying down, you notice thoughts of greed, dislike, or confusion—or of compassion, loving-friendliness, or appreciative joy—watch as the thoughts rise and fall. You cannot create, nor can you stop, the automatic occurrences of the rising and falling of movements, feelings, perceptions, thoughts, and consciousness. Keeping these things in mind as you move, notice the impermanence, unsatisfactoriness, and selflessness of all experience. In every posture and in every activity, be it reaching for a doorknob, walking through a mall, or lying down to sleep, continue to cultivate insight into these characteristics of the five aggregates.

You can refine your ability to see into the characteristics of the aggregates by practicing slow-movement meditation. Think of the slow-motion video replay of a sports game. When the action of the game is moving at normal speed, we miss many subtle details, but during the replay, we can see clearly the terrific block made by one player or the foul committed by another. Similarly, when we move slowly, as we do in slow walking meditation, we notice the many changes of posture that make up the action—lifting the heel, resting the foot, carrying it forward, moving it, touching the floor.

If you have been engaging for a while in sitting meditation focused

on the breath and decide to practice mindfulness of slow movement in
walking, here's what you do: *Walking meditation*
Stand up slowly, continuing to pay attention to the breathing process.
While you are standing up, be aware of the changes in your physical
sensations and perceptions. Notice that every part of the body has to
cooperate in order for you to stand up. While standing, continue to pay
attention to your breathing.

Now, while breathing in, lift the heel of one foot, and while breathing out, rest that foot on its toes. Next, while breathing in, lift the entire
foot and move it forward, and while breathing out, slowly lower it and
press it against the floor. Again, while breathing in, lift the heel of the
other foot, and while breathing out, rest it on its toes. While breathing
in, lift that entire foot and carry it forward, and while breathing out,
lower it and press it against the floor.

When you walk in this mindful way, paying attention to your
breathing, you begin to see how every part of the body from the head
to the toes is changing, cooperating, functioning together in the process
of walking. For instance, you see that the physical actions that make up
walking begin with mental intentions. You see the intention to lift the
foot, the intention to move it forward, and the intention to lower it and
touch the floor. Simultaneous with these intentions, actions are taking
place. Intention and action happen together so quickly that there is no
time to see the interval between an act and the thinking behind it.

Of course, nobody thinks of all these steps in the process of walking.
They just walk! Everything happens in a split second. Yet, when you
slow the sequence down and look at each action mindfully, you see that
many different actions must come together for walking to take place.
When the intention of walking arises in the mind, energy is created,
which is discharged through the body via the nervous system. Many
different nerve cells cooperate in conveying the message, and many
other body structures carry out the processes that are needed. Muscles
contract and extend, joints flex, and balance is maintained by other complex mechanisms.

In all this you see clear evidence of impermanence. For instance, you
intend to lift the right foot, but when you lift it, that intention is gone,
and as you lift it, the sensation you had before the lifting is gone. When

you rest the right foot on the toes, you have one sensation, and when you move it forward, that sensation is gone, and a new sensation arises.

You see that the mind is always changing as well. When your weight is evenly balanced, your mind may have a feeling of comfort and equilibrium. But then, as your weight shifts, that feeling changes. The mind waits for another comfortable moment to arise. But when that next moment of comfort and equilibrium arises, it too passes away. Each time a comfortable moment changes into an uncomfortable one, the mind is disappointed. The repetition of comfortable and uncomfortable moments makes you tired. Tiredness is a nagging kind of dissatisfaction that builds up slowly during any repeated sequence of changes.

While paying attention to the movements of walking, you are also aware of the ever changing flow of thoughts. While you are walking, you may experience fear, insecurity, tension, worry, lust, anger, jealousy, or greed. The thought may arise, "This is going very well. I hope everyone notices how well I'm doing." Such thoughts come from pride or craving for recognition. You have already learned how to take care of them. First you simply become mindful of them. If they persist you apply the methods for overcoming negative mind states that you practiced during sitting meditation. Then you proceed to cultivate wholesome mental activities by letting go of greed and hatred and by generating loving-friendliness, appreciative joy, and equanimity.

It is always important to take steps to overcome any negative states that arise. I remember a young meditation student confessing to me what happened while he was engaging in walking meditation behind a young woman. After the session ended, he approached me and said sadly, "Venerable Sir, there was a girl walking in front of me. All I could think of during the last period of walking meditation was what was inside her clothes! I could not pull my mind away from her." I met this same fellow again years later. His mind was still messy and undisciplined. Since he had not been able to apply the methods for overcoming the negative mind states that hindered his practice, he had not made much progress.

Walking mindfully can also help you see that this complex body-mind functions without any permanent entity behind it pulling the strings, without a single thing you can call "self" or "I" controlling the complex sequence of thoughts and actions that goes into everything you do.

How can walking lead to this insight? While you walk, you are mindfully observing your posture and the movement of your body. You are also aware of various feelings, thoughts, and states of consciousness as they arise. Whenever the thought "I am walking" arises, ask yourself, "What is this 'I'? Is it this body? Is it identical with the body or is it different from the body? Is it in the body or is it separate from the body? Is the body in the 'I'? Or is the 'I' in the body?" (Note that these are impersonal questions that investigate reality, unlike the doubt-inspiring question "Who am I?", which assumes that a self exists.)

You will not find any satisfactory answers to these questions. Your mind tells you that your "I" is the one who is lifting the right foot, sliding it forward, and pressing it to the floor. But it is also "I" who is standing, breathing, seeing, hearing, thinking, remembering, feeling, and engaging in multitudes of other activities at every moment. These movements and activities are changing so rapidly that you cannot notice them all. "I breathe in" is different from "I walk," which is different again from "I see" and "I remember" and "I feel sad." In none of these activities can you find an "I" that is independent of the things you do.

You will begin to see that "I" is a concept that we use for the sake of convenience to refer to an ever changing flow of experiences. It is not a single independent entity that exists in the body or the mind. The concept of "I" changes many times a day, depending on the activity "I" is engaged in. It does not exist on its own even for a minute. "I" exists only when you think of it. It does not exist when you do not think of it. Therefore "I" is as conditional as everything else.

Thus walking slowly and mindfully can be a complete meditation that shows how impermanence, dissatisfaction, and selflessness pervades every moment. These same techniques can be applied to the postures of sitting, standing, and lying down. Of course this is not the normal, ordinary way of moving. It is a special technique we use to train the mind. The point isn't merely to put the body into slow motion but to analyze the way the mind and body cooperate in producing the posture, and to see the impermanence, dissatisfaction, and selflessness of mind and body.

While we are paying close attention to the posture, we have a good opportunity to study what goes on in the mind, to see whether states such as greed, hatred, jealousy, or fear arise. These things become easier to spot when the mind is not distracted. Once you train yourself to watch for these negative states during meditation sessions on the various postures—standing, walking, sitting, and lying down—you can bring the same vigilance to every activity in everyday life.

Mindfulness of the Parts of the Body

Investigating the parts of the body helps end any mistaken notions you may have about the body. As you mentally dissect the body into its many parts, you come to see the body and its parts exactly as they are.

We do not ordinarily look at the body in this analytical way. We do not even think of the body's parts except when something goes wrong or when we suffer aches and pains. The Buddha referred to this meditation by a Pali word that means "going against the grain." By this he meant that in doing this meditation, we go against the normal way we think about the body.

Normally, people experience feelings of loathing when they think about certain parts of the body. They carry these parts inside their bodies very willingly and hold them very dear, but when they think about them, they feel disgust. Other people get attached to certain parts of the body, seeing them as beautiful and permanent, or they feel pride about their good looks, good health, or strength. This meditation can help get rid of these deluded notions. It helps us see the body as it is, without rejecting it or clinging to it.

The Buddha recommended that the meditator mentally dissect the body into thirty-two parts. Of these, twenty are solid or earthlike parts, and twelve are liquid. The twenty solid parts are head hair, body hair, nails, teeth, skin, flesh, sinews, bones, marrow, kidneys, heart, liver, diaphragm, spleen, lungs, intestines, bowels, undigested food, feces, and brain. The twelve liquid parts are bile, phlegm, pus, blood, sweat, fat, tears, grease, saliva, mucus, oil of the joints (synovial fluid), and urine.

In addition, the Buddha listed ten bodily processes associated with fire and with air. The four bodily processes associated with fire are the heat of digesting food, the heat of aging, the bodily burning sensation (when overheated), and the temperature of the body. The six processes associated with air are belching (which the Buddha called "up-going air"), passing gas ("down-going air"), air in the digestive tract, air in the pores of the body, the inhaling breath, and the exhaling breath.

In a way, this meditation is very much like the way a biologist looks at the body. A biologist dissecting an animal does not run away when the animal's liver or intestine is exposed. The biologist wants to see what this organ is and how it operates. Scientific objectivity helps the biologist view these parts just as they present themselves, without any added emotional or romantic notions. We should cultivate this same kind of emotional detachment as we perform this meditation.

To do this meditation, focus your attention on each of the parts of the body in turn, starting with the visible parts. When you consider the hair on the head, for example, ask yourself, "Did I have hair like this when I was five years old?" The answer, of course, is no. Then ask yourself what happened. As you realize immediately, the hair is changing, as are the other body parts, such as the nails, skin, teeth, and so forth. The meditation leads you to conclude that there is nothing stable about the body and its parts. Everything is changing. Everything is impermanent. This is reality.

Meditating on the body as a collection of ever changing parts also helps you to overcome the fetter of greed or clinging to the body. Not that you want to discard the body before you die! You do want to maintain the body, wash it, clothe it, protect it. But you can do these things without arrogance, without obsessive clinging. As you become aware of the disintegration of the body—its strength becoming feeble, its beauty becoming ugly, its health becoming diseased—you see that change happens to all bodies. You see that there is nothing permanent about the body to which you can become attached.

Instead of getting upset, you become humble in the face of this truth. The reality of the body's impermanence is so powerful, so crushing, so overwhelming that you automatically surrender. What else can you do? Can you run away from this truth? No. You have no choice but to accept it. Thus this meditation also helps you overcome the fetter of conceit in the existence of a permanent self. Moreover, you see that everyone faces the same fears of old age, sickness, and death. Seeing the universality of this condition helps you overcome your personal fear and develop tender compassion for the suffering of others.

Further, you gain inferential knowledge that if any part of your body becomes defective, is removed, or no longer works harmoniously with other parts, your body will function differently. This realization gives you insight into the compound and dependent nature of everything that exists.

When you compare your body with those of other people, you also see that what is true about your body is true of everyone else's. Your body gets old, falls sick, and grows weak. All bodies do this. What happens to your body due to hormonal changes, injuries, or other conditions happens to other people's bodies, too. Therefore it does not matter how beautiful or ugly, fat or thin, hairy or bald your body looks on the outside. All bodies function, grow, age, fall sick, decay, die, and decompose in similar ways. In this respect you and others are not different at all. This insight helps you to cultivate equanimity and to treat all living beings with compassion and loving-friendliness.

MINDFULNESS OF FEELINGS

We tend to think, "I feel!" without realizing feelings are impersonal phenomena. They come and go due to conditions that trigger them. When we understand the different kinds of feelings and the way they function, we can prevent the conditions that lead to very painful and confused mental states simply by relaxing and altering our attitudes. Our minds stay pleasant and clear. But this is just the beginning. When we see the true nature of feelings we become more detached and less reactive to whatever feelings arise. It is an exercise in letting go of greed and aversion. Letting go, we dig up the very root of our suffering and advance toward full enlightenment.

We often assume that persons or situations outside us are responsible for what we feel. However, mindfully watching our feelings teaches us that both pleasant and painful emotional feelings come not from the objects that we perceive but from our own mental state or attitude. You can prove this to yourself by remembering that when several different people see the same movie, they each have a different set of feelings about it. Thus we can stop blaming other people and external events for our sorrows and begin to look inside—where we truly have power to change things. This is what the Buddha's invitation to "come and see" means.

When you become familiar with your own feelings, you can also compare your feelings more easily to those of other people. You note that just as you develop various kinds of feelings based on circumstances, so do others. Just as your feelings pass away, so do those of others. The knowledge you gain from mindfulness about your own feelings is called "direct insight." The knowledge you gain from comparing your experiences with those of others is called "inferential understanding." Although there is no way of knowing for sure how others feel, inferential understanding helps you gain much insight into reality.

When we remember that all living beings have feelings, that they all experience emotional and physical pain, suffer from cold and hunger, and feel sad or lonely, we become less selfish and less inclined to defend our own feelings as right. We can listen patiently to complaints of pain without complaining. When we are mindful that all beings have the same feelings we do, how can we say or do something to hurt someone else?

In each moment the whole cycle of suffering is powered by the mind's unenlightened reactions to feelings. All living beings, without exception, feel, and all unenlightened beings suffer from their reactions to their feelings. Feeling arises from the periphery of the body due to contact with the outside world and also from deep in the mind due to contact with mental events. Thus when we talk about feelings in the context of the Four Foundations of Mindfulness, we do not distinguish between physical sensations ("the sun feels warm") and emotions ("I feel sad"). We use both meanings of the word feeling interchangeably.

From the moment our nerve cells began to develop, we experienced feelings. Feeling is present even for a baby in the womb. When the mother moves, the baby she carries inside feels the movement. When she sings, the baby hears her and is lulled. When she is angry, the baby feels her agitation and tension. When she laughs, the baby feels her delight. While we may not be able to recall these feelings, we experienced them.

Moreover, every aspect of our lives—our struggles, achievements, inventions, work, and very survival—depends on how we feel. The drive for food, clothing, medicine, shelter, sex, and physical comfort depends on feelings. Human beings have discovered, manufactured, or developed many things because of feelings. When we feel cold, we seek warmth. When we feel hungry, we look for food. We procreate according to our feelings. Even our thinking often starts with a feeling. We rationalize our emotional reaction to a situation by saying, "I have every reason to feel angry about what happened."

When a feeling is pleasing, greed arises; you want more. When a feeling does not please you, you react with aversion, rejecting it. When a feeling is neutral you tend to ignore it with a deluded quality of mind. As we have pointed out, greed, hatred, and delusion—or just greed, for short—is the source of all suffering. Mindfulness of feeling is an opportunity to explore this source, where we can let go of suffering.

Let's say you sit with the intention of watching the rise and fall of breath—along with feeling, perception, thoughts, or consciousness—for forty-five minutes. But after twenty-five minutes or so, pain arises in the middle of your back and your mind shifts to watching the pain. Sometimes these little aches and pains quickly go away when watched mindfully, but on this occasion the pain intensifies. Your mind resists the pain.

If you keep still and watch the pain, eventually it peaks and then breaks up. When the pain breaks, a pleasant feeling arises. You can observe the way the mind hangs onto that pleasant feeling, wanting more of it. Then some other kind of feeling replaces that pleasant feeling. As feelings arise and pass away you may notice how volatile feelings are. A pleasant feeling may stay pleasant briefly, but then it fades, and its loss brings painful feeling. A painful feeling hurts while it lasts, but when it has faded a pleasant sense of relief will arise.

When the mind loses interest in these feelings, you go back to watching the breath.

You can see that we do not need a special kind of sitting meditation in order to practice mindfulness of feelings. Rather, we carry on with our usual mindfulness meditation and observe the arising and passing of feelings in just the same way we observe the passing of thoughts. We continue this practice in our everyday life. Whether in sitting meditation or going about our daily life, whenever a feeling arises that is strong enough for the mind to be drawn to it, we examine it.

When we become mindful of our feelings, we no longer have to mindlessly react to them. We become more skillful. If a pleasant feeling arises, we can subdue the underlying tendency of pleasant feelings—greed. If a painful feeling arises, we can subdue the underlying tendency of that kind of feeling—aversion or hatred. If a feeling is neutral, we can recognize that fact and not allow the underlying tendency of neutral feelings—delusion—to emerge.

The Buddha described two broad categories of feelings: "worldly" and "unworldly." Worldly feelings are feelings with the underlying tendencies of greed, hatred, or delusion activated to some degree. These feelings lead directly into greed, hatred, or delusion. Worldly feelings inevitably arise in the pursuits of mundane, ordinary life such as enjoying pleasures, seeking wealth, looking for a companion, seeking a position, or building up recognition and power. The feelings that arise from such activities always trigger some amount of greed, hatred, or delusion.

The Buddha repeatedly warned his disciples that worldly pursuits and worldly feelings are dangerous due to these underlying tendencies. He urged us to become aware of the danger of the underlying tendencies and to abandon them. With mindfulness we stop ourselves from getting so carried away by the greed, hatred, or delusion. We make an effort to subdue these tendencies—by watching them. We pay attention to them with a relaxed mind, not trying to force anything, but simply letting go.

The moment we do this, we experience unworldly feelings. Unworldly feelings arise in the pursuit of the spiritual path of liberation. These feelings come with the underlying tendencies fully suppressed or—in the case of an enlightened being—eliminated. Whenever we transcend a worldly feeling we are left with an unworldly feeling.

Let us look at the pleasant, painful, and neutral aspects of both worldly and unworldly feelings. Worldly pleasant feelings are very familiar to us. Sense pleasures bring us a wealth of pleasant worldly feelings. For example, a delicious meal, an entertaining TV show, or a shiny new car usually evoke pleasant worldly feelings. Unless your mindfulness remains very strong, pleasant sensations of body and mind will be worldly, because we like these things and want to experience them more and more.

Unworldly pleasant feelings may be less familiar. They arise whenever we do something that propels us along the path to liberation. Consider, for example, the feelings of peace and happiness we get from deep concentration. The pleasant, peaceful feelings we experience when our mindfulness meditation practice is going well are also unworldly feelings.

When we use mindfulness to let go of a worldly pleasant feeling, such as the feeling that comes from eating tasty food, unworldly feelings arise. Be skeptical, however, of anyone who says you can mindfully enjoy sensual pleasures. That is not the Buddha's way. The Buddha taught us to mindfully let go of sense pleasures and enjoy the pleasant unworldly feelings that come from letting go. To let go, we remain mindful of the impermanent nature of these sensual pleasures. Thus we remain detached, and this detachment evokes unworldly pleasant feelings.

Whenever we let go of some greed, hatred, or delusion, pleasant unworldly feelings will arise. In fact, any action we take along the Buddha's eight steps may lead to the arising of some pleasant unworldly feelings. As our mindfulness develops, we experience unworldly pleasant feelings more often.

Imagine that you have some objects to which you are greatly attached, such as the belongings of some dear friend who died. Whenever you look at these objects, feelings of grasping or sadness arise, and you suffer. When you succeed in letting go of these objects it is a big relief, for then those feelings stop. You relax, and a pleasant feeling arises. It is as though you were gripping something, and the more you tightened your grip the more it hurt. Then you opened your hand and you felt great relief. Unworldly pleasant feelings arise because you let go of grasping.

Painful feelings can also be either worldly or unworldly. Worldly painful feelings lend themselves most easily to aversion. For example, painful feelings of anger or resentment may arise when our ambitions are blocked, such as when we are passed over for a promotion. The methods we have discussed for overcoming anger can help when such painful worldly feelings come up.

Unworldly painful feelings may arise when we are engaged in practicing the Buddha's path. Say that you have really understood the Buddha's message and want very much to free your mind from greed, hatred, and delusion. You have practiced meditation, observed all the precepts, and followed all the instructions. Yet, you feel that you are not making progress toward your goal. The frustrated and painful feeling you experience in this case is unworldly in nature.

However, unlike other kinds of painful feeling, this is wholesome. It does not come out of greed, hatred, or delusion. You may wonder, for example, "Where have I gone wrong? Why have I not gained the expected results attained by others? Maybe I am missing something; let me try again from the beginning." It becomes an urge to experiment and continue. Your disappointment does not lead to anger but creates impetus for more effort. It helps propel you toward liberation.

Neutral feelings can also be categorized as worldly or unworldly. In the context of worldly pursuits, a sluggish, unconcerned feeling pervades moments that do not have the highs and lows of pleasant or painful feelings. Delusion can thrive in these neutral worldly feelings. For example, if you do not know better, when neutral feeling arises, you may think, "Ah! This is the soul; this is how the soul feels in its neutral state, when it is not affected by other things."

When your mindfulness leads you to recognize that what you call the "self" or "soul" is always changing, always subject to impermanence, the feeling you get is neutral and unworldly. It is impartial, unbiased, and nondeluded. You feel alert and interested in seeing what will unfold next. You do not fall into this or that camp of emotion—neither desiring nor averse—but stay equanimous and mindful. The longer you remain in that state, the stronger mindfulness becomes.

Let's recall the example of meditating with lower back pain. At first there is aversion toward the pain, followed by pleasant feeling and grasping at pleasant feeling. If you continue to watch the feelings, you will see them change again and again. Eventually, on seeing the impermanence, you let go of your reactions of grasping and aversion. Then equanimity toward feelings will arise. This equanimous state is an unworldly neutral state.

To practice mindfulness of feelings, when a prominent feeling arises, we first notice whether this is a worldly feeling or an unworldly feeling. Then we know whether to let go of it or to pursue it.

If we are experiencing an unworldly feeling, we make an effort to cultivate the feeling. We note the causes of that feeling so that we can recreate similar causes in the future. Then we work to recreate the right conditions. Again and again we figure out the varying circumstances and actions that will lead to that unworldly feeling. We deliberately develop a habit of bringing up this kind of feeling.

On the other hand, if we see that we have a worldly feeling wrapped up in the underlying tendency of greed, hatred, or delusion, we make a strong effort to overcome these underlying tendencies of the feeling. We become very mindful not to get carried away with the unwholesome state that is arising from the feeling. We mindfully watch the worldly feeling without reacting, until it eventually subsides. In the process we can see the impermanence of everything involved: impermanence of the desirable (or undesirable) objects, of one's opinions regarding the situation, of one's own body and of one's ability to enjoy the pleasures involved, and the fleeting nature of the feelings themselves. By observing impermanence in this way, we can let go.

When we let go, the worldly feeling is replaced by a pleasant unworldly feeling, and we become mindful of the absence of greed, hatred, and delusion at that time. Then the mind may return to the breath, or it may continue to observe the changing unworldly feelings. Happiness arises. The mind settles down, becomes calm and peaceful, and happiness increases. Happiness leads to a deeper level of concentration.

Suppose, for instance, you wake up one morning feeling sad. Rather than becoming upset, you sit down in a quiet place, close your eyes, and spend some time watching your sadness without any presumption or worry, but paying total attention to this painful worldly feeling. If you allow yourself to become attached to the cause of your sadness, the painful feeling lasts longer. But if you watch your feeling, you notice the truth of your sadness. Then you learn to diminish greed, hatred, and delusion. When you accept the reality of change that takes place during every moment of feeling, you are reminded that, fortunately, even painful feelings are impermanent. Pleasant unworldly feelings arise.

Thus your general mood changes from sadness to a calm, happy, peaceful feeling. Now the mind is clear and can easily gain concentration.

Suppose on another day you feel particularly peaceful and joyful. You look at this unworldly pleasant feeling as it is, paying total attention to it for as long as it lasts. But you do not try to make the feeling permanent. So long as attachment does not arise, the feeling will continue to predominate, even for days. When it begins to fade, you let it go. As you continue to be mindful of your feelings, you learn that you cannot force a pleasant feeling to stay for however long you wish. Paradoxically, the harder you try to keep a pleasant feeling with you, the quicker it disappears. If you simply watch your feelings as they come and go, your mind relaxes and becomes more comfortable. You also maintain your emotional equilibrium more easily.

When we mindfully observe any feeling, it will peak and break. That feeling is then replaced by another feeling, which also peaks and breaks. If you begin with a pleasant feeling, the next feeling may be an unpleasant feeling, or a neutral feeling, or another pleasant feeling. The type of feeling you experience switches constantly. This switch from one type of feeling to another happens from one split second to the next. Groups of feelings—predominantly pleasant, predominantly unpleasant, or predominantly neutral—change from moment to moment. Trends of feelings change from hour to hour, day to day, and so forth. Observing any of these changes gives us insight into our true nature.

MINDFULNESS OF THE MIND

Mindfulness of the mind refers to watching various mental states arise and pass away—the greedy or nongreedy mind, the hateful or nonhateful mind, the ignorant or discerning mind, the contracted or expanded mind, the distracted or focused mind, the scattered or concentrated mind, the undeveloped or developed mind, the unliberated or liberated mind. You observe such states as they appear and disappear along with consciousness appearing and disappearing.

It's impossible to separate consciousness from the mind states and mental objects, because they arise and pass away together. You can, however, notice when consciousness has been affected by negative mental qualities such as greed, hatred, confusion, depression, or restlessness, or by positive qualities such as generosity, patience, or loving-friendliness.

You give each mental state total attention as it arises, without doing anything specific about it and without allowing yourself to get involved or to follow the thought or feeling. You simply watch as each state or quality rises and falls. This rising and falling is the nature of the entire mind. Every moment—in fact, many times every moment—mind arises, reaches its peak, and passes away. It is the same for any mind of any being in the universe. The more you observe this rising and falling of all mental qualities, the more volatile you know them to be. Seeing this volatility, you gain insight into the impermanent phenomena called "mind."

Thus the more you focus on mind itself, the less solid it seems. Like everything else that exists, it is always changing. Moreover, you discover, there is no permanent entity; no one is running the movie projector. All is flux, all is flow, all is process. In reality, who you are is simply this constant flow of changing moments of mind. Since you cannot control this process, you have no choice but to let go. In letting go, you experience joy and you taste for an instant the freedom and happiness that is the goal of the Buddha's path. Then you know that this mind can be used to gain wisdom.

MINDFULNESS OF MENTAL OBJECTS

Mindfulness of mental objects may sound like a new kind of meditation practice, but it is just another way of describing the insight practice that you are already doing. "Mental objects" refers to thoughts—which here means all conscious mental activities. Thoughts have several categories: there are fetters, hindrances, the five aggregates of existence, factors of enlightenment, and the Four Noble Truths. They may arise in any order.

In sitting meditation, while practicing with your intended object of meditation, such as the breath, you quickly become mindful of any thought that arises, such as the hindrance of doubt or an aspect of one of the aggregates. That mental object—the thought—becomes the new, temporary object of your meditation. You simply notice the mental object and watch it fade. Or, if it is unwholesome and it persists, you do whatever is necessary to get rid of it. As the mental object disappears, you note that it is characterized by impermanence, dissatisfaction, and selflessness. Then you return your attention to the breath or your chosen object of meditation. When the next thought arises, you repeat the process.

Note that you do not determine in advance what kinds of mental objects you will turn to during the meditation. Nor is there any need to categorize what arises, thinking, "I am observing a fetter." When observing wholesome mental objects such as joy, you do what you can to encourage such thoughts to keep coming, but you also continue to observe the impermanence, dissatisfaction, and selflessness of these states.

As we mentioned before, however, mindfulness meditation practice is not limited to the meditation cushion. In any posture, no matter what you may be doing, you can become aware of any mental activity as it arises. As you try to maintain continuous mindfulness every day, unwholesome mental activities eventually occur less frequently, and wholesome ones occur more frequently. Since you spend less time getting lost in negative thinking, it becomes easier and easier to stay abreast of the actions of the mind.

As you train yourself to be mindful for most of your waking hours, one day you will see that your mindfulness is steady and strong. Your mind is very clear, and you begin to see how everything you experience fits into the Four Noble Truths. When this happens, the Four Noble Truths have become the object of your mindfulness. You may recall an example of observing the Four Noble Truths from the section on "Mindfulness of Skillful Understanding" in step two.

As your mindfulness improves, you naturally begin to observe factors of enlightenment—the qualities of mind necessary to achieve the goal of the path. The Buddha practiced for many lifetimes to reach the utmost perfection of these factors in order to become a Buddha. The Seven Factors of Enlightenment are mindfulness, investigation, effort, joy, tranquillity, concentration, and equanimity. You have been cultivating these factors all along. As your mindfulness improves, they simply reach a higher level. The Seven Factors of Enlightenment are traditionally presented in the order in which they arise, because the development of each factor leads to the next.

When mindfulness is steady and strong, you notice its strength, and it becomes your object of meditation. You know that you are mindful. Thus mindfulness becomes a mental object of mindfulness. This awareness of your mindfulness sheds more light on your own experiences of form, feelings, perceptions, volitional formations, and consciousness, so that you can see them more clearly. Encouraged by this awareness, you continue your mindfulness training. Mindfulness is what you have been practicing all along as you have been developing on the path of the Buddha. Mindfulness is one of the cardinal factors of that path. Eventually, after much work, you come to a point at which your mindfulness becomes deeper, clearer, and stronger, and you know that your mindfulness is established. Now, mindfulness has been raised to the level of a factor of enlightenment.

With mindfulness you have been discriminating between wholesome and unwholesome objects. You have been observing the characteristics of objects that you experience, finding them characterized by impermanence, dissatisfaction, and selflessness. In the course of these efforts you have been developing habits of investigation into truth. With strengthened mindfulness, the wholesome desire arises to investigate impartially every experience you have. You become aware of this. Then your mental object is investigation of all phenomena of life. Your enhanced mindfulness acts like a flashlight to illuminate objects in the dark.

With the beam of powerful mindfulness focused on your experience of an object, you investigate and see that object's impermanent nature. As that object disappears, another object arises, revealing the same truth of impermanence, dissatisfaction, and selflessness. When the next experience arises, you may think, "This one will be permanent!" Yet your strong investigation reveals that it, too, is changing. As you continue to look for the truth and continue to find all experiences to share the same three characteristics, your investigation becomes a factor of enlightenment.

As everything you investigate continues to reveal this truth, zeal arises to see more. The mind is filled with energy. At this point your mindfulness is strong, as though crystallized. All along you have been making effort—to develop mindfulness, to remove unwholesome states, to encourage wholesome states, and to work hard to accomplish every step of the path. Now your readiness to make effort reaches its fruition: the enlightenment factor of energy.

You sense the energetic readiness of the mind to tackle any task, and energy becomes your mental object of mindfulness. The mind remains active yet relaxed. Wholesome desire arises to bring up this energized quality of mind again and again. Now with powerful mindfulness, powerful investigation, and powerful energy, you continue to investigate whatever object arises in the mind, seeing the three characteristics again and again. The more you energize yourself to see the truth, the more you become pleased, even joyful. You feel so pleased because you are no longer in conflict with reality. Thus the joy factor of enlightenment becomes the new object of mindfulness.

Joy yields to contentment, which leads to happiness. Happiness brings peace and tranquillity. Thus tranquillity arises as a factor of enlightenment. Continuing to see the same truth, on every level, in every conceivable experience, you relax. The mind was once in constant agitated motion like a flag on a mountain top. Now restlessness has given way. Calmness comes. Deep, powerful concentration arises. Earlier you may have had deep, powerful concentration; this is the same. But now the mind is ripening, and you can use this concentration to achieve stages of enlightenment. Thus concentration becomes a factor of enlightenment.

All the factors are in perfect harmony—mindfulness, investigation, energy, joy, tranquillity, and concentration. They all are in balance. At this stage the equanimity factor of enlightenment takes over. Seeing whatever arises in a very impartial, steady state, equanimity purifies each of the other factors. Before, there always was some subtle desire for things to be other than they are. You think, for example, "I wish this beautiful experience would continue." That subtle desire ends when the mind is in an equanimous state.

When impermanence is very clear, you don't hope that the next moment will not be impermanent. When the unsatisfactory, suffering nature of things becomes clear, you do not wish that the next moment will be satisfactory. When the impersonal, uncontrollable, selfless nature of things becomes clear, you have no expectation that the next moment might be different. With equanimity, the mind does not have even a trace of desire to see things in any way other than how they are. The mind is completely united with truth. This is how the Four Noble Truths line up with the Seven Factors of Enlightenment. You see suffering exactly as it is. You see the cause of suffering exactly as it is. You see the end of suffering exactly as it is. And the path that you have been developing all along up to now—this, too, you see exactly as it is.

Whenever each of these factors of enlightenment do not arise, you become aware of this. Whenever they do arise, you become aware of this and cultivate them, until you come to this level of perfection. When each of the Seven Factors of Enlightenment has been perfected, we achieve nibbana, perfect happiness, perfect peace. We can achieve this goal within this life. When we do, all suffering ceases. All questions come to an end. All anxiety, worry, fear, and tension disappear, never to return. There is no craving, no clinging to anything. We live in perfect harmony, perfect balance. All our senses are sharpened. We still eat, drink, talk, walk, and use our body and mind, but with full awareness, total mindfulness. Our morality does not make us think we are superior to others. Our concentration does not make us praise ourselves and disparage others. Our wisdom gives us perfect loving-friendliness, perfect compassion, and perfect appreciative joy. Enjoying perfect equanimity, we are never again troubled by life's ups and downs.

KEY POINTS FOR THE PRACTICE
OF SKILLFUL MINDFULNESS

- Mindfulness is paying moment-to-moment attention to what is. A mindful mind is precise, penetrating, balanced, and uncluttered. It is like a mirror that reflects without distortion whatever stands before it.

- Mindfulness grants you insight into the three characteristics of all existing things: impermanence, dissatisfaction, and the nonexistence of an eternal or unchanging self or soul.

- You can use any object to further your mindfulness, so long as it helps you gain insight into these three characteristics.

- The deep purpose of mindfulness is to open the wisdom eye, for insight into the true nature of reality is the ultimate secret of lasting peace and happiness.

- The Four Foundations of Mindfulness are mindfulness of the body, mindfulness of feelings, mindfulness of the mind, and mindfulness of mental objects.

- Three essential practices of mindfulness of the body are mindfulness of the breath, mindfulness of posture, and mindfulness of the parts of the body.

- Mindfulness of the breath can help you learn to focus, as the breath is easy to observe and always present.

- Uniting the mind with the breath puts the mind into the present moment. The breath also functions as a home base to which the mind can return after investigating other phenomena.

- Walking slowly and mindfully can be a complete meditation that reveals how impermanence, dissatisfaction, and selflessness pervade every moment. The same meditation can be used for other postures, such as sitting, standing, and lying down.

- Maintaining mindfulness of posture throughout the day trains the mind to see clearly the characteristics of the five aggregates.

- Meditating on the body as a collection of forty-two ever-changing parts and processes shows you that there is nothing permanent about the body to which you can become attached.

- Pleasant and unpleasant emotional feelings come from our own attitudes, therefore we can stop blaming others for how we feel.

- The whole cycle of suffering is powered by the mind's unenlightened reactions to the three kinds of feelings—grasping at pleasant feelings, rejecting unpleasant ones, and experiencing a deluded sense of "self" in neutral ones.

- "Worldly feelings" arise from mundane pursuits and have underlying tendencies toward greed, hatred, or delusion. "Unworldly feelings" arise from insight and lack any underlying tendencies.

- Mindfulness of feelings is part of our ordinary insight meditation practice. Seeing the impermanence of feelings, we learn to let go of the underlying tendencies of greed, hatred, and delusion, and to cultivate unworldly feelings.

- The Buddha did not teach us to "mindfully enjoy" sense pleasures. He taught us to mindfully let go of desire for pleasurable worldly feelings and to enjoy the pleasant unworldly feelings created by this detachment.

- When you cultivate mindfulness of mind, you notice the rising and falling of mental states, such as greedy and nongreedy states of mind, contracted and expanded states of mind, and so forth.

- Mindfulness of mental objects means noticing the arising and falling away of the five hindrances, the ten fetters, the five aggregates, the Four Noble Truths, and the factors of enlightenment.

- You can regard the factors of enlightenment as the fruits of mindfulness practice. As your mindfulness deepens, they arise in this order: mindfulness, investigation, energy, joy, tranquillity, concentration, and equanimity.

- When all of the factors of enlightenment have been perfected, we achieve nibbana, perfect happiness, perfect peace. We can achieve this goal within this life.

STEP 8
Skillful Concentration

SKILLFUL CONCENTRATION is the last essential step on the Buddha's path to happiness. When the mind is serene, peaceful, and concentrated, the hindrances that block our happiness do not arise. Moreover, when we sit in meditation, we are able to focus our concentrated mind on the mental objects that arise with consciousness. Concentration helps us pierce right through the superficial appearance of these objects to a clear perception of their impermanence, the dissatisfaction they bring, and their lack of a permanent or unchanging self or identity. With skilled concentration, our meditation practice accelerates, and we make rapid progress on the Buddha's path.

Generally, when we say that someone is "concentrating," we can mean anything from being engrossed in a television show to strategizing in a chess game to plotting a crime. But the concentration the Buddha taught as part of his Eightfold Path has three special characteristics: it is always wholesome; it goes into very deep and powerful levels of one-pointed focus; and it incorporates the use of mindfulness to develop wisdom.

This kind of concentration does not happen right away. Like any other skill it must be learned step by step. The mind must be trained. It may take anything from several sessions of sitting meditation to several years of effort to develop concentration that is wholesome, one-pointed, and mindful. Once we do achieve this full concentration, we must repeat the training steps over and over until we are able to bring up Skillful Concentration easily and at will.

We mentioned at the beginning the importance of finding a good teacher to guide your practice. A teacher can offer great assistance as you work to develop full concentration. Many questions may arise as you try to refine your ability. If a good teacher is not available, the next best thing would be to read books devoted entirely to the subject.

Furthermore, it is hard for the mind to settle down enough to reach full concentration so long as you continue dealing with the daily problems of ordinary life. We recommend that you set aside specific periods of time to practice full concentration, such as a week during which you will not be interrupted by duties. Attending a retreat focused on concentration practice may be the best way to begin.

WHOLESOME CONCENTRATION

Not all concentration is wholesome. Think of a cat waiting to pounce, focusing its attention on its prey. The cat has intense concentration, but it is not wholesome. The wholesome concentrated mind is free of greed, hatred, and delusion.

In everyday life, we may use strong concentration to solve a mathematical problem, to repair a car engine, or to prepare a complicated recipe. This kind of concentration can be wholesome if it is motivated by good thoughts such as generosity, loving-friendliness, or compassion. It will be unwholesome if motivated by unwholesome states such as greed, aversion, or cruelty.

Unwholesome states, including the five hindrances, are present in everyday concentration more often than you may realize. For instance, while you are trying to solving that math problem, you may be overly attached to getting a good grade on the exam; while repairing your car engine, you may be afraid of botching the job; while cooking your elaborate meal, you may be thinking angrily about a family member who will be eating it. The kind of concentration taught by the Buddha is always free of the hindrances.

In sitting meditation, too, if concentration has been established while any hindrance is present, it is unwholesome. For example, while sitting in meditation, you may achieve a little concentration while experiencing the hindrance of dullness and drowsiness. You may be in a half-asleep, half-awake state, dreaming pleasant thoughts. Later you may imagine that you reached some great attainment during your meditation. This is delusion, not wholesome concentration.

Practicing concentration when there is some resentment in your mind is also unwholesome. You'll be able to tell when your concentration practice has gone wrong in this way because you will experience tension, worry, or strain. Some meditators may even get a headache from forcing themselves to focus on their object of meditation despite the presence of irritation or some other kind of aversion. You should always practice Skillful Effort to overcome such obstacles and to create a wholesome state of mind before continuing. The worst mistake a meditator can make is to spend time in meditation concentrating upon grievances or other unwholesome thoughts. Of course, bringing mindful awareness to these states is wholesome insight meditation.

Thus the first step in establishing Skillful Concentration is to make sure your practice is wholesome by blocking hindrances from the mind. Here are the additional steps you should follow every time you sit with the intention of establishing Skillful Concentration:

- For the period of your meditation, give up all thoughts of attachment to situations, ideas, people, and habits. Do not think of your family, friends, relatives, job, income, bills, investments, properties, or responsibilities. Tell yourself, "I choose to spend this very special period of time to better myself. I did not sit down on this cushion to think all of my regular thoughts. I will make good use of this time."

- Do not worry about anything you may have left undone, or about things you may have done incorrectly, or about ways you may have offended someone. Remind yourself that the past is gone, and what is done cannot be undone.

- Spend a few minutes cultivating thoughts of loving-friendliness to make the mind feel pleasant and better able to concentrate. Then take three deep breaths.

- Focus the mind upon your chosen object of meditation such as the breath.

- Keep your mind in the present moment.

- Make unremitting effort to pull your mind together.

- If any of the five hindrances is present, overcome it using the methods you have learned. Cultivate the wholesome state of mind that is the opposite of any hindrance that is present. For example, if greed is present, cultivate the thought of letting go. Let the mind become light and bright.

- Once a hindrance has been overcome, refocus the mind upon the chosen object of meditation such as the breath.

- Remember, the goal of this session is to practice your concentration technique. At this point you should not look into the details of your experience but mindfully keep focusing on your primary object of meditation.

- Each time you establish wholesome concentration, it gets easier, and you should feel encouraged. No matter how short-lived or feeble the wholesome concentration may be, you have gained something by cutting through old habits and improving the mind.

While you are training the mind in concentration, you should feel happy about whatever level of wholesome concentration you have been able to achieve. In sitting meditation, wholesome concentration brings energy, some stability, and the beginnings of confidence in the practice. Joy arises because wholesome concentration keeps the hindrances suppressed.

Even in everyday life, a degree of wholesome concentration is necessary to living with good morality. Wholesome concentration helps you focus on positive thoughts, speech, and actions and abstain from unwholesome ones. Wholesome concentration allows you to deal with daily problems impartially, with an equanimous state of mind. The reverse is also true. Success in developing wholesome concentration depends upon a strong foundation of morality. As your sense of morality improves, so will your concentration.

The concentration we have been talking about up to now is what we might call "ordinary wholesome concentration." This kind of concentration is relatively easy to achieve. Yet, the insight that arises from ordinary wholesome concentration can transform lives. It turns you away from unwholesome thoughts, speech, and behavior. You lose interest in doing things that retard the liberation of mind. This is why the Buddha said that wholesome concentration spearheads all wholesome mental states.

When the Buddha was still Prince Siddhattha Gotama, his father, the king, prevented him from seeing anything that might encourage him in a spiritual direction. When the prince did finally see the four signs—an old person, an invalid, a corpse, and a renunciant spiritual practitioner—that marked a turning point for him. Pondering these four things, Siddhattha reached a state of concentration. Insight arose into the fact of suffering. So he resolved not to return to the comforts and pleasures of his father's palace but to seek a solution to human suffering.

The same can be true for us. When we look upon them with wholesome concentration, common, everyday things can trigger the mind to ponder more deeply. The insight that can come with ordinary wholesome concentration can convince you that you have been in the cycle of suffering for long enough and that it is time to begin a new page of your life. You gain a new vision and knowledge of the suffering in your life. You see the blindness of pursuing happiness through sense pleasures; you see through the satisfactions of material pleasure to their underlying stress and sorrow. You no longer try to rationalize misery as pleasure.

The way out of misery also becomes clear. Since ordinary wholesome concentration helps you see the truth of the Buddha's message, you are motivated to develop more profound states of concentration so that you can attain deeper insights.

THE STAGES OF FULL CONCENTRATION

The profound concentration that can lead to the deepest realizations is called "full concentration," or *jhana*. Full concentration is always wholesome and possesses one-pointed, undistracted focus. Note, however, that full concentration is not yet Skillful Concentration unless mindfulness is present. With full concentration, your progress toward enlightenment is accelerated.

We are talking about concentration here in a very special sense. Every time the mind focuses on any object, however insignificant, concentration arises. But usually we just notice the big picture, not the little bits that make it up. In the act of reading, for example, the eyes focus on one letter and then the next, or on one word and then the next, and then they send that information to the mind. But we do not read letter by letter or even word by word. The mind is so quick and its ability to concentrate so powerful that we take in whole lines or sentences.

If we slow the process down, we can become aware of each tiny moment of concentration. The goal of concentration practice is to sustain awareness so that concentration flows into each succeeding moment of mind, consecutively, without gaps. This level of awareness is difficult, however. A moment of mind is so small that it is almost unimaginable.

Someone asked the Buddha to give an example of a moment of mind. He replied that he could not give an example. He said it is impossible to describe the rapidity, the swiftness of the moment. Suppose, however, that there is a tiny and delicate spider web. Suppose, you bring a candle to burn it. How long would it take to burn the spider web? You can hardly bring the candle close to the web before it burns. He said that within such a short period of time, thousands and thousands of mind moments arise, mature, and pass away. With this illustration, the Buddha was saying that the rapidity of the mind is virtually inconceivable.

Each of these fleeting moments of mind consists of three even briefer mind moments: the rising moment, the peak moment, and the dying moment. Immediately after the dying moment, the next moment of mind arises, followed by its peak and dying moments. These three briefer moments make one complete mind moment. Ordinary concentration arises with only some of the mind moments—perhaps one in a billion. A powerfully concentrated mind can see all the way down to the level of the arising, peaking, and dying of individual mind moments. Once we directly observe the arising and passing of individual mind moments, we can no longer doubt the truth of the impermanence of all things, and we must let go. That is why we need a completely concentrated mind in order to see reality clearly enough to attain enlightenment.

Full concentration has a number of stages or levels. Actually, there are eight levels of full concentration or jhana that are accessible to people who are not yet enlightened, and any of them may be used to attain enlightenment. For simplicity, however, we will limit our discussion to the first four levels.

At least the first level of full concentration is needed in order to develop the mental power necessary for insight into things as they are. With the attainment of each of the next three levels, it becomes easier to see the truth. At the second level, concentration is much improved due to the absence of thinking processes. At the third level mindfulness becomes much more powerful, and at the fourth level even more so, being completely purified due to the presence of equanimity.

The First Level

To achieve the first level of full concentration, you must clear the mind of any of the hindrances and establish wholesome concentration. Then five mental factors must come together: "initial application of thought," "sustained application of thought," joy, happiness, and concentration.

Any of these five factors may arise, alone or combined, under various circumstances. For example, happiness arises whenever hatred disappears. When sleepiness fades, "initial application of thought" may arise. When restlessness and worry fade, joy may arise. Whenever there is a moment of ordinary wholesome concentration, joy will arise due to the absence of hindrances, and some of the other factors may arise, too.

It is a wonderful feeling when any of these five factors arise. You may think you are in heaven. But this marvelous feeling is not jhana, nor do you get to jhana by bringing these factors together randomly, one by one. A certain system must be followed to attain the first level of jhanic concentration.

This method begins with ordinary wholesome concentration. The joy that you find in this state leads to happiness. Joy and happiness are different emotions. Joy arises in hopeful anticipation of happiness. Happiness arises out of contentment when one's hopes have been fulfilled.

Here's an analogy that can help distinguish between joy and happiness:

You are walking in a desert. There's no water or trees or shade—just sand. On and on you walk, tired and thirsty. Then you see someone approaching with wet hair and clothes dripping with water. Delighted, you ask, "How come you're so wet?"

"I'm coming from an oasis right over there."

You walk toward the oasis. When you first see the water, you feel joy. As you get closer, your joy increases. Then, you dive into the water head first. You drink the water. Then you rest along the bank, feeling cool and calm. "Oh, what happiness! Happiness is like that."

Normally, people associate happiness with excitement. Say, for instance, somebody wins a lot of money in the lottery. That person will express excitement by kissing, hugging, crying, jumping up and down. That person thinks, "I'm so happy!" But this feeling is not true happiness. It is excitement. When true happiness arises, excitement disappears, and you feel relaxed and peaceful.

True happiness leads to tranquillity. As the mind calms down, it naturally becomes more concentrated. As your concentration deepens you can proceed to train the mind toward full concentration with these next steps:

- Keep the mind steadily focused upon the breath or another object of meditation. Do not, at this point, turn to examine other objects as they arise, such as sounds or thoughts. Let go of whatever comes up and return to the breath. Do this over and over, until the mind loses interest in all other things and stays with the object.

- Eventually the breath or other chosen object seems to fade and is replaced by a memorized impression of it. That mental image or feeling—called the "sign of concentration"—becomes your new object of meditation, and you stay with it.

- When that mental image also fades and the mind concentrates upon itself, you have reached the first level of full concentration.

How does this come about? As wholesome concentration deepens, the mind gradually loses interest in other things and stays with the object of meditation, such as the breath. As you continue to focus on this object, it becomes so subtle that you do not notice it at all. But at the place of focus, such as the tip of the nostril, the memory of the breath or other object of meditation continues. This memory turns into a very pleasant sensation called the "sign of concentration." This sign may appear as a visual image, perhaps like a light, or as some other sensation, such as soft touch. Exactly how this mental image appears is a very individual thing.

When you develop the sign, however it appears, stay with it. Use the same image each time you meditate. Do not tell anyone else your sign. Everybody's sign is different, and you will just make others confused. At the beginning of your practice, your inhalation and exhalation were the object of your meditation. Now you have the sign as the object of meditation. The Buddha urged his monks to "practice, develop, and fix" the sign. (A IV (Nines) IV.4) Practice achieving the sign of concentration many times, until you gain full control of it, so that whenever you want to experience it, the sign is available and you can unite your mind with it.

When it first appears in your practice, the sign of concentration appears to be static. Thus concentration can arise based on it. But as you pay total attention to the sign, you begin to see that the sign itself is changing every moment. Eventually, like all other conditioned phenomena, the sign itself fades away. When the sign also disappears, the mind has no object but itself to focus on, so the mind becomes concentrated within itself. In this moment, "initial application of thought" briefly occurs. This is the beginning of wholesome one-pointedness of mind.

When initial application of thought is sustained for a few seconds, "sustained application of thought" can arise. Now the mind stays steadily on the object. Because the mind is no longer wandering here and there, a more refined quality of joy arises, closely followed by a more refined happiness. These four factors trigger jhanic concentration. Now the five factors of the first level of concentration or jhana—initial application of thought, sustained application of thought, joy, happiness, and concentration—are functioning together as a unit.

People often ask me, "How do I know whether I have attained the first level of jhana?" The answer is simple: as we said earlier, only when all five factors are functioning in unison can you say that you have attained the first stage of full concentration or jhana. Imagine that you are looking for a rainbow. Before you find one you may see a red color here, or you may see green or blue colors over there, or some color combinations. They may be very beautiful, wonderful colors. But that is not the phenomenon of a rainbow. Until you have the right conditions of sunlight reflecting on the clouds, causing a prism to appear with all the colors lining up in the way that they must, you do not have a rainbow. Similarly, until the conditions come together and all of the five jhanic factors line up, you do not have full concentration.

Some people have the idea that the concentrated mind becomes blank. They imagine the mind of the meditator to be without feeling—just resting there like a stone. Nothing could be further from the truth. The mind in full concentration is not static but dynamic. In first jhana the mind has the following dynamic qualities:

- equanimity, a balanced, neither-painful-nor-pleasant feeling
- tranquillity, lack of concern with anything in the world, such as politics or your emotions
- one-pointedness
- the mental factors of contact, feeling, perception, volition, and life force
- zeal, decision, energy, and attention

The mind concentrated within itself has great, dynamic power. Like a whirlpool, it gathers ever greater force by focusing in on itself and creating a powerful vortex. This great power is called the "force of concentration." Think, for example, of hydroelectric power. When a large amount of water is forced through a small opening, the force of the concentrated water is so powerful that it can move turbines with enough force to light up a city. Yet, when the water is not focused upon an outer object, its power is gathered to itself. Similarly, when the mind has no distraction to cause it to focus on some outer or inner object, it gathers its force in on itself. Then the mind is like water forced through a small opening. Its force of concentration is so great that it can directly observe impermanence at the most minute, fundamental, subatomic level of

Skillful understanding

* To Know why we're doing it.
1. Choices we make lead
   To happiness or unhappiness

Skillful Understanding.

1. Cause → effect
2. 4 Noble Truths.

   1. Cause → effect
      A. Skillful vs unskillful

4 Noble Truths

Dissatisfaction

1. Life cycle

Aging - the pain cycle of
illness. "Pain sensations
are usually managable.
Dissatisfaction ē "what is"
is harder to overcome.

2. Ignorance is
"not knowing" or "wrong
Knowing."

3. Change
   All conditioned things
are 1. Impermanent
   2. unsatisfactory
   3. Not self

HI SHARON:

   I THINK IT IS A GOOD IDEA TO
STAY OVERNITE @ KEN'S & DRIVE
HOME ē YOU & MTN NEXT DAY.
SEE IF PATRICIA IS ABLE TO
STAY ONE MORE DAY.

            LOVE S

   HOPE YOU ARE DOING WELL
MY CURRENT KEY WORD IS
   ATTENTION TO THE MOMENT.

KARANĪYA METTA SUTTA

karanīyam atthakusalena
yam tam santam padam abhisamecca
sakko ujū ca sūjū ca
suvaco c'assa mudu anatimāni

santussako ca subharo ca
appakiccoca sallahuka-vutti
santindriyo ca nipako ca
appagabbho kulesu ananugiddo

na ca khuddam sāmacare kinci
yena vinnu pare upavadeyyum

sukhino vā khemino hontu
sabe sattā bhavantu sukhitattā

ye keci pānabhūtatthi
tasā vā thāvarā vā anavasesā
dighā vā ye mahant vā

body and mind. Full concentration is a wholesome state of such one-pointedness of mind.

This dynamic concentration is not the same as being "glued" to the object of meditation. That would be attachment, which would make the mind waver. Full concentration is not the mind uniting with the object; it is the mind uniting with itself. The object is merely used as a springboard into the mind. If the mind gets stuck on an object, that is not wholesome; it is concentration with attachment. Unfortunately, that is the kind of concentration some meditators practice, but it cannot bring liberation.

When you attain the first level of concentration for the first time, you are so suffused with joy and happiness that these positive states feel like an integral part of your body. They are like bath salts that dissolve so thoroughly into the bath water that you can no longer separate the salts from the water. Similarly, when your entire body is fully charged with joy and happiness, you cannot separate your sense of body from those feelings. Your feeling of peace is so great that you wish to stay in this state of concentration forever!

The Second Level

After attaining the first level of concentration, you are advised not to strive immediately for the second level. This would be a foolish and profitless spiritual ambition. Before you achieve the second level, you must bring the first level to perfection. If you are too eager, you are likely to fail to gain the second level and may find yourself unable even to regain the first.

The Buddha compared such an overeager meditator to a cow who, while still unfamiliar with her own pasture, sets out for new pastures. The foolish cow gets lost in the mountains without food or water and cannot find her way back home. This is not the time to go seek a new high. It is time to patiently train the mind.

Therefore, when you attain the first level of concentration, you should remember the steps you followed to attain it. This is where your mindfulness comes in. Mindfulness helps you remember the steps you followed to gain the first level of concentration. If concentration seemed to happen to you all of a sudden, without your going through these steps, then what you experienced was not full concentration. Some teachers might tell you that your have attained one of the levels of concentration. Test this perception for yourself. Do not simply accept the opinions that some people so freely pronounce.

Having reviewed the steps, you then mindfully determine to attain the first level again, determine to remain a little longer in that state of concentration, and determine when your period of concentration will end. Having made these three determinations, you follow the necessary steps and practice attaining the first level of concentration many times.

As you repeat this procedure over and over, you lose interest in the initial application of thought and the sustained application of thought. This change may occur in one sitting or over a number of sittings. Suppose, for example, you attain the first level of concentration fifty times, and every time, you find the initial application and the sustained application of thought a little less interesting. Then, in the fifty-first attainment, you skip these two factors completely and pay no attention to them because you have lost interest in them entirely. The moment this happens, these factors disappear, and you attain the second level of concentration.

In the second jhana there is no more thinking to disturb the mind and disrupt its one-pointed focus. The factors of jhana that remain are a stronger one-pointedness of mind, joy, and happiness. The joy and happiness of the second level of concentration are less exuberant and more refined, for they are no longer based on the mind feeling pleased at being relieved of the hindrances. Now the joy and happiness are based on concentration. There is also a new sense of confidence that comes from your achievements up to this point—confidence in your ability to proceed, confidence in the method, and confidence in the Buddha's message. Concentration is strengthened.

Imagine a cool lake fed only by a spring welling up from below. The fresh water from the spring mixes with the cool water of the lake, thoroughly suffusing and recharging it. The lake is cleansed yet remains undisturbed. Just as the springwater wells up into the lake, in the second level of jhana the pure joy and happiness born of concentration continuously pour into the mind. The mind is so soothed and the body so completely suffused with joy and happiness that no part remains untouched.

The Third Level

Using the same procedure as before, you repeat the second level of concentration many times. When you first attained the second level of concentration, the joy you experienced was wonderful and refreshing. Constant repetition, however, makes the joy seem monotonous rather than peaceful. Gradually, you begin to ignore it. As you ignore the factor of joy, it gradually fades away. The moment joy fades from your mind, you have attained the third level of concentration.

Equanimity becomes stronger, and so does concentration. This makes your mindfulness stronger and more stable. Your mind becomes suffused with deeper and subtler degrees of happiness. Think of a pond with water lilies growing just below the surface. These flowers are born in the water, remain underwater, and are fed from the water's depths. They are thoroughly saturated, inside and out, their every cell completely full of water. Similarly, in the third level of jhana, your body is completely saturated and filled with happiness. In the second level, there was a certain amount of activity or excitement, like the movement of the refreshing springwater pouring into the lake. But in the third level, you do not feel the need to be refreshed by happiness that seems to come from outside yourself. Your refined happiness has a quality of stillness because happiness is merged completely with the body and mind.

The Fourth Level

As before, you repeat the third level of concentration many times, until you lose interest in happiness as well. As happiness fades, your mindfulness becomes even more pure due to the presence of equanimity—the neither-painful-nor-pleasant feeling of perfect emotional balance. You begin to find that mindfulness and equanimity are even more peaceful than happiness. When you let go of happiness completely, you reach the fourth level of concentration, in which mindfulness is purified by the power of equanimity. You recall that there was also equanimity at the third level, but because you had not yet let go of happiness, equanimity was not yet powerful enough to purify mindfulness.

At the fourth level of concentration, the mind is completely quiet, tranquil, and stable. Because all negative mind states have been suppressed, the mind is imperturbable. The mental purity and clarity suffusing your body is like a soft, pure white cloth gently wrapped around you. The cloth is so pure and so gentle that you can barely feel it; but it protects you from insects, heat, wind, and cold. Similarly, when the mind is pure and clear, nothing can shake it into grasping or aversion. It remains equanimous. Even if the body experiences insect bites, cold, or heat, the mind remains unaffected. Even if someone pulls on your sleeve and talks to you, the mind ignores the intrusion, remaining concentrated and unperturbed.

At this point you have gained the real force of concentration. The mind has consolidated, become pure, bright, free of hindrances, and steady. It is malleable yet imperturbable, strengthened and sharpened for its most important task. When you focus that concentrated mind on an object, you see the object as it is. In other words, the perfectly concentrated mind can penetrate into the true nature of reality.

———————

These four stages of full concentration are so pleasant that you may wish to immerse yourself in them for pure enjoyment, without directing the mind toward insight. If you simply "bliss out" and fail to explore ways to use the concentration, however, you limit its power. Your concentration remains wholesome, and there is nothing wrong with it. But not putting your concentrated mind to good use is like receiving a gift of the world's fleetest thoroughbred racehorse and using it only for quiet pleasure rides around your neighborhood. Full concentration is too valuable a tool to waste. If, while concentrated, you use your mindfulness to see reality, concentration can help you achieve liberation.

MINDFULNESS OF SKILLFUL CONCENTRATION

There are three skillful approaches to sitting meditation. The first is to begin the session making an effort to attain full concentration. Once full concentration is achieved you use it to practice insight. That is, you use concentration to look into the impermanence, suffering, and self-lessness of your form, feelings, perceptions, volitional formations, and consciousness.

The second approach is to begin the sitting session with insight meditation. When you start with insight meditation, whenever an object has caught your attention, you watch until it fades, observing its impermanence, dissatisfaction, and selflessness. Then you relax and return to your primary object of focus, such as the breath. Each time you return to the breath, your concentration deepens. If any hindrance arises, you overcome it, and this also deepens your concentration. As your monkey mind slowly settles down, you lose interest in the objects that normally catch your attention. These objects slowly fade from awareness. Eventually the sign of concentration arises, then initial and sustained application of thought, and finally full concentration arises in the manner that we explained before. In that fully concentrated state you continue with your insight practice, watching the impermanence, suffering, and selflessness of form, feelings, perceptions, volitional formations, and consciousness.

A third approach is to begin with either insight meditation or the effort to attain concentration and switch back and forth between the two. For example, let's say you begin by focusing on the breath and ignore other objects in an effort to achieve concentration. If concentration does not become established, frustration arises, and you use insight practice to observe the changes in the feelings of frustration. When the frustration has subsided, you notice whatever other hindrances may have arisen. Once the mind has steadied, you return to deeper focus, ignoring objects as they arise, again making the effort to achieve full concentration. Thus in this third approach concentration and mindfulness act as a team gradually deepening your concentration and sharpening your insight. Eventually, one day, when insight is nearly complete in its ability to see, and concentration is nearly full, they unite.

Thus, regardless of how you begin your sitting sessions, mindfulness and concentration, used skillfully, eventually merge and work together. If you sit down to meditate and find that the hindrances are easy to overcome and the mind is quiet, it is good to begin with concentration. On the other hand, if the mind is racing, unable at first to settle down, then you should not try to develop full concentration but should begin the session with insight meditation. Or go back and forth between the two. Your decision whether to start with insight or with concentration depends upon the initial steadiness of your mind.

Regardless of your initial approach, once there is unity of full concentration and powerful mindfulness you use them to shake off the first three fetters. You see selflessness, thus losing your belief in a permanent, unchanging self. You see the meaninglessness of rites and rituals. You see the Four Noble Truths more clearly than ever before and lose all doubt in the Buddha's path to awakening. Having overcome these fetters, you enter the first stage of enlightenment.

Using the concentrated mind is a little like using a laser beam to burn a hard substance. To focus the beam effectively, you must use your eyes. If you keep looking around the room, you cannot focus the beam properly, and you end up either burning the wrong thing or not burning anything at all. Of course, if you fail to turn on the laser beam in the first place, nothing will get burned, even if you sit there looking at it all day!

In this analogy, the eyes are like your wisdom or insight. The laser beam is like the mind when concentrated. Wisdom and concentration work together. Without insight, the beam of concentration will be scattered, or it may focus on the wrong thing. Without the beam of concentration, the eyes of insight may see the object but not be able to burn through it. What is it that we want to burn? Our dirt. Our unwholesomeness of mind. We must see it with wisdom and burn it with a concentrated mind.

So, once you establish skilled concentration, what object do you focus on? You focus the wholesome one-pointed mind on the constant change of the components of your body and mind: physical form, feelings, perceptions, thoughts, and consciousness. You pay attention to the impermanence, dissatisfaction, and selflessness of these components. When you pay attention to any one of these components, you see that all of

them are always changing. You see the connection between impermanence and suffering caused by your clinging to impermanent, pleasant
experiences. You see that what is impermanent and subject to suffering
is selfless.

Seeing the impermanence, dissatisfaction, and selflessness of your
own form, feelings, perceptions, volitional formations, and consciousness
is the primary function of insight meditation. When that function is fulfilled, you will be liberated from clinging to these aggregates composing
the body and mind. With nothing left to cling to, you become free.

When meditators cultivate sufficient concentration guided by mindfulness, they can trace back their mental images of events, time,
thoughts, and previous behavior until they perceive the link between
the present continuous flow and the events, thoughts, and actions of the
past. That link is greed and ignorance. They see for themselves the relationship between impermanence, greed for impermanent things, and
suffering. The penetrating wisdom of the meditator also recognizes all
negativities in all dimensions and how and why they arise. Wisdom recognizes that all negativities come from grasping. It recognizes that this
grasping can end and that the way to end it is by ending one's own greed.

Through this knowledge, the meditator comprehends by personal
and direct experience that everything is impermanent, that clinging to
anything impermanent causes dissatisfaction, and that everything that
exists is without permanent substance. Gaining this threefold knowledge is the doorway to enlightenment.

Putting Concentration to Use

On the night of his enlightenment, the Buddha did not develop powerful concentration and then ignore it; he put it to use. In one heavily
charged, powerful moment, the three realizations of impermanence, dissatisfaction, and selflessness all came together and the Buddha achieved
his goal.

Putting the realizations of concentration to use is the key. It is said
that Alarakarama and Uddaka Ramaputta, two former teachers of
Siddhattha Gotama (the Buddha before his enlightenment), had attained
full concentration. However, they did not train themselves to focus their

attention on form, feelings, perceptions, volitional formations, and consciousness to see their true nature. Rather, they became attached to the pleasantness of concentration and thought that this pleasurable feeling was enlightenment.

Siddhattha Gotama said that his former teachers, like him, had faith, energy, mindfulness, concentration, and wisdom. Like him, their wisdom had helped them understand the danger of the hindrances and the need to overcome them. But unlike Siddhattha Gotama, the teachers did not see that they were using states of concentration merely to suppress hindrances, not vanquish them. And they did not discover the underlying fetters—the forces that bind human beings to repeated rebirth. Siddhattha Gotama alone had used his concentration to see clearly how the hindrances and fetters trap us.

What understanding did the Buddha reach? As you have learned, the five hindrances—greed, ill will, dullness and drowsiness, restlessness and worry, and doubt—get in the way of full concentration. And so, as you work to develop concentration, you push them out of the way. However, the fetters, from which the hindrances spring, continue to exist in your subconscious mind. The ten fetters, as you recall, are belief in a permanent self or soul, doubt, belief in the efficacy of rules and rituals, greed, hatred, desire for rebirth in material form, desire for rebirth in immaterial form, conceit, restlessness and worry, and ignorance. These unwholesome mind habits remain dormant during your period of concentration. Since the underlying fetters are still present in a dormant form, when you come out of concentration, the hindrances return. When you wish to regain the same level of concentration, you have to push the hindrances out of the way again, though as you train your mind, it becomes easier to get past them.

It's a bit like sweeping dust from a hard dirt floor. Even though you swept earlier, in a few days, the dust appears again. Bits of the floor's surface continually break off, crumble underfoot, and become a thick dust. To get rid of the dust you may sweep the whole building, or sprinkle the floor with water, or pour buckets of water that turn the floor to mud. Nevertheless, the dust will return. But if you dig down to bedrock and remove all the dirt, then pour concrete, dust and dirt will no longer be a problem. Digging up all the dust and dirt is like insight meditation overcoming the hindrances and fetters. Pouring concrete represents entering into enlightenment—making the mind firm, unmovable by worldly vicissitudes. Once you have done that, nothing can shake the mind.

Siddhattha Gotama's teachers, Alarakarama and Uddaka Ramaputta, did have wisdom. They knew of the dangers of sensual pleasure and the benefits of full concentration, so they temporarily got rid of the hindrances and attained full concentration. However, these attainments were not enough to liberate them from the fetters that bound them to repeated rebirth. Concentration alone cannot get rid of the fetters. To get rid of them, you have to combine full concentration with mindfulness and attention. Otherwise you may simply get attached to the pleasure of concentration, as did Siddhattha Gotama's teachers, and get nowhere.

The Buddha's wisdom was very special. With this wisdom he not only saw the dangers of sensual pleasure and the benefits of concentration, but he used that wisdom to go beyond full concentration. He used his wisdom to discover that the hindrances he had transcended in this concentrated state were merely a symptom of a much deeper, stronger problem: the fetters. He saw the way the fetters entangle and confuse the mind, creating a delusive reality and propelling onward the suffering sense of self. In his purified mindfulness in full concentration, he saw the way to transcend the fetters: to see the impermanence, dissatisfaction, and selflessness of all conditioned things. When you see these three characteristics in every aspect of your existence, then your greed, hatred, and delusion, along with the fetters, vanish forever.

Don't Fool Yourself!

When we try to use the Buddha's method in our practice, we must be careful not to fool ourselves. Some people report that when they enter deep concentration, they do not feel anything, hear anything, or have any thoughts. They say that they are absorbed so fully that they are not even aware that time is passing. Often at our retreats I have seen such meditators rocking back and forth like small trees swayed by the wind. Sudden descent into a nonfeeling state is not called concentration. It is called sleep! Some of them even snore. As soon as we ring the bell, these meditators come out of their "deep concentration" and say, "I had very wonderful meditation. I managed to attain the fourth stage of concentration today."

Don't fool yourself! This is pure delusion. If the meditator had reached any of the stages of full concentration, sleepiness would be banished and the mind would have all of the dynamic qualities mentioned above. Full concentration is achieved deliberately. You notice clearly what steps you took to get there. Thus you can repeat the steps again later. Full concentration comes in stages, and only when it is combined with mindfulness can it propel you along the path toward enlightenment.

Also, don't fool yourself into thinking that concentration is the same as enlightenment. Enlightenment is not so quick and easy. You must go through the process of suppressing hindrances, gaining concentration, and combining that concentration with insight to destroy the hindrances and fetters. No matter how long you sit in concentration—even in the most powerful level of concentration—without destroying the fetters, you cannot attain even the first stage of enlightenment.

Finally, don't fool yourself into thinking that mindfulness alone is sufficient to take you to enlightenment. You cannot say, "I do not care for concentration or morality. I simply want to practice mindfulness." Mindfulness cannot be taken out of context or isolated from the other steps of the Buddha's path. People who do not practice the rest of the steps often find that they are unable to end their lust, hatred, and ignorance and thus are not successful in their mindfulness practice.

Be Patient

People who struggle to gain concentration in order to help their insight meditation sometimes worry when they cannot concentrate. Don't feel discouraged! It can take many years to reach full concentration. If your practice of awareness is guided by mindfulness, you can be content whether or not you gain full concentration. Don't try to force it. Each time you meditate, you are getting closer to concentration. How long it takes depends upon how often you meditate and how well you practice the other steps of the path.

Some days you may have better concentration and some days better mindfulness. If you have gained full concentration in the past but did not practice it every day, and did not fully master it, then you may sometimes have difficulty when you try to achieve it again. It may even seem impossible, if latent hindrances have become active, or if you have become involved in unwholesome activities. On days when concentration is more difficult, you should simply be mindful of your active state of mind without worrying or verbalizing that you cannot concentrate. The mindful observation of what is happening sharpens your penetrating wisdom into the reality of your experience. So long as you keep practicing all the other steps of the path and keep trying—without attachment—to gain concentration, you can trust that Skillful Concentration will come eventually, and that by using this powerful tool, you will achieve ultimate happiness.

KEY POINTS FOR MINDFULNESS OF SKILLFUL CONCENTRATION

The key points for gaining happiness through Skillful Concentration are the following:

- Skillful Concentration has three characteristics: it is wholesome, one-pointed, and it functions with mindfulness.

- The Buddha gave us a step-by-step, gradual training method for attaining Skillful Concentration.

- Wholesome concentration is concentration free of greed, hatred, and delusion. It is free of the five hindrances.

- To develop skilled concentration, first practice wholesome concentration by overcoming the hindrances. Keep the attention on the breath or other chosen object and do not observe new objects that may arise.

- After you have been practicing wholesome concentration for a while, your breath becomes very subtle and seems to disappear. The memory of the breath at the place of focus, such as the tip of the nostril, turns into a pleasant sensation called the "sign of concentration."

- "One-pointedness" refers to the mind concentrated upon itself after the sign of concentration has disappeared. One-pointed mind is a factor of full concentration or *jhana*.

- The first level of full concentration is marked by initial application of thought, sustained application of thought, joy, happiness, and concentration functioning in unison. It is very pleasant.

- At least the first level of full concentration is necessary to achieve enlightenment.

- Once you know how to attain the first level of concentration, determine to attain this level again, how long you will stay at the first level, and when you will exit from concentration.

- Practice attaining the first level of concentration many times until you master it.

- The second level of concentration arises when you have attained the first level so many times that you lose interest in the initial and sustained application of thought, and cause these applications of thought to disappear by ignoring them.

- The third level of concentration occurs when frequent repetition of the second level causes the mind to lose interest in the joy of concentration. As joy fades away, happiness is refined and deepened, and mindfulness and equanimity become more prominent.

- The fourth level of concentration arises when you lose interest in happiness, and your mindfulness becomes purified by deep equanimity.

- In full concentration the mind is full of wholesome and powerful dynamic qualities, not inert like a stone or like someone who is asleep.

- Full concentration gives the quality and strength needed for insight meditation practice.

- No matter how long you remain in the most powerful level of full concentration, that alone will not bring enlightenment. To achieve enlightenment, you must remove the fetters.

- You may begin a sitting meditation session with cultivating full concentration or with mindfulness practice, depending upon the steadiness of the mind that day. Or, you may switch back and forth between the two.

- No matter how you started the session, full concentration and mindfulness must come together to create powerful insight.

- Powerful insight is necessary to see the impermanent, suffering, and selfless nature of all experience. Insight allows you to see the role that greed plays in causing suffering and to let it go.

- Full concentration alone or mindfulness alone cannot bring enlightenment. Enlightenment can happen only when full concentration combines with mindfulness to break the fetters through insight.

- It can take a few days or many years to reach full concentration. Don't be discouraged if it comes slowly, and don't try to force it.

The Promise of the Buddha

THE DIVISION of the Buddha's path into eight steps does not imply that it's a vertical ladder. It's not necessary to master one step before moving on to the next. The path is more like a spiral. When you set out on the path, you have a certain amount of understanding of all eight steps. As you keep practicing, the steps become clearer and clearer in your mind, and you progress to the next stage.

There are, however, several useful ways to think about the path as a whole. For one thing, it's clear that greed, hatred, and delusion are the three most powerful unwholesome factors and the source of all kinds of suffering. Opposing these are the three most powerful aspects of the path: Skillful Understanding of the Buddha's teaching; Skillful Effort to overcome greed, hatred, and delusion; and the practice of Skillful Mindfulness as the means of overcoming those states. These three factors—understanding, effort, and mindfulness—support each other and work together to move you along the path.

Understanding the Buddha's teaching takes effort. It is certainly much easier not to strive, not to change, just to take life for granted, and to continue in whatever patterns of thought and behavior have become your comfortable habits. Yet the Buddha taught that as long as people do not understand the truth, they will pretend they have no problems, or despair that their problems are unsolvable.

Yet, if you make the effort, you will understand much. Mindfulness can help. In fact, without mindfulness, you will never understand

anything! You can make effort; you can struggle; but if you do not have
mindfulness, you will never progress in your understanding. Through
mindfulness you can understand the truth of dissatisfaction, its cause,
its end, and the path leading to its end. Moreover, when you practice
mindfulness, you make the effort to keep the mind clear of greed, hatred,
and delusion. Thus practicing mindfulness requires effort, and the
combination of mindfulness and effort frees the mind from misunderstanding.

The other steps of the Buddha's path also rely on these three factors.
Skillful Thinking, Skillful Speech, Skillful Action, Skillful Livelihood,
and Skillful Concentration can be cultivated only with the support of
understanding, effort, and mindfulness. Without Skillful Understanding, you will not see why it is important to work on improving these
other aspects of your life. Without Skillful Effort, you will find it impossible to progress toward your goal of positive change. And Skillful
Mindfulness is the supreme tool of awareness and attention that helps
you combat your negativities and strive toward perfection.

Another way of thinking about how the eight steps of the path work
together is to group them into three clusters: morality, concentration,
and wisdom. Each cluster pushes you toward the practice of the next
and toward a more comprehensive understanding of the path as a whole.
How does this work?

The first cluster begins with a certain amount of understanding.
You understand, for instance, how greed causes dissatisfaction, so you
begin to practice generosity. You also understand how hatred and cruelty cause suffering to you and to others, so you decide to practice
loving-friendliness and compassion. These three thoughts—generosity,
loving-friendliness, and compassion—are skillful thoughts. You have to
be wise to cultivate these positive thoughts. That wisdom comes from
Skillful Understanding. Therefore, Skillful Understanding and Skillful
Thought are grouped together as the wisdom aspect of the path.

The second cluster grows out of the first. When you look at your life
with wisdom, you see how peaceful and happy you are when you think
and act in positive ways. Your wisdom also helps you understand that
the dissatisfaction you experience is caused by your greed and attachment and that when you eliminate these causes, your dissatisfaction

ends. This understanding motivates you to improve various aspects of your outward behavior. Since you see that lying, malicious words, harsh language, and gossip cause pain, you avoid these types of negative speech and resolve to speak politely and meaningfully. Since you see how much pain and dissatisfaction is caused by killing, stealing, drinking, and sexual misconduct, you avoid these negative actions. Instead, you appreciate the lives of other beings and try to spare them; you respect other people's property; you avoid alcohol and act appropriately in your sexual behavior. Since you understand the suffering caused by wrong livelihood, you seek a wholesome way of making your living that supports your spiritual practice. The outward changes implied by Skillful Speech, Skillful Action, and Skillful Livelihood are clustered together as the morality aspect of the path.

The third cluster is based on your understanding that outward changes alone will not end your dissatisfaction and suffering. You see that actions begin with thoughts and that unwholesome thoughts themselves cause you tremendous suffering. Therefore, you try to train and discipline your mind. When you start to watch your mind, you see that in spite of your good intentions, harmful thoughts of greed, hatred, delusion, and doubt arise again and again in your consciousness. You see further that the only way to combat these mental traps is to apply sincere and diligent effort to avoid negative thought patterns, to overcome them when they do arise, and to cultivate and maintain positive thoughts. Moreover, you see that mindfulness is essential for positive change, both external and internal. Developing mindfulness is not easy without concentration, for it is concentration that helps you see things as they really are. These three—Skillful Effort, Skillful Mindfulness, and Skillful Concentration—are grouped as the concentration aspect of the path.

So, round and round you go, practicing the eight steps of the path. With each round, your greed, hatred, and delusion are reduced. With each round, your understanding of the truths of dissatisfaction, its cause, its end, and the way to end it deepens. No matter where you start the path, the steps link up and support one another. No matter what your level of understanding at the beginning, the result of the path is the same—the end of suffering and, ultimately, the highest degree of peace and happiness.

ENLIGHTENMENT

Some people ridicule the idea of enlightenment. In Internet chat rooms where the Dhamma is discussed, I have observed that people use derogatory terms—even angry and profane words—to describe enlightenment. Perhaps they misunderstand what enlightenment is. Enlightenment is nothing less than extinguishing the burning pain caused by greed, hatred, and delusion. It is putting out once and for all the fire of birth, growth, decay, death, sorrow, lamentation, grief, and despair.

The people who ridicule enlightenment may fear that when they extinguish this fire, they will be left with nothing to live for, in the cold darkness of despair. They may be confusing this painful internal fire with the fire that initiated civilization, or with the fire of electricity. But when the painful fire of delusion is extinguished, what prevails is not the frigid air of a pitch-black winter night. It is not a grim, lifeless state. Not at all. When the fire of greed, hatred, delusion, birth, growth, decay, death, sorrow, lamentation, pain, grief, and despair is extinguished, the result is total peace, total calm, total tranquillity, total inexpressible happiness, while the mind and senses are, at the same time, 100 percent clear, pure, and energized. Enlightenment is inner light, inner brightness, inner warmth.

From having laid down the burden of all the psychic irritants—greed, hatred, and delusion—the mind and body feel buoyant. We are not accustomed to feeling so light. We are used to having a heavy head, a heavy heart, a heavy body. The prospect of having such a light heart makes us feel a little nervous. We're afraid that this lightness will make us light-headed. Our heaviness, our suffering, is so familiar that we fear becoming disoriented if we let go.

Something like that happened to a friend of mine. His job transferred him to another office and he moved to an apartment next to a busy train station. When he first moved to this new apartment, he could not sleep for many nights because of the noise of the trains and the crowds of people coming and going. A few years later he was transferred to another office and had to move again. His new apartment was very quiet. Again, for many nights, he could not sleep. He had grown so used to the noise and commotion that he actually needed it to relax and fall asleep! Like my friend, we get so used to our heavy and uncomfortable habits of mind that we fear we will miss them when they're gone.

Our situation also reminds me of a man I read about when I lived in Washington, D.C. This fellow was serving a life sentence for committing murder. Because of his good conduct in prison, after ten years, he became eligible for parole. One day, a newspaper reporter interviewed him. "You must be very happy that you are eligible for parole," the reporter commented.

"No, no, please don't talk about parole," the man replied with some agitation. He said that he felt comfortable with life in prison. He enjoyed privileges such as watching television, and prison life did not have the insecurities of life outside. But, I asked myself, had he really become so accustomed to the violence of prison life, the endless restrictions, the tyranny of the guards? Had he forgotten the joy of living beyond the prison walls, the feeling of fresh air, the beautiful open spaces, the good food, and the freedom to meet other free people? Had he become so attached to conditions inside that freedom seemed strange and unappealing?

People who ridicule enlightenment are like that man in jail. They cling to what they have. They don't want to leave the comforting familiarity of their discomfort. But they don't know what they're missing.

Enlightenment is not something you wish for. It is the state that you end up in when all your wishes come to an end. As the Buddha said,

> What use is there for a well
> If there is water everywhere?
> When craving's root is severed
> What should one go about seeking?
> (Ud VII.9 [translated by Ireland])

When you know you are missing something, you keep looking for it. When you have each and every thing you ever wished for, you don't seek any more. Because you have attained perfect peace, perfect harmony, you are content to allow everyone else to live in peace and harmony.

At the end of the *Great Discourse on the Four Foundations of Mindfulness (Maha-Satipatthana Sutta)*, the Buddha guaranteed that if somebody practices mindfulness meditation exactly in the manner it is prescribed, then that individual attains enlightenment within this lifetime. If not fully enlightened because of some subtle fetters holding the person back, then he or she will at least become a nonreturner, reaching the third stage of enlightenment. (D 22)

The Buddha did not mean to imply that enlightenment can be achieved by a person who practices only some limited part of the path. Enlightenment requires that you develop thoroughly every aspect of morality, concentration, and wisdom. Moreover, in making this rather astonishing promise, the Buddha did not mean that casual, occasional practice—working at it every now and then—would be sufficient. He meant that to achieve enlightenment, your practice must be characterized by relentless dedication, energy, and perseverance. In order for you to gain concentration, your efforts must be supported by perfectly clear morality. Your concentration must be wholesome and one-pointed. This powerful concentration must be cultivated with equally powerful mindfulness. Then, supported by pure morality and skilled concentration, the wisdom that brings liberation takes place.

Still, some people find the Buddha's words to be an unrealistic promise. I wonder what grounds they have to challenge it. Are they like a person who hates to have wet feet and doubts that anyone can swim as fast as Olympic swimmers? Or like someone who has never run even a step and doubts that anyone can finish a twenty-six-mile marathon? Of course the Buddha's promise must seem unrealistic to someone who has never sat on a meditation cushion or tried to watch the breath for one minute! And it may seem like a hollow promise to those who have sat in meditation for many years but have never practiced all of the eight steps comprising morality, skilled concentration, and wisdom.

Meditation requires sincere discipline. You undertake the discipline of meditation not to impress anybody but to free your mind from the suffering caused by your own negativities. If you approach the Buddha's path like a hobby or a game, it will not work. The eight steps of the Buddha's message are not something that you learn about and then put into practice only when you need them....Come to think about it, you do use the eight steps only when you need them—but you need them every single moment of your life!

Your mindfulness of the eight steps of the Buddha's path, however, does not have to be perfect in order for you to start the practice. If your mindfulness of the path should lapse, don't worry. Simply become mindful of the unmindfulness as soon as you are able. Your success as you begin to walk the path depends on whether you maintain a strong intention to be mindful at all times, not whether you are actually able to do so. As you keep reminding yourself to be mindful, your lapses become fewer and fewer, until mindfulness of the path becomes automatic. If you make that kind of effort, you will progress quickly. Then you'll be the kind of student the Buddha had in mind when he made his promise.

"COME AND SEE"

This book offers only the essential guidelines for following the path. As your practice deepens, if you refer back to it again and again, you may find that it continues to serve as a useful guide at any level of understanding. But, it has not explained everything you will need to know about the Dhamma, about practice, about your own experience, and about what you will achieve. Different individuals have different backgrounds, education, intuitions, understandings of the Dhamma, and levels of spiritual growth. Moreover, the questions that you have tomorrow will be very different from the ones you have today.

Even the Buddha could not come up with one discourse that covered every exigency for every person. That is why he gave many thousands of Dhamma sermons. This book has presented a summary of these and some explanation of their most significant points. You will fill in the rest through your practice. The present moment is your teacher. Turn it into your own personal laboratory. Pay attention. Investigate. You alone can generate wisdom in yourself. You do this by pursuing what is skillful.

A rather skeptical audience once demanded that the Buddha tell them why they should believe him, when they had heard so many other holy men claiming to possess all the truth. The Buddha responded that they should not believe anything just because someone somewhere said it is true. Sources such as hearsay, documented reports, traditional beliefs passed down over many generations, scriptures considered to be holy, words of a highly respected and credible teacher, and teachings from someone you think of as your guru—all lack any guarantee of truth. The Buddha said that these things should not be accepted on faith.

The Buddha then said that truth cannot be uncovered through reasoning, either. He said you should not believe something just because it appears to be logical, or seems to take you closer to your goal, or appeals to your inclinations, or appears true after you have engaged in reflective reasoning. Why? Because the Dhamma still has an aspect that none of these things, not even reflective reasoning, can catch: your own experience.

The Buddha gave one general standard for what we should accept. This standard is not based on any kind of faith or reasoning. Rather, he said, when contemplating an action, ask yourself whether, based on your own experience, such an action would be harmful to anyone, including yourself. If it is harmful, it is not skillful, and the action should not be done. If it is beneficial to everyone, including you, and if people who are wise would approve it, then it is skillful, and the action should be done. (A I (Threes) VII.65)

The Buddha later elaborated that once a deed is done, you should reexamine it. You should ask yourself, "How well did that deed actually go? Was it really skillful?" If not, and you "reap the results with tearful eyes," the action should be avoided in the future. If it is skillful, and you "reap the results with cheerful eyes," the action should be done repeatedly. (Dh 67–68) If you pay close attention and stay honest with yourself about what you know to be true, then—without having to believe anything anybody else has said—you begin to choose actions that develop your purity and wisdom and that bring increasing happiness. Only you hold the key to your liberation. The key is your willingness to look within and decide what actions are skillful for bringing happy results.

Do you want to see the Dhamma? Look at your experience. Use your experience as a mirror reflecting the Dhamma. All the impersonal patterns of the universe are there. In your day-to-day life and in your moment-to-moment existence, you can see all there is to see anywhere: cause and effect, impermanence revealed by the constant flow of changes on every level, suffering wherever there is clinging, and the fact that no matter how hard you try to track it down, no self can be found in any of them.

Do you want to know about your experience? Look at the Dhamma. There you see all the impersonal elements and patterns that make up "you." There, too, you see that what you experience is the same, in its essence, as what is experienced by any other being. Dhamma is thrust in your face everywhere you turn. Even watching a bug struggling in a pot of water, for example, can spark your insight into the reality of the fear of death shared by you and all beings. The entire Dhamma is revealed in every experience in your life, every moment, every day. It is right there to be seen, with no blind faith or theoretical reasoning necessary. From this kind of rigorous observation, you gain confidence in the practice and proceed along the path.

Until you have become deeply familiar with the path and see the Dhamma in your own experience, the knowledge gained from this book will remain theoretical. If I were pointing up toward the North Star, you might stare at me and wonder, "Why is he pointing like that? Shouldn't he point over here? Or maybe over there?" How would you explain a star to someone who has never looked upward at night? Until you tilt your head enough to be able to see the stars and then follow the directions for examining the sky until you manage to pick out the North Star, there will be doubt in your mind. This doubt gives rise to all kinds of questions. But when you catch sight of the North Star and observe for yourself the way everything else revolves around it, then you have no such doubt.

Similarly, until you glimpse the goal, you will have many questions about the path, about the teaching, about your own practice, and about why I have said certain things in this book. How can words explain what Nibbana is like, given that Nibbana is nonexperiential? Experience happens through our senses, and whatever labels we could use to describe nonexperiential states are misleading, as they are based on sensory experience. We just have to follow the steps of the path all the way to the end and see for ourselves.

Have you ever tried to point at something for a cat to see? The more you point, the more the cat will want to sniff your finger. The cat will never look beyond the finger. If you finish this book and say, "Is that all there is? Where is ultimate truth? I didn't get anything out of this," you are like that cat. Look beyond the words of this book. Use the kinds of actions suggested by the Buddha to propel yourself into another way of understanding. Walk the path for yourself. This path is spread across all the experiences of your life as you cultivate increasing skillfulness in thought, word, and deed.

When you have skillfully and thoroughly followed the steps for purifying your mind, you will finally catch sight of the truth of the impermanence of all experience, of the suffering that follows from clinging to what is impermanent, and of the lack of self in all things subject to impermanence and suffering. You will see how greed holds together all suffering experience. At that moment you see for yourself, and all your questions cease.

If you don't believe in the greater goals described in this book, that is okay; it still may be useful to you. Just use this book to help you keep asking questions about your own experience. Try to learn something from everything that happens to you. The Buddha often said, "Come and see!" He meant, come and look inside your own body and mind to see the truth, the Dhamma. You won't find it anywhere else.

Suggested Further Reading

Being Nobody, Going Nowhere: Meditations on the Buddhist Path.
Ayya Khema. Boston: Wisdom Publications, 1988. Straightforward
advice and explanation on basic Buddhist ideas by a Western nun.

Breath by Breath, The Liberating Practice of Insight Meditation. Larry
Rosenberg. Boston: Shambhala Publications, 1988. Explains how to
cultivate tranquility and deep insight through breath awareness,
based on the *Anapanasati Sutta*.

The Buddha's Ancient Path. Ven. Piyadassi Thera. Kandy: Buddhist
Publication Society, 1974. The central teachings of the Buddha
explained with stories and illustrations from the Pali Canon and its
commentaries.

Buddhism for the New Millennium. London: World Buddhist Foundation, 2000. Collection of essays by eminent Buddhist scholars on
Buddhism's past development and future challenges; includes some
modern exploratory scholarship.

*Connected Discourses of the Buddha: A New Translation of the
Samyutta Nikaya.* Translated by Bhikkhu Bodhi. Boston: Wisdom
Publications, 2000. The canonical source for many of the core Buddhist
ideas. Heavily and expertly annotated.

The Dhammapada. Translated by Thanissaro Bhikkhu. Barre: Dhamma
Dena Publications, 1998. The Buddha's classic verses providing the
essence of the Dhamma, rendered by a Western monk with the ear
of a poet.

The Experience of Insight: A Simple and Direct Guide to Buddhist Meditation. Joseph Goldstein. Boston: Shambhala Publications, 1983. Lucid instruction by a leading Western teacher.

The First Discourse of the Buddha. Dr. Rewata Dhamma. Boston: Wisdom Publications, 1997. An explanation of the Four Noble Truths.

Great Disciples of the Buddha: Their Lives, Their Work, Their Legacy. Nyanaponika Thera, Hellmuth Hecker, and Bhikkhu Bodhi. Boston: Wisdom Publications, 1997. The life stories of twenty-four of the Buddha's original disciples, drawn from the canonical scriptures.

The Jhanas in Theravada Buddhist Meditation. Henepola Gunaratana. Kandy, Sri Lanka: Buddhist Publication Society, 1998. An explanation of the stages of meditative concentration. (Wheel Publications, 351–53)

Journey to the Center: A Meditation Workbook. Matthew Flickstein. Boston: Wisdom Publications, 1998. An accessible workbook, with hands-on exercises, guided meditations, and space for journal entries.

Landscapes of Wonder: Discovering Buddhist Dhamma in the World Around Us. Bhikkhu Nyanasobhano. Boston: Wisdom Publications, 1998. A beautiful and inspiring collection of essays by an American monk who takes us beyond the obvious to the sublime.

Long Discourses of the Buddha: A Translation of the Digha Nikaya. Translated by Maurice Walshe. Boston: Wisdom Publications, 1996.

Lovingkindness: The Revolutionary Art of Happiness. Sharon Salzberg. Boston: Shambhala Publications, 1995. A leading Western teacher on the heart practice of *metta*, or lovingkindness.

Living in the Light of Death: On the Art of Being Truly Alive. Larry Rosenberg. Boston: Shambhala Publications, 2000. Shows how intimacy with aging and mortality can be a means to liberation, using a text known as the *Five Subjects for Frequent Recollection*.

Middle Length Discourses of the Buddha: A New Translation of the Majjhima Nikaya. Translated by Bhikkhu Ñanamoli and Bhikkhu

Bodhi. Boston: Wisdom Publications, 1995. The richest and most comprehensive collection of the Buddha's teachings.

Mindfulness in Plain English. Bhante Henepola Gunaratana. Boston: Wisdom Publications, 1993. The bestselling guide that has introduced thousands to the liberating practice of mindfulness.

The Path of Serenity and Insight. Ven. Henepola Gunaratana. Delhi: Motilal Banarsidass, 1985. Thorough analysis of the jhanas based upon the scriptures and exegetical literature of Theravada Buddhism.

Swallowing the River Ganges: A Practice Guide to the Path of Purification. Matthew Flickstein. Boston: Wisdom Publications, 2001. Engaging commentary on the *Visuddhimagga,* the classic fourth-century Theravada manual of meditation and Buddhist practice.

Voices of Insight. Edited by Sharon Salzberg. Boston: Shambhala Publications, 1999. Teachings from the spectrum of leading Insight Meditation teachers in the West, including Bhante Gunaratana.

What the Buddha Taught. Ven. Walpola Rahula. New York: Grove Press Books, 1974. A comprehensive yet succinct and easy-to-read presentation of the Buddha's basic teachings, providing an important basic manual for all students of Buddhism.

When the Iron Eagle Flies: Buddhism for the West. Ayya Khema. Boston: Wisdom Publications, 2000. Illuminates the practical implications of dependent origination with clarity and humor.

The Wings to Awakening. Ven. Thanissaro Bhikkhu. Barre, MA: Dhamma Dana Publications, 1996. Explains how to develop the skills leading to enlightenment, structured around seven sets of core teachings; includes extensive passages translated from the Pali Canon.

The Word of the Doctrine (Dhammapada). Translated by K.R. Norman. Oxford: Pali Text Society, 1997. A translation of the Buddhist classic with an introduction and notes.

Index

of the Buddha 25, 38, 84, 170, 185,
217, 239
factors of 216, 217–20
"false" 26, 48–49, 63, 240, 242
fetters and. *See* fetters, the ten
full concentration and 227–29, 232,
238–39
nibbana 47, 48, 49, 220, 255
path to. *See* Eightfold Path, the
stages of 152–53, 154, 175–78, 252
See also insight
ethics. *See* morality

factors of enlightenment, the seven
216, 217–20
fasting 124–25. *See also* precepts,
eight training
fear 19, 57, 63–65, 113
of death 33, 86–87, 111, 255
feelings 44, 208–15
mindfulness of 213–15
as the source of suffering 209, 210
worldly and unworldly 211–13
fetters, the ten 151–58, 216, 240–41
overcoming 161, 173–78, 207–8,
238, 240–41, 242
relationship to hindrances 156,
158–59, 240
and stages of enlightenment
152–53, 175–78, 238, 252
See also hindrances, the five
Four Foundations of Mindfulness
197–220, 251. *See also* mindfulness; Skillful Mindfulness
Four Noble Truths 11, 25, 30–54, 178,
217, 220. *See also* dissatisfaction;
Eightfold Path
full concentration (jhana) 227–36
and attachment 233, 236, 239–240
difference from Skillful Concentration 227–28, 239–40
force of 232–33, 236

four levels of 229–36
jhanic factors 229, 231–32, 234, 235
sign of 230, 231, 237
training methods 224, 225–26, 230
See also concentration, Skillful
Concentration

generosity 7, 15, 58–60, 84
See also renunciation
greed. *See* craving

happiness 4–6, 31, 47, 130, 190
categories of 6–8
of concentration 212, 214, 233,
234–36
joy, excitement and 229–30
mind as source of 194–95
path to. *See* Eightfold Path
permanent. *See* enlightenment
and wholesome choices 149, 150,
151, 254
See also full concentration, jhanic
factors
hatred. *See* anger; aversion
hindrances, the five 158–61
concentration and 223, 224–26,
229, 240–41
relationship to fetters 156, 158–59,
240
working with 159, 161, 167–73,
187–89, 240–41
See also fetters, the ten

ignorance 34, 41, 44, 239
as a fetter 151–53, 155, 157, 177
and rebirth 33–34, 51
ill will 28, 70, 98, 158,160. *See also*
anger; hindrances, the five
impermanence 35–37, 168, 195–97,
238–39
of the body 202, 207
defense against 61

About the Author

Venerable Henepola Gunaratana was ordained at the age of twelve as a Buddhist monk in Malandeniya, Sri Lanka. In 1947, at age twenty, he was given higher ordination in Kandy. He received his education from Vidyasekhara Junior College in Gumpaha, Vidyalankara College in Kelaniya, and Buddhist Missionary College in Colombo. Subsequently he traveled to India for five years of missionary work for the Mahabodhi Society, serving the Harijana ("Untouchable") people in Sanchi, Delhi, and Bombay. Later he spent ten years as a missionary in Malaysia, serving as religious advisor to the Sasana Abhivurdhiwardhana Society, the Buddhist Missionary Society, and the Buddhist Youth Federation of Malaysia. He has been a teacher in Kishon Dial School and Temple Road Girls' School and principal of the Buddhist Institute of Kuala Lumpur.

At the invitation of the Sasana Sevaka Society, he came to the United States in 1968 to serve as general secretary of the Buddhist Vihara Society of Washington, D.C. In 1980, he was appointed president of the Society. During his years at the Vihara, from 1968 to 1988, he taught courses in Buddhism, conducted meditation retreats, and lectured widely throughout the United States, Canada, Europe, Australia, New Zealand, Africa, and Asia. In addition, from 1973 to 1988 Venerable Gunaratana served as Buddhist chaplain at The American University.

He has also pursued his scholarly interests by earning a Ph.D. degree in philosophy from The American University. He has taught courses on Buddhism at The American University, Georgetown University, and the University of Maryland. His books and articles have been published in

Malaysia, India, Sri Lanka, and the United States. His book *Mindfulness in Plain English* has been translated into many languages and published around the world. An abridged Thai translation has been selected for use in the high school curriculum throughout Thailand.

Since 1982 Venerable Gunaratana has been President of the Bhavana Society, a monastery and retreat center located in the woods of West Virginia (near the Shenandoah Valley), which he co-founded with Matthew Flickstein. Venerable Gunaratana resides at the Bhavana Society, where he ordains and trains monks and nuns, and offers retreats to the general public. He also travels frequently to lecture and lead retreats throughout the world.

In 2000, Venerable Gunaratana received an award for lifetime outstanding achievement from his alma mater, Vidyalankara College.

Also from Wisdom Publications

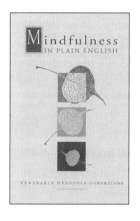

MINDFULNESS IN PLAIN ENGLISH
Venerable Henepola Gunaratana
208 pages, 0-86171-064-9, $14.95

"A masterpiece. I cannot recommend it highly enough." —Jon Kabat-Zinn, author of *Wherever You Go, There You Are*

"One of the best nuts-and-bolts meditation manuals. If you'd like to learn the practice of meditation, you can't do better."—Brian Bruya, Religion Editor, Amazon.com

"*Mindfulness in Plain English* lives up to its title… With a very modern and inviting writing style, the language is loose and free, and occasionally humorous… An excellent resource for anyone wishing to begin or further meditative studies." —*Today's Librarian*

"Wonderfully clear and straightforward."—Joseph Goldstein, author of *Insight Meditation: The Practice of Freedom*

"Of great value to newcomers…especially people without access to a teacher."—Larry Rosenberg, author of *Living in the Light of Death: On the Art of Being Truly Alive*

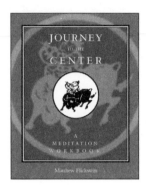

JOURNEY TO THE CENTER
A Meditation Workbook
Matthew Flickstein
Foreword by Bhante Henepola Gunaratana
224 pages, 0-86171-141-6, $15.95

"This is a book to do rather than simply to
read, a book to work with slowly and
intensely but also joyfully."
—NAPRA ReView

"The workbook format makes the meditations easy to follow, simple
to do, and very effective. Flickstein leads readers to uncover unconscious memories, discover new, positive ideas, and open the way to
change. *Journey to the Center* is a guide to successful living."
—*New Age Retailer*

SWALLOWING THE RIVER GANGES
A Practice Guide to The Path of Purification
Matthew Flickstein
Foreword by Bhante Henepola Gunaratana
208 pages, 0-86171-178-5. $16.95

"With astounding simplicity and clarity,
Matthew Flickstein has created a guidebook for
earnest students of vipassana. But don't let the
simplicity fool you. This is a monumental
synthesis of the Buddha's teachings from the
standpoint of one who has walked the path."—Ginny Morgan,
meditation teacher and Director, Mid-America Dharma

"An inspiring, splendidly detailed, and user-friendly guidebook for
navigating the subtle complexities of the Buddha's path to spiritual
freedom. Matthew Flickstein writes with sharp clarity and contagious
enthusiasm that draws one back to the sitting cushion again and
again."—Steve Shealy, Ph.D., meditation teacher and psychologist

LANDSCAPES OF WONDER
Discovering Buddhist Dhamma
in the World Around Us
Bhikkhu Nyanasobhano
192 pages, 0-86171-142-4, $14.95

"The essays in *Landscapes of Wonder* are prose meditation, and what prose it is! Nyanasobhano describes a country walk and it becomes an investigation of impermanence. He reads the paper and reflects on the mind and its search for distraction... This book reveals a literary power rare among writers on Buddhism... This is an inspiring book, to read with pleasure and contemplate with care." —*dharmalife*

LESSONS FROM THE DYING
Rodney Smith
Foreword by Joseph Goldstein
224 pages, 0-86171-140-8, $16.95

Are a person's perceptions and values altered when facing the end of life? Do the dying see the world in a way that could help the rest of us learn how to live? This book takes us into the lessons of the dying. Through the words and circumstances of the terminally ill, we become immersed in their wisdom and in our own mortality. The dying speak to us in direct and personal ways, pointing toward a wise and sane way to live.

"In the tradition of the *Tibetan Book of the Dead* and Elizabeth Kübler-Ross, Rodney Smith's work finds a gold mine of wisdom behind the mask of death and grief's convulsions... There are books about death and grieving. This is a book about transforming life." —*Amazon.com*

Wisdom's Teachings of the Buddha Series

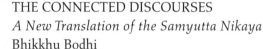

THE CONNECTED DISCOURSES
A New Translation of the Samyutta Nikaya
Bhikkhu Bodhi
2080 pages in 2 volumes, 0-86171-168-8,
Clothbound, $120.00

A complete translation of the *Samyutta Nikaya*—one of the most inspiring compilations in the Buddhist canon—containing all of the important short suttas on such major topics as the Four Noble Truths, dependent origination, the seven factors of enlightenment, and the Noble Eightfold Path.

THE MIDDLE LENGTH DISCOURSES
A New Translation of the Majjhima Nikaya
Bhikkhu Ñanamoli and Bhikkhu Bodhi
1424 pages, 0-86171-072-X, Clothbound, $60.00

"[This] brilliant, scholarly, and eminently readable version of *The Middle Length Discourses* sets a benchmark for translations of the Buddha's words into English."—Joseph Goldstein, author of *Insight Meditation: The Practice of Freedom*

THE LONG DISCOURSES
A Translation of the Digha Nikaya
Maurice Walsh
656 pages, 0-86171-103-3, Clothbound, $45.00

An invaluable collection of the teachings of the Buddha that reveal his gentleness, compassion, and penetrating wisdom. These thirty-four discourses are among the oldest records of the Buddha's original teachings.

About Wisdom

WISDOM PUBLICATIONS, a not-for-profit publisher, is dedicated to making available authentic Buddhist works for the benefit of all. We publish translations of the sutras and tantras, commentaries and teachings of past and contemporary Buddhist masters, and original works by the world's leading Buddhist scholars. We publish our titles with the appreciation of Buddhism as a living philosophy and with the special commitment to preserve and transmit important works from all the major Buddhist traditions.

If you would like more information or a copy of our mail-order catalog, please contact us at:

Wisdom Publications
199 Elm Street
Somerville, Massachusetts 02144 USA
Telephone: (617) 776-7416 • Fax: (617) 776-7841
Email: sales@wisdompubs.org • www.wisdompubs.org

The Wisdom Trust

As a not-for-profit publisher, Wisdom Publications is dedicated to the publication of fine Dharma books for the benefit of all sentient beings and dependent upon the kindness and generosity of sponsors in order to do so. If you would like to make a donation to Wisdom, please do so through our Somerville office. If you would like to sponsor the publication of a book, please write or e-mail us for more information.

Thank you.

Wisdom Publications is a nonprofit, charitable 501(c)(3) organization affiliated with the Foundation for the Preservation of the Mahayana Tradition (FPMT).